BEST RECIPES
of the
GREAT FOOD
COMPANIES

BEST RECIPES

of the

GREAT FOOD

COMPANIES

JUDITH ANDERSON

🔟 TEN SPEED PRESS
Berkeley, California

1☯

TEN SPEED PRESS
P.O. Box 7123
Berkeley, California 94707

Text design by Sarah Levin
Cover design by Fifth Street Design
Typesetting by Recorder Typesetting

FIRST PRINTING 1992

Library of Congress Cataloging-in-Publication Data

Best recipes of the great food companies / by Judith Anderson.
    p.   cm.
   Includes index.
   ISBN 0–89815–459–6
   1. Cookery. I. Anderson, Judith, 1940- .
TX714.B464 1992
641.5—dc20   91–34824
            CIP

Printed in the United States of America

   2 3 4 5 — 96 95 94 93 92

CONTENTS

PREFACE

This book celebrates the marvelous contributions made by our great American food companies to our diets, nutrition, and dining pleasures. The recipes included in it are the crowning achievements of years of testing by the most qualified home economists in the United States. Some are classics that have been enjoyed for years. A few were so innovative when they were introduced that they started new trends. Many are new, designed for today's lighter dietary interests.

These are the kinds of foods people really cook and eat. The recipes are easy to prepare and require ingredients that are readily available in supermarkets everywhere.

Stories of the origins of our important foods and recipes and of our major brand-name products included in this cookbook will make interesting dinner-time conversation. In researching the histories of these companies, products, and recipes, I discovered that Americans today regularly enjoy foods that were reserved exclusively for royalty and the privileged upper classes in other times and places. These histories tell of many of the great discoveries and innovations that have led to our incredible variety of food products from around the world, the ease with which we prepare food, and the excellent nutrition available to us in our varied diets.

The companies included in this book became great because they offered so much to our food heritage. *Best Recipes from the Great Food Companies* extols their achievements.

Note: Microwave ovens vary in wattage and power output. Cooking times in some recipes may need to be adjusted.

ACKNOWLEDGEMENTS

BEATRICE CHEESE, INC. COUNTY LINE and TREASURE CAVE are registered trademarks of BEATRICE CHEESE, INC. Thanks for permission to use recipes go to Tom Hickey and Katherine Coupoulous.

BORDEN, INC. EAGLE BRAND, MEADOW GOLD, BENNETT'S, ORLEANS, REALEMON, COCO LOPEZ, DOXSEE, SNOW'S, LITE-LINE, VIVA, CREAMETTE, CLASSICO, WYLER'S, STEERO, KRUNCHER'S!, COUNTRY STORE, CARY'S, NONE SUCH, and MAPLE ORCHARDS are registered trademarks and MACDONALD'S is a common law trademark. The photos and recipes featuring such trademarks are used with the permission of Borden, Inc. Thank you Annie Watts.

CAMPBELL SOUP COMPANY CAMPBELL'S, VLASIC, and FRANCO-AMERICAN are registered trademarks of CAMPBELL SOUP COMPANY. Permission was granted to use recipes. Thank you to Justine Good and Donna Skidmore.

CPC INTERNATIONAL INC. HELLMANN'S, BEST FOODS, SKIPPY, SUPER CHUNK, KARO, MAZOLA, MUELLER'S, TWIST TRIO, ARGO, KINGSFORD'S, MAZOLA, SAHARA, and THOMAS' are registered trademarks of CPC International Inc. Recipes and photos are courtesy of Best Foods, a division of CPC International Inc. Thanks go to Elizabeth Strauss.

DOLE FOOD COMPANY Dole is a registered trademark of DOLE FOOD COMPANY. Recipes and photos courtesy of Dole Test Kitchens.

DURKEE-FRENCH FOODS FRENCH'S and DURKEE are registered trademarks of DURKEE-FRENCH FOODS, a Division of Reckitt & Colman Inc. Permission was granted to use recipes and photos. Thanks to Elizabeth Erman.

GENERAL MILLS, INC. SUPERMOIST, BISQUICK, GOLD MEDAL, SOFTASILK, and GOLDEN GRAHAMS are registered trademarks of GENERAL MILLS, INC. Recipes are used with permission of GENERAL MILLS, INC. Thank you to Mary Bartz, Gretchen Beede, and Judy Lund.

HERSHEY FOODS CORPORATION HERSHEY'S, REESE'S, SKOR, and MINICHIPS are registered trademarks of HERSHEY FOODS CORPORATION. All recipes are used with permission. Thank to you Cheryl Reitz and Bonnie Glass.

JFC INTERNATIONAL, INC. DYNASTY is a registered trademark of JFC INTERNATIONAL, INC. All recipes used with permission. Thank you to Diane Plocher.

KELLOGG'S® KELLOGG'S CORN FLAKES®, RICE KRISPIES®, ALL-BRAN®, are trademarks of Kellogg Company. Recipes and photos courtesy of Kellogg Kitchens™.

KRAFT GENERAL FOODS, INC. PHILADELPHIA BRAND, MIRACLE WHIP, SAUCEWORKS, JELL-O, CASINO, BIRDS EYE, PARKAY, VELVEETA, BREAKSTONE'S, BAKER'S, GERMAN'S, ANGEL FLAKE, CALUMET, DREAM WHIP, COOL WHIP, POST, and GRAPENUTS are registered trademarks of KRAFT GENERAL FOODS, INC. Recipes and photos are used with permission. Thank you to Denise Henderson, Kathy Knuth, Lisa K. Van Riper, and Maryellen Clark.

LAWRY'S FOODS, INC. is a registered trademark of Lawry's Foods, Inc., Los Angeles, CA 90065. Recipes are used with permission. Thanks to Maribeth Drogosz.

LINDSAY INTERNATIONAL, INC. on behalf of Lindsay Olive Growers is appreciated for their contribution of recipes and photos. LINDSAY is a registered trademark. Thanks to Eric M. Boyle for permission to use recipes and photos.

McCORMICK & COMPANY, INC. McCORMICK/SCHILLING and BON APPÉTIT are registered trademarks of McCORMICK & COMPANY, INCORPORATED. Permission received to use recipes and photos. Thank you to Diane Hamel.

NESTLÉ FOOD COMPANY LIBBY'S, CONTADINA, and CARNATION are registered trademarks. Libby's is a division and Contadina Foods, Inc. a subsidiary of NESTLÉ FOOD COMPANY. Recipes are used with permission. Thank you to Vivian Manuel and Mary Ann Bydlon.

NABISCO FOODS GROUP NABISCO, SPOON SIZE, BLUE BONNET, WRIGHT'S, ORTEGA, REGINA, GREY POUPON, A.1., DAVIS, FLEISCHMANN'S, EGG BEATERS, CREAM OF WHEAT, BRER RABBIT, ROYAL, COLLEGE INN, and NILLA are registered trademarks of NABISCO FOODS GROUP. Recipes and photos are used with permission. Thank you to Catherine Marschean-Spivak.

OSCAR MAYER FOODS CORPORATION d/b/a/ LOUIS RICH COMPANY and KEMP SEAFOOD COMPANY. Oscar Mayer and Louis Rich are registered trademarks of Oscar Mayer Foods Corporation. Louis Kemp is a trademark of Oscar Mayer Foods Corporation. Recipes and photos are courtesy of Oscar Mayer Foods Corporation. Thanks to Shelagh Hackett Thomee.

PEPPERIDGE FARM, INC. PEPPERIDGE FARM is a registered trademark of PEPPERIDGE FARM, INC. Recipes are used with permission. Thank you to Elizabeth Gabriele.

PET INCORPORATED PET, UNDERWOOD, OLD EL PASO, NACHIPS, PROGRESSO, PET-RITZ, HOLLYWOOD, and LA CREME are registered trademarks of PET INCORPORATED. Recipes are used with permission. Thank you to Fran Sharp and Roberta Phillips.

RAGÚ FOODS CO. RAGÚ and ADOLPH'S are registered trademarks of RAGÚ FOODS CO. Recipes are used with permission. Thanks to Rosemary Smalberg.

SARGENTO CHEESE COMPANY, INC. SARGENTO and PREFERRED LIGHT are registered trademarks of SARGENTO CHEESE COMPANY, INC. whose photos and recipes are used with permission. Thank you to Barbara Ganon.

THOMAS J. LIPTON CO. LIPTON, WISH-BONE, and CUP-A-SOUP are registered trademarks of the Thomas J. Lipton Co., Englewood Cliffs, New Jersey 07632. KNOX is a registered trademark of Knox Gelatine, Inc., Englewood Cliffs, New Jersey 07632. IMPERIAL is a registered trademark of Lever Bros., New York, N.Y. 10022. All photos and recipes are used with permission. Thanks to Anna Marie Cesario and Ronda Di Guglielmo.

PARTY BEVERAGES

PIÑA COLADA PUNCH

BORDEN, INC.

Makes about 4 quarts

Ice ring (optional; see below)
1 can (20 ounces) crushed pineapple, undrained
2 cans (15 ounces each) Coco Lopez® Cream of Coconut

1 can (46 ounces) pineapple juice, chilled
2 cups light rum (optional)
1 bottle (32 ounces) club soda, chilled

Prepare ice ring in advance. In blender container, combine crushed pineapple and cream of coconut; blend until smooth. In large punch bowl, combine pineapple mixture, pineapple juice, and rum, if desired. Just before serving, add club soda and ice ring or block of ice.

To make ice ring: Fill ring mold with water to within 1 inch of top rim; freeze. Arrange pineapple chunks and maraschino cherries on top of ice. Gradually pour small amount of cold water over fruits; freeze.

MAI TAI PUNCH

DOLE FOOD COMPANY

Makes 25 servings, 4 ounces each

3 quarts Dole® Pineapple Juice
¼ cup lemon juice
¼ cup lime juice
½ cup sugar

1 cup dark rum *or* orange juice
1 cup light rum *or* sparkling water
2 cups sparkling water

Combine fruit juices and sugar. Stir until sugar dissolves. Add rum. Chill. Just before serving, pour over block of ice in punch bowl. Add sparkling water and stir gently.

Serve in punch cups.

SUNNY HOLIDAY PUNCH

DOLE FOOD COMPANY

Makes about 4 quarts

1½ quarts Dole® Pineapple Juice, chilled
1 quart mineral water, chilled
1 can (6 ounces) frozen orange juice concentrate

1 Dole® Lemon *or* lime, thinly sliced
2 cups fresh strawberries *or* drained frozen strawberries
1 bottle (750 milliliters) chilled champagne

Combine all ingredients in a punch bowl.

SIR TEA
The Story of Sir Thomas Lipton

The rags-to-riches story of Sir Thomas Lipton begins in a walk-up tenement in Glasgow, Scotland, in 1850. There Lipton was born of Irish parents. After quitting school at age ten so that he could supplement the pinched family coffers, he started working in a stationery store where he was an unusually hard worker from the start and took in every detail about the steps required to retail successfully and to achieve customer satisfaction.

Around this time, droves of immigrants were sailing to America, where the streets were paved with gold, they had heard. Some came to stay, others to make their fortunes or to learn how Americans succeeded before returning to their homeland. Lipton saw the Statue of Liberty at age fifteen, with eight dollars pushed deeply in his pocket.

He moved around the vast, young country, holding manual jobs in New York City, New Orleans, and South Carolina. He liked Americans, and they liked him. He watched the people of the thriving marketplaces and learned how shrewd businessman competed. Enthusiastically, he absorbed all the skills he would need to become a great success when he returned to Glasgow to open his grocery store at age twenty-one.

Lipton's ability to keep the customers' interests as his highest priority made him so successful that he was able to build that first grocery store into the largest company in Great Britain. What made a customer want to purchase again, he wanted to know. How could he save the consumer money, yet offer the highest-quality product available?

By the time he approached his thirtieth year, Lipton owned a chain of more than twenty stores. At forty, he was a millionaire, even before he had sold a single ounce of the tea that would make his name a household word in all tea-drinking countries.

Tea drinking had long been an expensive habit enjoyed only by the elite because the long voyage around the Cape of Good Hope had kept the price of importing the dried leaves high. The opening of the Suez Canal in 1869 shortened the distance to tea-growing countries and brought the price to a level that allowed the masses to consume the brew.

Brokers streamed through Lipton's office trying to convince him to carry the product. He was thinking. Wanting to eliminate the middlemen and keep the price down for his customers, he decided to buy his own estates in Ceylon. At this time, stores kept tea in huge chests and sold it to customers by the individual scoop, with each order individually weighed. Questions of cleanliness, accuracy of weight measurement, and freshness were always in customers' minds. Lipton's genius was to package the blended product in pound, half-pound, and quarter-pound containers. Customers were impressed with this innovation, and demand exploded. In India and Ceylon, Lipton expanded with more tea plantations, then with coffee and cocoa plantations. Later he built a meat-packing business in Chicago. Never having forgotten his respect for Americans, in 1915 he formed the Thomas J. Lipton Company of the United States. Lipton® tea boxes now depict a charming likeness of Thomas Lipton wearing a yachtsman's cap and holding a teacup.

Besides being famous in our country as "Sir Tea," Lipton was America's favorite good sport. He had tried to win the America's Cup in the international yacht race five times with five different green-hulled yachts named *Shamrock*. Each time he failed. But his good-natured and chivalrous comments with the press after each failure caused his popularity with the American public to skyrocket. After his last failure in 1930, he told reporters, "It's no use, I can't win, I can't win." Americans were so affected that they contributed thousands to buy the captivating man a gold Tiffany-designed loving cup.

Thomas Lipton had been knighted and made a baronet in recognition of his philanthropy. But his response to this outpouring of affection by the American people was most emotional. "Although I lost, you make me feel as though I had won."

FIRESIDE PUNCH

THOMAS J. LIPTON CO.

Makes about 5 servings

1½ cups cranberry juice cocktail
1½ cups water
4 Lipton® Cinnamon Apple *or* Gentle
   Orange Herbal Tea Bags

2 tablespoons brown sugar
Cinnamon sticks for garnish (optional)

In medium saucepan, bring cranberry juice and water to a boil. Add herbal tea bags; cover and brew 5 minutes. Remove tea bags; stir in sugar. Garnish with cinnamon sticks.

REDHOT MARY

DURKEE-FRENCH FOODS

Makes about 1 quart

4 cups vegetable juice cocktail
2½ tablespoons lemon juice
4 teaspoons French's®
   Worcestershire Sauce

2 teaspoons Durkee® RedHot Cayenne
   Pepper Sauce, or to taste
½ teaspoons prepared horseradish
Celery for garnish

Combine all ingredients; pour over ice cubes. Serve in a tall glass garnished with celery stalk.

RICH AND CREAMY COCOA

PET INCORPORATED

Makes 4 servings

2 cups hot water
¼ cup unsweetened cocoa powder
¼ cup sugar
¼ teaspoon salt
¼ teaspoon ground cinnamon

⅛ teaspoon ground nutmeg
2 cups Pet® Evaporated Milk
6 large marshmallows
¾ teaspoon vanilla.

In heavy saucepan, mix hot water, cocoa, sugar, salt, cinnamon, and nutmeg. Cook over medium heat until mixture comes to a boil, stirring frequently. Boil 5 minutes, stirring frequently. Reduce heat and add evaporated milk and marshmallows. Heat slowly until marshmallows are dissolved, stirring constantly. Add vanilla. Remove from heat and beat 1 minute with rotary beater.

   Serve at once.

SNACK MIXES

PEANUT BUTTER SNACK MIX
Durkee-French Foods

8

ZESTY CRUNCH MIX
Durkee-French Foods

8

MICROWAVE BEEF JERKY
Nabisco Foods Group

9

CINNAMON AND SPICE TRAIL MIX
Nabisco Foods Group

9

HOLIDAY TRAIL MIX
Dole Food Company

10

PEANUT BUTTER SNACK MIX

DURKEE-FRENCH FOODS

Makes about 7 cups

2 tablespoons butter *or* margarine
⅓ cup creamy peanut butter
2 cans (1½ ounces *each*) Durkee®
    Potato Sticks

2 cups toasted oat cereal
2 cups bite-size shredded wheat
1 cup chocolate chips

Preheat oven to 350°F. Melt butter and peanut butter in 9-by-13-inch baking dish in oven, about 4 minutes. Stir in potato sticks, oat cereal, and shredded wheat. Bake 20 minutes, stirring after 10 minutes. Cool potato-stick mixture to room temperature. Stir in chocolate chips.

ZESTY CRUNCH MIX

DURKEE-FRENCH FOODS

Makes about 8 cups

2 tablespoons butter *or* margarine
2 tablespoons Durkee® RedHot Cayenne
    Pepper Sauce
¼ cup grated Parmesan cheese

2 cans (1½ ounces *each*) Durkee®
    Bar-B-Q Potato Sticks
2 cups mini pretzels
2 cups peanuts
2 cups corn chex cereal

Preheat oven to 250°F. Melt butter in 9-by-13-inch baking dish in oven. Stir in pepper sauce and Parmesan cheese. Add remaining ingredients, 1 at a time, stirring after each addition. Bake 45 minutes, stirring every 15 minutes.

MICROWAVE BEEF JERKY
NABISCO FOODS GROUP

Makes about ½ pound

1 pound flank steak
2 tablespoons Wright's® Natural Hickory Seasoning

2 tablespoons soy sauce
1 tablespoon seasoned salt
¼ teaspoon ground red pepper

Trim meat of all visible fat. Slice beef across grain into ⅛-inch strips; place in nonmetal dish. Blend remaining ingredients; pour over meat, stirring to coat well. Cover; chill at least 8 hours, stirring occasionally. Arrange a third of the meat strips on microwave-safe rack or paper-towel-lined microwave-safe plate; cover with paper towel. Microwave at HIGH five minutes; turn over strips.

Microwave 3 to 3½ more minutes or until meat is well cooked and firm, but not crisp. Repeat with remaining beef strips. Cool completely. Cover and store in refrigerator for up to 1 week.

CINNAMON AND SPICE TRAIL MIX
NABISCO FOODS GROUP

Makes about 5 cups

¼ cup Blue Bonnet® Margarine
¼ cup honey
4 cups Spoon Size® Shredded Wheat
¼ cup sugar
1 teaspoon ground cinnamon

⅛ teaspoon ground nutmeg
½ cup dark seedless raisins
⅓ cup dried apricots, chopped
⅓ cup dried apples, chopped

In large skillet, over medium-high, heat margarine and honey until margarine melts. Stir in cereal, tossing to coat well; cook and stir for 2 minutes until cereal is toasted. Remove from heat; let stand 5 minutes.

In large bowl, combine sugar, cinnamon, and nutmeg; stir in prepared cereal, tossing to coat well. Stir in dried fruit; cool. Store in airtight container.

HOLIDAY TRAIL MIX

DOLE FOOD COMPANY

Makes 11 servings, ½ cup each

1 box (8 ounces) Dole® Chopped Dates
1 cup Dole® Whole Almonds, toasted
1 cup Dole® Raisins

1 cup dried banana chips
1 cup dried apricots
½ cup sunflower seed nuts

Combine all ingredients. Store in closed container in refrigerator. Will keep 2 weeks.

To toast almonds: Preheat oven to 350°F. Place almonds in a shallow pan and bake for 10 minutes. Toasting time will vary depending on the size of the almonds.

BREAKFAST DELIGHTS

GOOD MORNING PUMPKIN PANCAKES
Libby's, Nestlé Food Company
12

PB&J FRENCH TOAST
Best Foods, a division of CPC International Inc.
12

ZUCCHINI-APPLE BREAKFAST CAKE
Nabisco Foods Group
13

FRUIT SWIRL COFFEE CAKE
General Mills, Inc.
14

GOOD MORNING PUMPKIN PANCAKES

LIBBY'S, NESTLE FOOD COMPANY

Makes about 16 pancakes

2 cups biscuit mix
1½ cups (12-ounce can) *undiluted* Carnation® Evaporated Milk
½ cup Libby's® Solid Pack Pumpkin
2 eggs
2 tablespoons firmly packed light brown sugar

2 tablespoons vegetable oil
2 teaspoons ground cinnamon
1 teaspoon ground allspice
1 teaspoon vanilla extract

Combine all ingredients in a medium bowl. Beat until smooth. Pour ¼ to ½ cup of batter onto heated and lightly greased griddle. Cook until edges are dry. Turn; cook until golden. Serve with syrup, honey, or jam.

PB&J FRENCH TOAST

BEST FOODS, A DIVISION OF CPC INTERNATIONAL INC.

Makes 4 sandwiches

8 tablespoons Skippy® Creamy *or* Super Chunk® Peanut Butter
4 tablespoons jelly

8 slices bread
1 egg
¼ cup skim milk

Spread peanut butter and jelly on 4 bread slices; top with remaining 4 slices. In shallow bowl, beat egg with milk. Dip both sides of each sandwich into egg mixture. Cook in greased hot skillet or on griddle over medium heat until browned on both sides.

ZUCCHINI-APPLE BREAKFAST CAKE

NABISCO FOODS GROUP

Makes 24 servings

1¼ cups Nabisco® 100% Bran
1½ cups all-purpose flour
2 teaspoons Davis® Baking Powder
1 teaspoon baking soda
1 teaspoon pumpkin pie spice
1½ cups firmly packed brown sugar
¾ cup Fleischmann's® Margarine, melted

¾ cup Egg Beaters® 99% Real Egg
  Product
2 teaspoons vanilla extract
2 cups shredded zucchini
1 cup chopped apple
Confectioners' Sugar Glaze (see
  below)

Preheat oven to 350°F. Mix bran, flour, baking powder, baking soda, and pumpkin pie spice. With mixer, beat brown sugar, margarine, egg product, and vanilla until smooth. Stir in zucchini, apple, and bran mixture. Spread batter in greased and floured 13-by-9-by-2-inch baking pan. Bake 40 to 45 minutes or until toothpick inserted comes out clean. Cool in pan 10 minutes. Remove from pan; cool on wire rack. Drizzle with Confectioners' Sugar Glaze; cut into squares to serve.

CONFECTIONERS' SUGAR GLAZE

2 teaspoons water

⅓ cup confectioners' sugar

Blend.

FRUIT SWIRL COFFEE CAKE

GENERAL MILLS, INC.

Makes 30 bars or 18 squares

1½ cups sugar
½ cup margarine *or* butter, softened
½ cup shortening
1½ teaspoons baking powder
1 teaspoon vanilla

1 teaspoon almond extract
4 eggs
3 cups Gold Medal® All-Purpose Flour
1 can (21 ounces) cherry, apricot, or
    blueberry pie filling
Glaze (see below)

Preheat oven to 350°F. Generously grease jelly-roll pan, 15½-by-10½-by-1 inch, or 2 square pans, 9-by-9-by-2 inches. Beat sugar, margarine, shortening, baking powder, vanilla, almond extract, and eggs in large bowl on low speed, scraping bowl constantly. Beat 3 minutes on high speed, scraping bowl occasionally. Stir in flour. (Note: If using self-rising flour, omit baking powder.) Spread two-thirds of batter in jelly-roll pan or one-third in each square pan. Spread pie filling over batter. Drop remaining batter by tablespoonfuls onto pie filling.

Bake about 45 minutes or until light brown. While warm, drizzle with Glaze. Cut coffee cake in jelly-roll pan into 2½-by-2-inch bars; cut coffee cake in square pans into 2¾-inch squares.

GLAZE

1 cup confectioners' sugar

1 to 2 tablespoons milk

Mix thoroughly.

BRUNCH DISHES

CHEESY BRUNCH CASSEROLE

Kraft General Foods, Inc.

16

CHEESY VEGETABLE CASSEROLE

Pet Incorporated

16

TOSTADA CASSEROLE

Beatrice Cheese, Inc.

17

MOZZARELLA SAUSAGE AND PEPPER BAKE

Beatrice Cheese, Inc.

17

SPINACH QUICHE

Pet Incorporated

18

MUFFIN QUICHES

Durkee-French Foods

18

MINI ITALIAN QUICHES

Durkee-French Foods

19

BRUNCH QUESADILLAS WITH FRUIT SALSA

Sargento Cheese Company, Inc.

20

CHEESY BRUNCH CASSEROLE

KRAFT GENERAL FOODS, INC.

Makes 8 to 10 servings

18 slices (1 regular loaf) white *or* wheat bread, cubed
1 cup broccoli florets
⅓ cup chopped red bell pepper

2 packages (8 ounces each; 4 cups total) Kraft® Natural Shredded Sharp Cheddar Cheese
8 eggs
3 cups milk
½ cup Parkay® Margarine, melted

Preheat oven to 350°F. In greased 13-by-9-inch baking dish, layer half each of the bread, broccoli, bell pepper, and cheese. Repeat layers. In large bowl, beat eggs. Add milk and margarine, beating until smooth. Pour evenly over casserole. Bake 50 minutes to 1 hour or until golden brown.

Preparation time: 20 minutes   *Cooking time:* 1 hour

CHEESY VEGETABLE CASSEROLE

PET INCORPORATED

Makes 4 servings

2½ cups broccoli florets
2½ cups cauliflower florets
½ cup carrot slices
2 tablespoons butter
1 tablespoon all-purpose flour
1 can (12 fluid ounces) Pet® Evaporated Milk

1 cup (4 ounces) shredded Cheddar cheese
¼ cup Progresso® Italian Style *or* Plain Bread crumbs
¼ cup Progresso® Grated Parmesan Cheese

Steam broccoli, cauliflower, and carrots just until tender. Place in a 1½-quart casserole. In medium saucepan, melt butter. Gradually stir in flour and cook over low heat until mixture is bubbly. Remove from heat and gradually stir in evaporated milk. Cook on medium-high heat until mixture thickens and begins to boil. Remove from heat and stir in Cheddar cheese until melted. Pour cheese sauce over vegetables and stir to mix. Combine bread crumbs and Parmesan cheese; sprinkle over top of vegetables. Place under broiler until top is lightly browned, about 1 to 2 minutes. Serve immediately.

TOSTADA CASSEROLE

BEATRICE CHEESE, INC.

Makes 6 to 8 servings

1 pound lean ground beef
1 cup salsa (mild, medium, or hot)
½ teaspoon ground cumin
Salt to taste
5 green onions, thinly sliced
3 cups (12 ounces) County Line®
   Shredded Taco Cheese
1 can (16 ounces) refried beans

1 can (2¼ ounces) pitted, sliced ripe
   olives, drained
Shredded lettuce
Chopped tomato
Sour cream
Guacamole
Tortilla chips

Preheat oven to 350°F. Lightly grease 3-quart casserole. In skillet, brown beef. Drain any fat. Add salsa, cumin, and salt. Simmer until thick and all liquid has been absorbed. Place meat mixture in casserole. Top with onions, 2 cups cheese, refried beans, olives, and remaining 1 cup cheese. Bake 30 minutes. To serve, spoon each casserole portion on a bed of shredded lettuce and top with chopped tomato, sour cream, and guacamole. Serve with tortilla chips.

   For real convenience, assemble ahead and refrigerate until ready to bake.

MOZZARELLA SAUSAGE AND PEPPER BAKE

BEATRICE CHEESE, INC.

Makes 8 servings

2 tablespoons olive oil
2 green peppers, seeded and thinly sliced
2 cloves garlic, minced
1¼ pounds mild or spicy Italian sausage,
   sliced into 1-inch circles

1 jar (32 ounces) meatless spaghetti
   sauce
1 package (16 ounces) rigatoni *or* ziti,
   cooked and drained
3 cups (12 ounces) County Line®
   Shredded Mozzarella Cheese

Preheat oven to 350°F. In large skillet, heat oil and sauté peppers and garlic until peppers are crisp-tender. Remove and set aside. Sauté sausage circles until brown. Drain any fat. Combine peppers, garlic, sausage, spaghetti sauce, pasta, and 2½ cups cheese in 4-quart casserole. Cover and bake 40 to 45 minutes. Top casserole with remaining ½ cup cheese. Bake, uncovered, only until cheese melts, about 5 minutes.

SPINACH QUICHE

PET INCORPORATED

Makes 6 to 8 servings

3 tablespoons finely chopped onion

2 tablespoons butter

I package (10 ounces) frozen chopped spinach, cooked and drained

I cup (4 ounces) shredded Swiss cheese

¼ cup grated Parmesan cheese

I tablespoon all-purpose flour

I Pet•Ritz® Deep Dish Pie Crust Shell

I ½ cups light cream

3 eggs, slightly beaten

½ teaspoon Worcestershire sauce

I teaspoon salt

¼ teaspoon ground white pepper

¼ teaspoon marjoram leaves

¼ teaspoon basil leaves

Preheat oven and baking sheet to 375°F. In small skillet, sauté onion in butter until translucent; remove from heat and cool slightly. Add spinach, cheese, and flour; spoon into frozen pie crust. Combine remaining ingredients; blend well. Pour egg mixture over spinach mixture. Bake 40 to 45 minutes or until knife inserted in center comes out clean. Let stand 10 minutes before serving.

MUFFIN QUICHES

DURKEE-FRENCH FOODS

Makes 18 muffins

I ½ cups milk

3 large eggs

I ⅓ cups buttermilk baking mix

I cup (4 ounces) shredded Cheddar cheese

I cup shredded zucchini

3 tablespoons French's® Yellow Mustard

I tablespoon instant minced onion

I tablespoon imitation bacon bits

⅛ teaspoon ground nutmeg

Paprika

Preheat oven to 375°F. Beat together milk and eggs. Add remaining ingredients except paprika; stir well to mix. Spoon lightly into greased muffin-pan cups using ¼ cup batter for each. Sprinkle tops with paprika. Bake 20 to 25 minutes or until knife inserted in center comes out clean. Cool in pan 5 minutes; loosen edges with spatula and invert. Serve warm.

MINI ITALIAN QUICHES
DURKEE-FRENCH FOODS

Makes 6 servings, 2 mini quiches each

1 (9-inch) folded refrigerated unbaked
   pie crust
1 cup (4 ounces) shredded mozzarella
   cheese
4 large eggs

1 cup half-and-half
1 tablespoon flour
1 teaspoon Durkee® Italian Seasoning
½ teaspoon Durkee® Garlic Powder
½ teaspoon Durkee® Onion Powder

Preheat oven to 400°F. On lightly floured board, roll dough into 15-inch circle; cut 12 circles from crust using 4-inch cookie cutter (reroll dough if necessary). Grease twelve 2-inch muffin or tart tins with vegetable cooking spray; line tins with pastry. Place on baking sheet. Divide cheese evenly among tins. In medium bowl, combine eggs, half-and-half, flour, and seasonings. Pour egg mixture over cheese, filling tins about three-fourths full. Bake 30 to 40 minutes or until crust is browned. Remove from tins and cool.

VARIATION

Pastry can be placed in 9-inch pie plate. Continue recipe as above. Bake, uncovered, at 400°F for 45 to 50 minutes.

BRUNCH QUESADILLAS WITH FRUIT SALSA

SARGENTO CHEESE COMPANY, INC.

Makes 4 servings

1 pint fresh strawberries, hulled and
  diced
1 fresh ripe Anjou pear, cored and diced
1 tablespoon chopped fresh cilantro
1 tablespoon honey
4 (8-inch) flour tortillas

2 teaspoons light margarine, melted
1 cup (4 ounces) Sargento® Preferred
  Light® Fancy Shredded Mozzarella
  Cheese
2 tablespoons light sour cream for
  garnish

Combine first 4 ingredients to make Fruit Salsa. Set aside. Brush 1 side of each tortilla with melted margarine. Place brushed side down and sprinkle *2 tablespoons* cheese on half of each tortilla. Top with *⅓ cup* salsa (drain and discard any liquid that has formed from the fruit) and remaining 2 tablespoons of cheese. Fold tortilla in half. Grill folded tortillas in a dry preheated frying pan until light golden brown and crisp, about 2 minutes. Turn and brown other side. Remove to a serving plate or platter. Cut each tortilla in half.

Serve with remaining Fruit Salsa and garnish of sour cream. Serve immediately.

EXTRAORDINARY
SANDWICHES

FRUIT OF THE ANCIENTS
The Story of Olives

Growing wildly, the silvery gray olive plant of prehistory was a low, thorny shrub. First cultivated more than five thousand years ago in Egypt for its oil, the plant developed in stature to become a tree, bearing a nearly inedible, hard, yellowish-green fruit. The people of the Nile learned the secrets of extracting oil and pickling the fruit in brine or in a lime mixture to make it edible. One tree provided a family with nutritious food and essential oil for cooking, skin and hair moisturization, and lamp and stove fuel.

According to Greek legend, humans first learned that the olive could be transformed into a savory morsel when a bountiful branch dipped in a river and the salty water leached the fruit's natural bitterness. The gift from Pallas Athene, goddess of wisdom and the arts, became sacred. To destroy an olive tree was deemed a sacrilege. A crown of olive branches became the highest honor the Greek state could bestow. Unbeknownst to the Greeks, the olive tree actually does approach immortality: Two-thousand-year-old trees are still producing fruit today.

The Roman legions brought the olive tree and knowledge of oil extraction and fruit processing to the Mediterranean countries. To this day, the peoples of Greece, Italy, Portugal, and Spain extract the fruity oil to export and use in all their cooking. Even their pastries include the distinctively flavored olive oil.

Sixteenth-century Peruvians and Chileans saw the first olive trees planted in the New World. The original California olive trees are believed to have been planted at the first Franciscan mission in San Diego in 1775; eventually the trees were cultivated throughout California in all twenty-one Franciscan missions.

California's rich soil and sunny climate have proved to be ideal for olive growing and have made the state one of the world's premier growing regions. At first, California olives were grown only for their oil, but olive growers began canning the fruit in the early twentieth century.

A grower-owned cooperative, the Lindsay Ripe Olive Company, was formed in 1916. Now known as Lindsay Olive Growers, this cooperative has become the world's largest canner of ripe olives. Lindsay has developed olive making into a fine art form through its years of experience. The olives that will become green Spanish olives, the type usually stuffed with a red pimiento pepper, and those selected for curing in the distinctive California black ripe style are harvested by hand between mid-September and November. Two different curing processes transform the fruit into the two distinct products.

Savory Pepper-Herb Cheesecake

COURTESY OF SARGENTO CHEESE COMPANY, INC.

Tortilla Pizzas
COURTESY OF DURKEE-FRENCH FOODS

Florentine Crescents
COURTESY OF KRAFT GENERAL FOODS, INC.

Olive batches vary in such qualities as size, ripeness, and sugar content of the fruit. Just as the wine maker uses specialized knowledge to develop grape harvests into fine and consistent wine, the olive maker draws on expertise to consistently bring out exactly the right color, texture, and flavor qualities in the green fruit.

Green Spanish olives are fermented in brine in a manner similar to that used for making a pickle from a cucumber. California black olives receive special treatment indeed. The olive maker determines exactly what degree of curing will purge the natural bitterness, soften the texture, and develop the tantalizing flavor in each batch. Natural air bubbles are filtered through the curing tanks to oxidize the olives, thus changing the California-style "ripe" olive from green to black, the natural color of a fully ripe olive.

The specially cured California black olive is an exquisite and unique ingredient that blends easily in recipes without overpowering other food flavors. For example, California black olives combined with delicately flavored foods such as smoked salmon will not be overwhelming. California black olives are also an excellent food for the diet-conscious individual. The low amount of fat they contain is monounsaturated, the fat that is beneficial to health, and the largest black olive contains only 12 to 13 calories. For these reasons, the fruit of the ancients remains a favorite for visual appeal, taste, and texture in today's light recipes.

NEW ORLEANS MUFFULETTA

LINDSAY INTERNATIONAL, INC.

Makes 6 servings

½ cup Lindsay® Pimiento-Stuffed Green Olives, drained and chopped
½ cup Lindsay® Extra Large Pitted Ripe Olives, drained and chopped
½ cup chopped celery
½ cup chopped, mixed, pickled vegetables
⅓ cup olive *or* salad oil
¼ cup snipped parsley
3 tablespoons lemon juice

1 clove garlic, minced
1 teaspoon dried oregano, crushed
Several dashes freshly ground pepper
1 loaf (1½ pounds) Italian bread
4 ounces thinly sliced Genoa salami
4 ounces sliced provolone *or* mozzarella cheese
4 ounces sliced cappicola *or* fully cooked ham

Combine first 10 ingredients. Cover; chill, tossing several times. Drain, reserving liquid. Cut bread in half horizontally. Remove a ½-inch-thick slice from cut side of bottom. Brush cut sides of remaining bread with reserved liquid. Layer bottom half with salami, cheese, cappicola, and olive mixture. Cover with top half of bread.

REUBEN SANDWICHES

OSCAR MAYER FOODS CORPORATION

Makes 4 sandwiches

1 cup well drained sauerkraut
¼ cup Thousand Island dressing
2 packages (½ pound each) Louis Rich®
    Turkey Pastrami

16 slices sandwich rye bread
8 slices (4 by 4 inches) Swiss cheese
Butter

Combine sauerkraut with dressing. Trim slices of meat to fit bread. To assemble each sandwich, place 1 slice meat (and trimmings) on bread slice, spread with 2 tablespoons sauerkraut mixture, top with cheese slices and another slice of turkey pastrami, and cover with bread. Butter outsides of sandwiches. Grill slowly on both sides until bread is toasted and cheese is melted.

VARIATIONS

Party Reuben: Makes about 8 sandwiches. Use snack rye bread and cut slices of meat and cheese in half. Serve hot or cold.

Oven Reuben: Make 4-at-a-time and serve 4-at-a-time by baking sandwiches open-faced in the oven. Preheat oven to 400°F. Place 4 slices of bread in 9-inch square pan and top each with 2 slices turkey pastrami. Add a layer of drained sauerkraut and top with a cheese slice. Bake 15 minutes.

ZORBA'S POCKET SANDWICH

OSCAR MAYER FOODS CORPORATION

Makes 8 sandwiches

1 medium cucumber, thinly sliced
1 medium onion, thinly sliced
12 pitted ripe olives, sliced
¾ cup low-cal Italian dressing
1 package (8 ounces) Oscar Mayer®
    Cotto Salami

1 package (8 ounces) Oscar Mayer®
    New England Brand Sausage
8 lettuce leaves
4 pita breads (6- to 7-inch diameter),
    cut in half

Combine salad ingredients. Cover; refrigerate at least 1 hour. For each sandwich, place 2 meat slices and 1 lettuce leaf in pita pocket. Add salad mixture.

TURKEY WALDORF PITAS

BEST FOODS, A DIVISION OF CPC INTERNATIONAL INC.

Makes 4 sandwiches

4 loaves (2 ounces each) regular-size
  Sahara® Pita Bread
I cup diced cooked turkey
I apple, diced
⅓ cup sliced celery

¼ cup roasted sunflower seeds (optional)
½ cup Hellmann's® *or* Best Foods®
  Mayonnaise
I teaspoon lemon juice
I teaspoon chopped crystalized ginger
Lettuce leaves

Cut one-third off each pita. Combine turkey, apple, celery, and sunflower seeds. Stir in mayonnaise, lemon juice, and ginger. Spoon into lettuce-lined pitas.

SPORTS FAN'S SOUPER SANDWICH

THOMAS J. LIPTON CO.

Makes about 8 servings

I envelope Lipton® Onion Recipe
  Soup Mix
I container (16 ounces) sour cream
½ cup chopped pitted ripe olives
½ cup chopped sweet pickles
2 loaves unsliced round bread
  (about 9-inch diameter)

Lettuce
1½ pounds thinly sliced
  cooked roast beef
½ pound thinly sliced Swiss cheese
2 tomatoes, sliced
2 green peppers, cut into rings

In medium bowl, combine soup mix, sour cream, olives, and pickles; chill. Cut thin lengthwise slice off top of each loaf of bread; reserve tops. Hollow out center of each loaf, leaving ¼-inch shell. Spread ¾ cup mixture into each shell. Place lettuce on top mixture, lining sides. Evenly layer roast beef, cheese, tomatoes, and green peppers; top with remaining mixture. To serve, replace reserved tops and cut into wedges.

SPECIAL SAN FRANCISCO PITA POCKET

LAWRY'S FOODS, INC.

Makes 8 servings

1 package (10 ounces) frozen chopped spinach
¾ pound lean ground beef
½ pound fresh mushrooms, sliced
½ cup chopped onion
3 tablespoons butter or margarine
¾ teaspoon dill weed

½ teaspoon Lawry's® Seasoned Salt
½ teaspoon Lawry's® Garlic Powder with Parsley
½ teaspoon Lawry's® Seasoned Pepper
2 cups (8 ounces) grated cheese, half Cheddar and half Jack
4 pita breads, cut in half

To microwave: Make slit in spinach package; place package, slit side up, on paper towel. Microwave on HIGH 5 minutes. Remove spinach from package; squeeze liquid from spinach. In microwave-safe pie plate or dish, microwave ground beef on HIGH 6 to 7 minutes, stirring once or twice. Drain fat. In 13-by-9-by-2-inch microwave-safe baking dish, microwave mushrooms, onion, and butter on HIGH 8 to 10 minutes. Stir in seasonings. Microwave on HIGH 3 minutes, stirring once. Stir spinach and cooked ground beef into mushroom-onion mixture. Fold in cheese. Cover with waxed paper and microwave on HIGH 3 minutes. Wrap pita breads loosely in plastic wrap microwave on HIGH 30 seconds to warm. Open pita breads and fill with meat mixture. Serve immediately with fresh fruit.

VARIATION

Substitute ground turkey for ground beef. Microwave on HIGH 4 to 5 minutes, stirring twice.

PARTY PINWHEEL SANDWICHES

THOMAS J. LIPTON CO.

Makes 10 dozen pinwheel sandwiches

1 envelope Lipton® Onion Recipe
   Soup Mix
1 container (16 ounces) sour cream

2 loaves unsliced white *or* pumpernickel
   bread, sliced lengthwise (8 slices each)
Festive Fillings (choose any 2 from
   below)

Blend soup mix with sour cream; chill. Trim crust from bread, flatten bread with rolling pin. Spread 1 filling mixture evenly on 8 slices of bread; roll, starting at narrow end, jelly-roll style. Repeat with remaining filling and bread. Wrap in waxed paper or plastic wrap and chill. To serve, cut into ½-inch slices.

To freeze and thaw: Tightly wrap pinwheels in waxed paper or plastic wrap, then heavy-duty aluminum foil; freeze. To serve, partially thaw frozen rolls; unwrap and cut into ½-inch slices. Continue thawing at room temperature for 1 hour.

FESTIVE FILLINGS

Blue Cheese Walnut Filling: Combine 1 cup sour cream mixture, 2 ounces crumbled blue cheese, and ½ cup finely chopped walnuts.

Fruity Curry Filling: Combine 1 cup sour cream mixture, ¾ teaspoon curry powder, ½ cup raisins, ½ cup finely chopped apple, and 1 tablespoon milk.

Ham and Cheese Filling: Use 1 cup sour cream mixture. Top each prepared slice with 1 thin slice cooked ham, then Swiss or American cheese. Place quartered dill pickle across end of bread; roll up starting at pickle end.

Wine, Cheese, Olive Filling: Combine 1 cup sour cream mixture, ¾ cup shredded Cheddar cheese, and 2 tablespoons red wine. Place 3 ripe olives across one end of each prepared slice; roll starting at olive end.

CALIFORNIA TUNA SANDWICH SPREAD

THOMAS J. LIPTON CO.

Makes about 2½ cups

1 can (6½ ounces) chunk-style tuna, drained and flaked
2 teaspoons lemon juice
2 cups Lipton® California Dip (see below)

Bread slices
Cucumber for garnish
Tomato wedges for garnish
Potato chips for garnish

Blend tuna with lemon juice, then combine with California Dip; chill thoroughly. Spread mixture on bread slices. Garnish sandwiches with cucumber slices, tomato wedges, and potato chips.

CALIFORNIA DIP:

Makes about 2 cups

1 envelope Lipton® Onion Recipe Soup Mix

1 container (16 ounces) sour cream

Blend together.

TUNA BRUSCHETTA

SARGENTO CHEESE COMPANY, INC.

Makes 4 servings

1 cup (4 ounces) Sargento® Preferred Light® Fancy Shredded Mozzarella Cheese
1 can (3½ ounces) water-packed tuna, well drained and flaked
4 plum tomatoes, seeded and chopped

2 tablespoons minced onion
2 teaspoons minced fresh parsley
½ teaspoon dried oregano
4 slices Italian bread (6-by-½-inch each)
2 tablespoons olive oil
2 cloves garlic, halved

Combine, cheese, tuna, tomatoes, onion, parsley, and oregano. Set aside. Brush both sides of bread with olive oil and rub surface with cut side of garlic. In a dry, preheated frying pan, grill bread until light golden brown. Turn and top each toasted surface with one-fourth of the cheese mixture. Continue to grill until cheese melts and bread is golden brown on bottom. Serve immediately.

APPETIZERS

TOASTED ALMOND PARTY SPREAD
Kraft General Foods, Inc.
31

CHUNKY-NUTTY CHICKEN BALL
Pet Incorporated
31

PINEAPPLE-ALMOND CHEESE SPREAD
Dole Food Company
32

CHICKEN LIVER-PIMIENTO SPREAD
Lindsay International, Inc.
32

THE UNDERWOOD STORY
The Story of Red Devil and Canning
33

GREAT BALL OF FIRE
Pet Incorporated
34

HUMMUS-TOPPED PITAS
Lindsay International, Inc.
35

TWO-ALARM MEATBALLS
Durkee-French Foods
35

WARM MUSHROOM & BACON DIP
Thomas J. Lipton Co.
36

BLUSHING SHRIMP DIP
Borden, Inc.
37

JIM BOWIE CAJUN DIP
Beatrice Cheese, Inc.
37

CLASSIC NACHO DIP
Kraft General Foods, Inc.
38

FIESTA DIP
Durkee-French Foods
39

TWO-CHEESE PESTO DIP
Sargento Cheese Company, Inc.
39

SAVORY PEPPER-HERB CHEESECAKE
Sargento Cheese Company, Inc.
40

GUACAMOLE
Thomas J. Lipton Co.
41

GUACAMOLE BITES
Pepperidge Farm, Inc.
41

HOT NACHO BEAN APPETIZER
Pet Incorporated
42

TOASTED ALMOND PARTY SPREAD

KRAFT GENERAL FOODS, INC.

Makes 2⅓ cups

1 package (8 ounces) Philadelphia® Brand Cream Cheese, softened
1½ cups (6 ounces) shredded Casino® Natural Swiss Cheese
⅓ cup Miracle Whip® Salad Dressing
⅓ cup sliced almonds, toasted

2 tablespoons chopped green onion
⅛ teaspoon ground nutmeg
⅛ teaspoon pepper
Additional sliced almonds, toasted, for garnish (optional)

Preheat oven to 350°F. Combine all ingredients; mix well. Spread mixture into 9-inch pie plate or quiche dish. Bake 15 minutes, stirring after 8 minutes. Garnish with additional toasted sliced almonds, if desired.

Serve with assorted crackers or toasted bread cut-outs.

Preparation time: 10 minutes   *Cooking time:* 15 minutes

VARIATION

Omit nutmeg and pepper.

To toast almonds: Preheat oven to 350°F. Place almonds in a shallow pan and bake for 10 minutes. Toasting time will vary depending on the size of the almonds.

CHUNKY-NUTTY CHICKEN BALL

PET INCORPORATED

Makes 1 ball

1 can (4¼ ounces) Underwood® Chunky Chicken Spread
1 package (3 ounces) cream cheese, softened

½ cup raisins
½ cup chopped celery
½ cup chopped pecans

In small bowl, combine chicken spread, cream cheese, raisins, and celery. Form into ball and roll in finely chopped pecans. Chill.

PINEAPPLE-ALMOND CHEESE SPREAD

DOLE FOOD COMPANY

Makes 4 cups

1 package (8 ounces) cream cheese, softened
4 cups shredded sharp Cheddar cheese
½ cup mayonnaise
1 tablespoon soy sauce
2 cans (8 ounces each) Dole® Crushed Pineapple, drained
1 cup chopped toasted Dole® Almonds
½ cup finely chopped green bell pepper
¼ cup minced green onion *or* chives
Celery stalks
Assorted crackers

Beat together cream cheese, Cheddar cheese, mayonnaise, and soy sauce until smooth. Stir in pineapple, almonds, bell pepper, and green onion. Use to stuff celery stalks or heap in a bowl surrounded by crackers, with a knife for spreading. Serve at room temperature.

CHICKEN LIVER-PIMIENTO SPREAD

LINDSAY INTERNATIONAL, INC.

Makes about 2 cups

½ pound chicken livers, finely chopped
2 tablespoons chopped onion
1 tablespoon butter *or* margarine
1 can (2.25 ounces; ½ cup) Lindsay® Sliced Ripe Olives, drained
2 hard-cooked eggs, finely chopped
¼ cup chopped pimiento
¼ cup plain yogurt
1 teaspoon Dijon mustard
¼ teaspoon garlic salt
Several dashes Worcestershire sauce
Snipped parsley
Party rye bread or crackers

Cook chicken livers and onion in butter about 5 minutes or until livers just begin to lose their pink color. Remove from heat; drain. In a mixing bowl, combine the cooked livers and onion, olives, eggs, pimiento, yogurt, mustard, garlic salt, and Worcestershire sauce. Cover the mixture and chill at least 3 hours. Sprinkle with snipped parsley just before serving. Serve spread with party rye bread or crackers.

THE UNDERWOOD STORY
The Story of Red Devil and Canning

America's oldest registered trademark, a thick-set red devil with cloven hooves, first glowered from an Underwood can label in 1867. Over the years the figure has evolved into a slimmed-down, smiling-and-dancing devil wearing slippers and waving a pitchfork.

UNDER🔱WOOD

Like the devil, William Underwood's canned-food business has changed dramatically. Underwood opened his first shop doors on Boston's bustling Russian Wharf in 1822 to sell his preserved and canned fruits, meats, condiments, and other delicacies. His biggest challenge was overcoming the housewife's suspicion of the tin canister.

The canning industry had begun only thirteen years earlier when an obscure French confectioner, chemist, or cook named Francois or Nicolas Appert—historical records differ—won a 12,000-franc prize awarded by Napoleon Bonaparte for inventing a process for preserving foodstuffs needed by Napoleon's troops on the march. After fifteen years of persistently experimenting with glass that only shattered, Appert had finally produced a successful method for preserving food by heating it inside hermetically sealed jars. Using this same method, an Englishman, Bryan Donkin, obtained a patent in 1810 for preserving foodstuffs in tin canisters.

Along with the discoveries of fire, agriculture, and the wheel, canning is one of humankind's greatest breakthroughs. It has alleviated our former dependence on the variable annual harvest, which all too regularly meant famine and starvation. Before canning, people carried cows, goats, chickens, sheep, pigs, and a menagerie of other farm animals in cages and pens aboard ships to provide fresh milk and meat.

Until Louis Pasteur's findings regarding microorganisms more than half a century later, no one understood that canning worked because the extreme heat used in the process killed the bacteria that caused spoilage. Hence, canning methods were inconsistent. Some food producers used quick techniques that resulted in spoilage. William Underwood insisted on using a slow and careful cooking process, however, because he knew this would ensure that all of his fine products would be safe to use.

Underwood's reputation for healthy and tasty products spread. People tried new foods, and their health improved substantially. Diets that had consisted mostly of meat, cheese, and alcohol now included fruits, vegetables, and milk, with their additional nutritive values.

By the mid-1800s, Underwood's canned seafood, meats, fruits, and vegetables were being traded in the West Indies, South America, the Far East, and the countries of the Mediterranean. Clipper ships carried tins of canned meat and fruit to the gold-seeking forty-niners. It is said that the first California gold nugget smuggled east was hidden in an empty Underwood salmon can.

Business took a turn in the late 1860s when Underwood was severed from its large Southern market by the Civil War. Hoping to capture more of the Northern market, Underwood used a secret family recipe, a lively combination of spices, to season canned meats in a process called deviling. The recipe popularized a new lunchtime food, the sandwich, and remains a secret to this day.

William Lyman, William Underwood's grandson, developed the Underwood tradition of food-preservation safety further when he worked with biologist Samuel Prescott of the Massachusetts Institute of Technology to refine the food-sterilization process. The perfected process transformed food processing from an art into an exacting science and influenced the entire industry.

Underwood joined the Pet Inc. family of products in 1982.

GREAT BALL OF FIRE

PET INCORPORATED

Makes one 2-cup cheese ball

1 cup (4 ounces) shredded Cheddar cheese
1 package (3 ounces) cream cheese, softened
1 can (4¼ ounces) Underwood® Deviled Ham

2 tablespoons finely chopped scallions
3 tablespoons Old El Paso® Chopped Green Chilies
⅓ cup chopped walnuts
Crackers

In small bowl, combine Cheddar cheese, cream cheese, ham, scallions, and chilies; mix well. Shape mixture into a ball. Roll in chopped nuts. Wrap in plastic wrap; chill. Remove from refrigerator to soften slightly before serving. Serve with crackers.

HUMMUS-TOPPED PITAS

LINDSAY INTERNATIONAL, INC.

Makes 8 appetizers

1 can (15 ounces) garbanzo beans
3 tablespoons lemon juice
Several dashes hot pepper sauce
1/4 cup chopped onion
1 clove garlic, minced
2 teaspoons cooking oil
1/2 cup sesame seed, toasted
1/4 cup tahini (sesame seed paste)

1/4 cup chopped green pepper
4 small pita-bread rounds
1 1/2 cups shredded lettuce
1 1/2 cups (6 ounces) crumbled feta cheese
1 medium tomato, chopped
1 can (2.25 ounces; 1/2 cup) Lindsay® Sliced
 Ripe Olives, drained

Preheat oven to 350°F. Drain beans, reserving 3 tablespoons liquid. Place beans, liquid, lemon juice, and pepper sauce in a blender container or food processor; cover and blend or process until pureed. Cook onion and garlic in oil until tender. Stir together bean mixture, onion mixture, sesame seed, tahini, and green pepper. Split pita rounds horizontally; bake 5 minutes. Top with lettuce and 1/2 cup bean mixture. Add cheese, tomato, and olives.

TWO-ALARM MEATBALLS

DURKEE-FRENCH FOODS

Makes about 30 meatballs

1 pound ground beef
1 egg
1/4 cup dried breadcrumbs
1/2 teaspoon Durkee® Garlic Salt
2 tablespoons Durkee® RedHot Cayenne
 Pepper Sauce

2 tablespoons French's® Worcestershire
 Sauce
1 tablespoon butter
1 tablespoon cornstarch
1/2 cup water
2 tablespoons ketchup

Preheat oven to 375°F. Combine ground beef, egg, breadcrumbs, garlic salt, *1 1/2 teaspoons* pepper sauce, and *1 tablespoon* Worcestershire sauce. Mix thoroughly and shape into 1-inch meatballs. Bake 15 minutes. In saucepan, melt butter; blend in cornstarch. Add water, ketchup, *1 1/2 tablespoons* pepper sauce, and *1 tablespoon* Worcestershire sauce. Simmer until thickened. Add meatballs and heat through.

WARM MUSHROOM & BACON DIP

THOMAS J. LIPTON CO.

Makes about 2 cups

6 slices bacon
½ pound mushrooms, thinly sliced
2 medium cloves garlic, finely chopped
1 envelope Lipton® Golden Onion Recipe Soup Mix
⅛ teaspoon pepper
1 package (8 ounces) cream cheese, softened

½ pint (8 ounces) sour cream
Assorted sliced breads or crackers
Parsley for garnish (optional)
Additional mushrooms for garnish (optional)
Additional bacon for garnish (optional)

In medium skillet, cook bacon; remove and crumble. Reserve 2½ tablespoons drippings. Add mushrooms and garlic to reserved drippings and cook over medium heat, stirring occasionally, 5 minutes or until mushrooms are tender and liquid is almost evaporated. Add soup mix and pepper, then cream cheese; combine thoroughly. Simmer, stirring constantly, until cream cheese is melted. Stir in sour cream and bacon; heat through. Garnish, if desired, with parsley and additional mushrooms and bacon. Serve with breads.

To microwave: In 2-quart casserole, arrange bacon; loosely cover with paper towel. Microwave at HIGH (100% Power) 6 minutes or until done, turning casserole once; remove bacon and crumble. Reserve 2½ tablespoons drippings. Add mushrooms and garlic to reserved drippings and microwave, uncovered, 2 minutes or until mushrooms are tender, stirring once. Add soup mix and pepper, then cream cheese; combine thoroughly. Decrease heat to MEDIUM (50% Power) and microwave, uncovered, stirring frequently, 3 minutes or until cream cheese is melted. Stir in sour cream and bacon. Microwave, uncovered, at MEDIUM 3 minutes or until heated through, stirring once. Garnish and serve as above.

VARIATION

Also terrific with Lipton® Onion Recipe Soup Mix.

BLUSHING SHRIMP DIP

BORDEN, INC.

Makes about 2½ cups

1 package (3 ounces) cream cheese, softened
¼ cup mayonnaise *or* salad dressing
1 container (8 ounces) Borden® *or* Meadow Gold® Sour Cream
½ cup Bennett's® Cocktail Sauce

1 can (4¼ ounces) Orleans® Shrimp, drained and soaked as label directs
2 tablespoons chopped green onion
1 teaspoon ReaLemon® Lemon Juice from Concentrate

In small mixer bowl, beat cheese and mayonnaise until smooth. Stir in remaining ingredients. Chill.

Serve with assorted fresh vegetables or potato chips. Refrigerate leftovers.

JIM BOWIE CAJUN DIP

BEATRICE CHEESE, INC.

Makes 10 to 12 servings

¼ cup butter *or* margarine
1 cup chopped onion
2 cloves garlic, minced
1 can mushroom soup
1 package (12 ounces) package small frozen shrimp
8 ounces (2 cups) County Line® Cheddar Cheese, shredded

1 can (4 ounces) chopped mushrooms
2 packages (10 ounces each) frozen chopped broccoli
1 tablespoon hot pepper sauce
1 teaspoon salt
1 cup cashews *or* pecans, chopped
1 can (6 ounces) water chestnuts, sliced

Melt butter in 3-quart saucepan. Sauté onion and garlic until tender; add soup, shrimp, cheese, mushrooms, broccoli, pepper sauce, salt, nuts, and water chestnuts. Cook over low heat for 15 minutes.

Serve in chafing dish or other heated server with Melba toast, toasted bread, or crackers.

VARIATION

Substitute horseradish for hot pepper sauce for a different taste. If famished guests eat too fast, melt another stick of butter and another package of County Line® Cheddar Cheese.

CLASSIC NACHO DIP

KRAFT GENERAL FOODS, INC.

Makes 3 cups

½ cup chopped onion
2 tablespoons Parkay® Margarine
1 pound Velveeta® Pasteurized Process
  Cheese Spread, cubed

1 jar (8 ounces) salsa
2 tablespoons chopped cilantro

Sauté onions in margarine, reduce heat to low. Add remaining ingredients; stir until cheese spread is melted. Serve hot with tortilla chips or vegetable dippers, if desired.

To microwave: Microwave onions and margarine in 1½-quart bowl on HIGH 1½ minutes or until tender. Add remaining ingredients; mix well. Microwave on HIGH 5 minutes or until thoroughly heated, stirring after 3 minutes. Serve hot with tortilla chips or vegetable dippers, if desired.

VARIATIONS

Substitute 1 can (14½ ounces) tomatoes, chopped and drained, for salsa.

Substitute 1 can (10 ounces) tomatoes and green chilies, chopped, drained, for salsa.

Substitute Velveeta® Mexican Pasteurized Process Cheese Spread with Jalapeño pepper, cubed, for Velveeta® Pasteurized Process Cheese Spread.

Substitute Velveeta® Light Pasteurized Process Cheese Spread, cubed, for Velveeta® Pasteurized Process Cheese Spread.

Substitute Parkay® Soft Diet Reduced-Calorie Margarine for Parkay® Margarine.

Preparation time: 10 minutes

FIESTA DIP

DURKEE-FRENCH FOODS

Makes about 2 cups

2 packages (8 ounces *each*) cream
  cheese, softened
1 package (1¼ ounces) French's® Taco
  Seasoning Mix
1 tablespoon Durkee® RedHot Cayenne
  Pepper Sauce
¼ cup milk

Shredded lettuce
Green onion, sliced
Ripe olives, sliced
Tomato, chopped
Cheese, shredded
Tortilla chips

Beat together cream cheese, taco seasoning mix, pepper sauce, and milk in food processor or electric mixer. Spoon dip into small serving bowl; place on platter. Surround with lettuce and sprinkle generously with green onion, ripe olives, tomato, and cheese. Serve with tortilla chips.

TWO-CHEESE PESTO DIP

SARGENTO CHEESE COMPANY, INC.

Makes 2 cups

1 cup light sour cream
½ cup light mayonnaise
½ cup finely chopped fresh parsley
¼ cup finely chopped walnuts
1 clove garlic, minced
1½ teaspoons dried basil *or* 3 tablespoons
  fresh minced basil

½ cup (2 ounces) Sargento® Preferred
  Light® Fancy Shredded Mozzarella
  Cheese
2 tablespoons Sargento® Grated
  Parmesan Cheese

Combine all ingredients. Cover and refrigerate several hours or overnight. Serve with assorted fresh vegetable dippers.

SAVORY PEPPER-HERB CHEESECAKE

SARGENTO CHEESE COMPANY, INC.

Makes 10 servings

CRUST

1¼ cups fresh dark rye *or* pumpernickel breadcrumbs (about 2 slices, processed in blender or food processor)

3 tablespoons melted margarine

FILLING

1 container (15 ounces) Sargento® Light Ricotta Cheese

½ cup half-and-half

2 tablespoons flour

2 eggs

⅓ cup chopped mixed fresh herbs (such as basil, mint, tarragon, rosemary, thyme, oregano, and parsley)

¼ cup chopped fresh chives *or* green onion tops

1½ teaspoons finely shredded lemon peel

½ teaspoon cracked black pepper

¾ teaspoon salt

Preheat oven to 350°F. Lightly grease sides of 8- or 9-inch springform pan. Combine crust ingredients; press evenly over bottom of pan. Chill while preparing filling.

In bowl of electric mixer, combine ricotta cheese, half-and-half, and flour; blend until smooth. Add eggs, 1 at a time; blend until smooth. Blend in fresh herbs, chives, lemon peel, pepper, and salt. Pour into crust; bake 30 to 35 minutes or until center is just set. Remove to wire cooling rack; cool to room temperature.

GUACAMOLE

THOMAS J. LIPTON CO.

Makes about 2½ cups

1 cup Lipton® California Dip (see below)
1 medium avocado, mashed
1 medium tomato, chopped
1 can (4 ounces) chopped green chilies,
   drained

¼ teaspoon garlic powder
⅛ teaspoon hot pepper sauce
2 tablespoons chopped cilantro

In medium bowl, blend all ingredients; cover and chill.

CALIFORNIA DIP

Makes about 2 cups

1 envelope Lipton® Onion Recipe
   Soup Mix

1 container (16 ounces) sour cream

Blend together and chill.

GUACAMOLE BITES

PEPPERIDGE FARM, INC.

Makes 24 hors d'oeuvres

1 package (9½ ounces) Pepperidge Farm®
   Frozen Mini Puff Pastry Shells
1 medium ripe avocado, peeled, pitted,
   and cubed
⅓ cup mayonnaise
1 tablespoon lime juice
1¼ teaspoons minced garlic

¾ teaspoon chili powder
½ teaspoon salt
⅓ cup canned green chilies, minced
Dash cayenne pepper *or* Tabasco sauce
Cucumber or tomato, finely chopped,
   for garnish

Prepare pastry shells according to package directions.

    Coarsely mash avocado. Mix with mayonnaise, lime juice, garlic, chili powder, salt, green chilies, and cayenne pepper. Spoon avocado mixture into pastry shells, mounding high. Garnish with cucumber or tomato. Serve cold.

HOT NACHO BEAN APPETIZER

PET INCORPORATED

Makes appetizers for 6 to 8 people

1 box (7½ ounces) Old El Paso® Nachips Tortilla Chips

3 cups (12 ounces) shredded Cheddar cheese

1 can (16 ounces) Old El Paso® Refried Beans

1 jar (16 ounces) Old El Paso® Thick 'n Chunky Salsa, drained

1 cup sour cream

1 cup guacamole

1 medium tomato, chopped, for garnish

½ cup sliced ripe olives, for garnish

Preheat oven to 350°F. On large ovenproof platter, arrange half of the chips; top with 1½ cups cheese; repeat layers. Place platter in oven for 10 minutes or until cheese is melted; remove platter from oven. Meanwhile, in a saucepan, combine beans and salsa; heat until steaming. Pour bean mixture into a shallow 1½-quart bowl. Spoon sour cream on half of bean mixture. Spoon guacamole on remaining half of bean mixture. Garnish with chopped tomatoes and sliced olives. Dip hot nachos into bean mixture.

To microwave: On a microwave-safe platter, assemble chips and cheese as directed above and microwave on HIGH 4 minutes, rotating platter one-quarter turn every minute. In a shallow 1½-quart microwave-safe bowl, microwave beans and salsa on HIGH 2 minutes, stirring once. Continue as above.

DELUXE NACHO PLATTER

THOMAS J. LIPTON CO.

Makes about 8 servings

2 tablespoons butter *or* margarine
½ cup chopped onion
½ cup chopped green pepper
2 cups water
1 package Lipton® Rice & Sauce—
   Spanish
½ teaspoon ground cumin (optional)
2 cups (about 8 ounces) shredded
   Cheddar cheese

1 can (4 ounces) chopped green chilies,
   drained
1 bag (7 ounces) corn tortilla chips
1 cup chopped tomato
½ cup sliced pitted ripe olives
Chili peppers for garnish (optional)
Avocado, sliced, for garnish (optional)
Sour cream for garnish (optional)
Fresh cilantro for garnish (optional)
Additional cheese for garnish (optional)

In medium saucepan, melt butter and cook onion with green pepper over medium-high heat, stirring occasionally, 3 minutes or until tender. Stir in water, Rice & Spanish Sauce, and cumin, and bring to a boil. Reduce heat and simmer, stirring occasionally, 10 minutes or until rice is tender. Stir in 1 cup cheese and chilies until cheese is melted; let cool slightly.

In large, round, shallow, broilerproof baking dish or pie plate, layer half of the chips, rice mixture, tomato, olives, and ½ cup cheese; repeat layering, ending with remaining cheese. Broil 1 minute or until cheese is melted. Garnish, if desired, with chili peppers, sliced avocado, sour cream, fresh cilantro, and additional cheese.

To microwave: In 2-quart microwave-safe round casserole, microwave butter, onion and green pepper, uncovered at HIGH (100% Power) 3 minutes. Stir in water, Rice & Spanish Sauce, and cumin; microwave 14 minutes or until rice is tender. Stir in 1 cup cheese and chilies. Let stand, covered, 5 minutes. In glass pie plate or on 9- or 10-inch glass plate, layer nachos as above. Microwave 2 minutes or until cheese is melted, turning plate once. Garnish as above.

TORTILLA PIZZAS

DURKEE-FRENCH FOODS

Makes 32 wedges

3 tablespoons butter *or* margarine,
  softened
4 (10-inch) flour tortillas
2 cups (8 ounces) shredded mozzarella
  or Monterey Jack cheese

¼ cup chopped green onions
1 tablespoon Durkee® RedHot Cayenne
  Pepper Sauce (or more, to taste)

Preheat oven to 400°F. Lightly butter the top side of each tortilla and arrange on an ungreased baking sheet. Toast in oven for 5 minutes or until lightly golden. In a small bowl, combine cheese, onions, and pepper sauce; sprinkle on each tortilla. Broil 5 minutes or until cheese is bubbly. Using a pizza cutter, cut tortilla into 8 wedges.

PEPPERONI PIZZA HORS D'OEUVRE

BEST FOODS, A DIVISION OF CPC INTERNATIONAL INC.

Makes 32 hors d'oeuvre

4 Thomas'® English Muffins
1 can (10¼ ounces) marinara sauce

1 package (4 ounces) shredded
  mozzarella cheese
1 package (4 ounces) sliced pepperoni

Split English muffins by scoring with tines of fork and gently pull apart. Toast. Spread sauce on 8 muffin halves. Sprinkle with cheese and arrange 4 pepperoni slices on each muffin half. Broil 4 to 5 inches from source of heat 2 to 3 minutes or until cheese bubbles and browns. Cut each muffin into 4 wedges.

FLORENTINE CRESCENTS

KRAFT GENERAL FOODS, INC.

Makes 32 appetizers

1 package (10 ounces) Birds Eye®
Chopped Spinach, thawed and well
drained
1 cup (4 ounces) Casino® Shredded
Natural Swiss Cheese

½ cup (2 ounces) Kraft® Grated Parmesan
Cheese
½ cup Miracle Whip® Salad Dressing
¼ teaspoon ground nutmeg
2 cans (8 ounces each) refrigerated quick
crescent dinner rolls

Preheat oven to 375°F. Mix spinach, cheese, salad dressing, and nutmeg until well
blended. Unroll dough; separate into 16 triangles. Cut each triangle lengthwise,
forming 32 triangles. Spread each triangle with 1 rounded teaspoonful of spinach
mixture. Roll up, starting at wide end. Place on greased cookie sheet. Bake 11 to
13 minutes or until golden brown.

Preparation time: 15 minutes   *Cooking time:* 13 minutes per batch

GOLDEN HAM PUFFS

BEATRICE CHEESE, INC.

Makes 24 rounds or 48 quarters

1 cup ground cooked ham
2 teaspoons prepared mustard
1 teaspoon horseradish sauce
¼ cup mayonnaise
1 teaspoon grated onion
1 teaspoon baking powder

2½ cups grated County Line® Cheddar
Cheese
1 egg, beaten
1 teaspoon grated onion
1 teaspoon baking powder
12 slices bread

In small bowl, stir together ham, mustard, horseradish sauce, mayonnaise, onion,
and baking powder. In another small bowl, stir together cheese, egg, onion, and
baking powder. Set aside. Toast 12 slices of bread and cut into 24 rounds with 1½-
inch food cutter, or cut crusts off bread and quarter. Spread ham mixture onto
bread rounds, then cheese mixture. Place on metal baking pan under broiler until
mixture puffs up and turns slightly brown, about 5 minutes.

PATÉ MAISON

LINDSAY INTERNATIONAL, INC.

Makes 1 loaf

½ turkey breast (2 pounds), skinned and boned
3 ounces pork fat or salt pork, cut up
2 beaten eggs
⅓ cup dry white wine
¼ cup brandy
4 teaspoons vinegar
¾ teaspoon salt
½ teaspoon dried thyme, crushed

½ teaspoon dried basil, crushed
¼ teaspoon dried savory, crushed
⅛ teaspoon pepper
¾ pound ground pork
¾ pound ground veal
4 slices bacon
½ cup Lindsay® Medium Pitted Ripe Olives, drained
3 or 4 bay leaves

Preheat oven to 350°F. Cut strips of turkey to make 1½ cups of meat; set aside. Grind remaining turkey and pork fat or salt pork through fine blade of food grinder or in a food processor. Combine eggs, wine, brandy, vinegar, salt, thyme, basil, savory, and pepper. Add ground-turkey mixture, pork, and veal; mix well. Lay bacon crosswise in bottom and up sides of 9-by-5-by-3-inch loaf pan. Press in half of the ground-meat mixture; arrange turkey strips and olives atop. Spoon in remaining ground-meat mixture. Top with bay leaves. Cover with foil. Bake about 1¾ hours. Remove from oven. Drain off fat; replace foil. Place the bottom of another 9-by-5-by-3-inch pan atop the hot loaf. Press very firmly to compact mixture; fill the empty pan with dry beans. Chill overnight. Remove bay leaves. Turn the pâté onto a serving plate and slice.

FRUIT OF KINGS
The Story of Pineapple and James Dole

The New World gold that Columbus discovered in Guadeloupe in 1493 was a pineapple: a fragrant, golden fruit shaped like a pine cone with a beautiful, spiny crown. The fruit and plant proved impossible to ship unspoiled on the long voyage back to Spain. Little more than a century later, living plants or shoots were successfully transported to Asia. In 1640 the emperor of China sent Oliver Cromwell pineapple plants through the East India Company.

The rare pineapple became highly prized in the Old World during the seventeenth century. Grown in hothouses at great expense, they adorned the sumptuous banquet tables of the elite and were considered a status symbol. The Spanish copied the West Indies natives, who put pineapples and pineapple tops near the entrances of their huts as welcome signs, by carving pineapple motifs above their doorways and on their gateposts. Caricaturists used pineapple art to symbolize the excesses of high living during the Napoleonic wars.

In the 1880s, a sea captain brought a variety of pineapple, the Smooth Cayenne, from Florida for cultivation in Hawaii. In 1899, James Dole, a recent Harvard graduate, arrived on the islands at this fortuitous time to seek adventure and fortune. At first, he wasn't quite certain how he would do this, but he soon proposed to "extend the market for the Hawaiian Pineapple into every grocery store in the United States."

There were many detractors of Dole's pioneering efforts. Sugar was the crop of Hawaii. Most certainly, the pineapple fruit couldn't withstand long ocean voyages.

Determined, Dole started with several hundred plants on sixty acres north of Honolulu. At Wahiawa he built his first cannery to preserve the fruit, then convinced the American Can Company to build a manufacturing plant nearby to save the cost of shipping cans. A young Dole engineer, Henry Ginaca, cut production costs further by inventing a machine to peel, core, and cut flawless pineapple cylinders at the rate of one hundred per minute.

By 1922 Dole had purchased the island of Lanai for $1.1 million. Lanai was barren except for the five-foot cacti Dole pushed over to make room for fields and roads. He tapped into underground water and built a dry dock for shipping pineapple to his canning facilities in Honolulu. Lanai City, with houses, stores, schools, and a hospital, was developed for the labor pool.

To familiarize Americans with canned pineapple, Dole's first ads proclaimed, "It Cuts With a Spoon—Like A Peach." Two company engineers discovered the process for extracting tangy pineapple juice in 1934, just in time for mixing with post-Prohibition gin.

Dole died in Hawaii in 1958, leaving behind his complete organization to place the rare and exotic fruit of Old World courts on the dining tables of every American household.

ALOHA CHICKEN WINGS
DOLE FOOD COMPANY

Makes 25 servings, 2 pieces each

25 chicken wings
3 tablespoons cider vinegar
2 tablespoons garlic salt
1 tablespoon onion powder
1 teaspoon ground ginger

1 teaspoon paprika
1 can (20 ounces) Dole® Crushed
   Pineapple
1 cup ketchup
¼ cup brown sugar, packed
¼ cup soy sauce

Preheat oven to 400°F. Have butcher cut wings at joints into 3 pieces. Discard bony end of wing tip or reserve for another use (such as in soup). Arrange remaining chicken parts in single layer in well-oiled baking pans. Prick skin with fork. Combine vinegar, garlic salt, onion powder, ginger, and paprika to make a baste; brush over chicken. Bake 30 minutes. Turn once. Combine pineapple and juice with ketchup, brown sugar, and soy sauce. Spoon sauce over wings. Continue roasting 15 minutes more. Turn wings; spoon on more sauce. Roast 15 minutes more, or until done. Remove wings to serving platter. Serve immediately or refrigerate until serving time. Wings may be reheated in oven or over hot coals on a grill.

BUFFALO WINGS

THOMAS J. LIPTON CO.

Makes 24 wings

24 chicken wings (about 4 pounds)
1 envelope Lipton® Golden Onion
   Recipe Soup Mix
½ cup Imperial® Margarine, melted
2 tablespoons white vinegar
2 tablespoons water

2 cloves garlic
1½ to 2 teaspoons ground red pepper
1 teaspoon ground cumin
1 cup Wish-Bone® Chunky Blue Cheese
   Dressing
Celery sticks (optional)

Cut tips off chicken wings (save tips for soup). Halve remaining chicken wings at joint.

In food processor or blender, process soup mix, margarine, vinegar, water, garlic, pepper, and cumin until blended; set aside.

Broil chicken 12 minutes or until brown, turning after 6 minutes. Brush with half of the soup mixture, then broil 2 minutes or until crisp. Turn, then brush with remaining soup mixture and broil an additional minute. Serve with dressing and, if desired, celery sticks.

VARIATION

Substitute Lipton® Onion Recipe Soup Mix for Lipton® Golden Onion Recipe Soup Mix.

BREADS & MUFFINS

BLACK BREAD
McCormick & Company, Inc.
52

PEANUT BUTTER HEALTH BREAD
Best Foods, a division of
CPC International Inc.
53

PINEAPPLE-ORANGE WALNUT BREAD
Dole Food Company
53

PIZZA BREAD
Lindsay International, Inc.
54

SILO BREAD
Beatrice Cheese, Inc.
55

MEXICAN HOT PEPPER BREAD
Kellogg Company
56

WHEAT GERM BISCUITS
Nestlé Food Company
56

BRAN-RAISIN MUFFINS
Nestlé Food Company
57

APPLE STREUSEL MUFFINS
Libby's, Nestlé Food Company
58

APPLE-RAISIN BRAN MUFFINS
Nabisco Foods Group
59

APPLESAUCE CHEDDAR MUFFINS
Sargento Cheese Company, Inc.
59

PINEAPPLE CARROT RAISIN MUFFINS
Dole Food Company
60

LEMON POPPY SEED MUFFINS
Borden, Inc.
60

BANANA MUFFINS
Kellogg Company
61

PEACHY BRAN MUFFINS
Kellogg Company
61

PEANUT BUTTER CEREAL MUFFINS
Best Foods, a division of
CPC International Inc.
62

ORANGE BRAN MUFFINS
Best Foods, a division of
CPC International Inc.
62

BRAN BATTER ROLLS
Kellogg Company
63

BLACK BREAD

MCCORMICK & COMPANY, INC.

Makes 2 loaves

½ cup cornmeal
2 cups water
¼ cup butter, cut in pieces
1 ounce unsweetened chocolate
½ cup dark molasses
1½ teaspoons salt

2 tablespoons McCormick/Schilling®
  Caraway Seed
2 teaspoons instant coffee
¼ cup lukewarm water
1 package (¼ ounce) active dry yeast
5½ cups flour

Preheat oven to 350°F. In saucepan, combine cornmeal and water. Cook, stirring, over medium heat until mixture comes to a boil. Simmer 1 minute. Remove from heat. Add next 6 ingredients. Stir well. Cool to lukewarm. Combine lukewarm water and yeast. Let stand 5 minutes. Stir into cornmeal mixture. Beat in 4½ cups flour, ½ cup at a time. Place dough on well-floured surface and knead in remaining flour. Continue kneading until dough is smooth and elastic, about 5 minutes. Butter inside of large bowl. Place dough in bowl. Turn dough until entire surface is lightly buttered. Cover with towel. Set in warm, draft-free place and let rise 1½ hours, or until double in size. Punch dough down. Knead 2 minutes on floured surface. Divide dough in half and shape each half into small loaf. Place each in a buttered 2¼-by-3½-by-7½-inch loaf pan. Cover with towel and let rise 40 minutes. Bake 1 hour or until loaves shrink away from sides of pan. Cool on wire racks.

PEANUT BUTTER HEALTH BREAD

BEST FOODS, A DIVISION OF CPC INTERNATIONAL INC.

Makes 1 loaf

2 cups flour
I cup quick oats
I tablespoon baking powder
I teaspoon salt
I cup Skippy® Creamy *or* Super Chunk®
   Peanut Butter

¾ cup firmly packed brown sugar
I egg
1⅔ cups milk
I cup raisins

Preheat oven to 350°F. In medium bowl, stir flour, oats, baking powder, and salt. In large bowl with mixer at medium speed, beat peanut butter and brown sugar until smooth. Beat in egg. Gradually add milk. With mixer at low speed, beat in dry ingredients until smooth. Stir in raisins. Pour into greased 9-by-5-by-3-inch loaf pan. Bake 70 to 75 minutes or until toothpick inserted in center comes out clean. Cool in pan 10 minutes. Remove and cool completely on wire rack.

PINEAPPLE-ORANGE WALNUT BREAD

DOLE FOOD COMPANY

Makes 1 loaf, 28 servings

I cup walnut pieces
2 cups flour
I teaspoon baking powder
I teaspoon baking soda
¼ teaspoon salt
¾ cup sugar

¼ cup margarine
I egg
Zest and juice from I Dole® Orange
I can (8¼ ounces) Dole® Crushed
   Pineapple, undrained
I cup Dole® Raisins

Preheat oven to 350°F. Pulverize walnuts in blender. Combine nuts with flour, baking powder, baking soda, and salt. Beat sugar and margarine until light and fluffy. Beat in egg, 1 tablespoon orange zest, and ¼ cup orange juice. Stir in one third flour mixture until blended. Stir in one half undrained pineapple. Repeat, ending with flour. Stir in raisins. Pour batter into greased 9-by-5-inch loaf pan. Bake 65 to 70 minutes until toothpick inserted in center comes out clean. Cool in pan 10 minutes. Turn out onto wire rack to cool completely.

PIZZA BREAD
LINDSAY INTERNATIONAL, INC.

Makes 2 pizzas

1 package (16 ounces) hot roll mix
2 cans (8 ounces each) pizza sauce
2 cans (2.25 ounces each; 1 cup total) Lindsay® Wedged Ripe Olives, drained
1 cup Lindsay® Pimiento-Stuffed Green Olives, drained and sliced

2 cans (4 ounces each) mushroom stems and pieces
6 tablespoons thinly sliced green onion
Shredded mozzarella *or* grated Parmesan cheese

Preheat oven to 400°F. Prepare the hot roll mix according to package directions, except decrease water by ¼ cup when dissolving the yeast and stir ¼ cup of the pizza sauce into the flour mixture. Turn the dough out onto a lightly greased surface; knead in ripe olives. Cover dough; let rise until double. Punch down; divide in half. Pat each half of the dough onto a greased 12-inch round baking pan. Let rise in a warm place for 30 minutes.

Spread remaining pizza sauce over the dough. Sprinkle each pizza with half the green olives, half the mushrooms, and half the green onion. Sprinkle with desired amount of mozzarella or Parmesan cheese. Bake 20 to 25 minutes or until edges begin to pull away from sides of the pan. Cut into thin wedges and serve immediately.

*Sweet Potato Soup
with Scallops*

COURTESY OF McCORMICK / SCHILLING SPICES

Market Salad

COURTESY OF SARGENTO CHEESE COMPANY, INC.

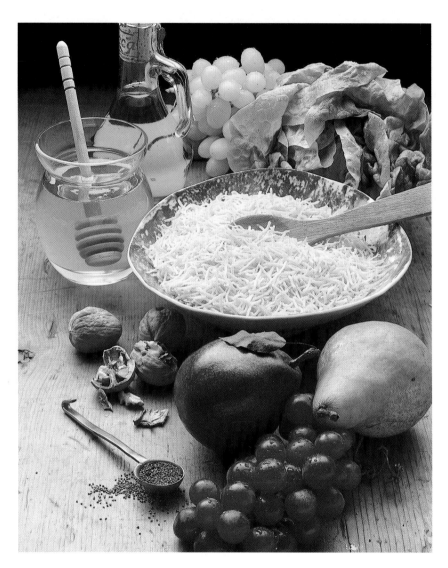

Poppy Fruit Salad

COURTESY OF SARGENTO CHEESE COMPANY, INC.

SILO BREAD
BEATRICE CHEESE, INC.

Makes 2 loaves

1 cup finely chopped onions
1¼ cups water
1 package active dry yeast
4 cups all-purpose flour
2 tablespoons sugar

1 teaspoon salt
1 teaspoon onion salt
¼ cup vegetable oil
2 eggs, slightly beaten
2 cups grated County Line® Extra Sharp
  Cheddar Cheese

Preheat oven to 375°F. In small saucepan, cook onion in 1 cup water until tender; set aside to cool. Dissolve yeast in remaining ¼ cup warm water. Mix flour, sugar, salt, and onion salt. In large bowl, mix together 2 cups sifted flour mixture, cooked onion, yeast, vegetable oil, and eggs. Add remaining 2 cups flour mixture. Turn out onto floured board. Knead until smooth and elastic (about 10 minutes). Divide into 2 equal portions. Roll each portion of dough into a 17-by-5-inch rectangle; sprinkle with 1 cup cheese each. Roll up; place end side down into a 1-pound greased coffee can. Cover cans with plastic lids or aluminum foil and set in warm place until dough rises to top of cans (about 1 hour). Remove covering. Bake 20 to 25 minutes. Let stand in can 5 minutes. Remove bread from cans. Serve warm.

MEXICAN HOT PEPPER BREAD

KELLOGG COMPANY

Makes 2 loaves

5 to 6 cups all-purpose flour

4 cups KELLOGG'S CORN FLAKES®
cereal, crushed to 1 cup

1 tablespoon sugar

1 tablespoon salt

2 packages active dry yeast

1½ cups milk

⅓ cup vegetable oil

2 eggs

1½ cups (6 ounces) shredded sharp
Cheddar cheese

½ cup finely chopped onion

¼ to ½ cup finely chopped hot chili pepper

2 tablespoons margarine *or* butter,
melted

Preheat oven to 250°F. In large bowl of electric mixer, stir together 2 cups flour, crushed cereal, sugar, salt, and yeast. Set aside. In small saucepan, combine milk and vegetable oil. Place over low heat until very warm (120°F to 130°F).

Gradually add to cereal mixture and beat until well combined. Add eggs. Beat on medium speed for 2 minutes. Stir in cheese, onion, and pepper. By hand, stir in enough remaining flour to make a stiff dough. On well-floured surface, knead dough about 5 minutes or until smooth and elastic. Place in greased bowl, turning once to grease surface. Cover lightly. Let rise in warm place until double in volume (about 1 hour). Punch down dough. Divide in half. Turn into 2 well-greased 1½-quart round casseroles. Cover and let rise in warm place until double in volume. Bake 25 to 35 minutes or until done. To prevent overbrowning, cover loosely with foil during last few minutes. Remove from casseroles. Place on wire racks. Brush with melted margarine. Cool completely.

WHEAT GERM BISCUITS

NESTLÉ FOOD COMPANY

Makes 8 servings

1¾ cups buttermilk baking mix

⅓ cup wheat germ

⅔ cup *undiluted* Carnation®
Evaporated Milk

Preheat oven to 450°F. Combine ingredients. Knead 10 times on floured surface. Roll to ½-inch thickness. Cut into 3-inch rounds. Bake on ungreased cookie sheet 8 minutes.

BRAN-RAISIN MUFFINS

NESTLÉ FOOD COMPANY

Makes 16 to 18 muffins

Boiling water
¾ cup raisins
⅓ cup oil
I slightly beaten egg
I cup liquid Carnation® Nonfat Dry Milk
I tablespoon lemon juice
I cup flour

½ cup sugar
¾ cup unprocessed bran
2 teaspoons baking powder
I teaspoon baking soda
½ teaspoon salt
¼ teaspoon cinnamon

Preheat oven to 400°F. Pour boiling water over raisins; let stand 10 minutes. Drain. Combine oil and egg in small bowl. Combine liquid nonfat milk and lemon juice. Stir into egg mixture. Combine flour, sugar, bran, baking powder, baking soda, salt, and cinnamon. Make a well in center of flour mixture. Pour in milk mixture all at once, stirring just until dry ingredients are moistened. Stir in raisins. Spoon into buttered muffin-pan cups, filling two-thirds full. Bake 15 minutes.

To freeze: Allow muffins to cool completely on wire racks. Place in heavy plastic bag; seal. Freeze.

To heat in conventional oven: Wrap 1 or 2 frozen muffins in foil. Heat at 350°F. for 15 minutes, or until heated through.

To heat in microwave oven: Microwave 1 frozen muffin, uncovered, 1 minute on MEDIUM (1½ minutes for 2 muffins).

APPLE STREUSEL MUFFINS

LIBBY'S, NESTLE FOOD COMPANY

Makes 18 muffins

2½ cups all-purpose flour
2 cups granulated sugar
1 tablespoon pumpkin pie spice
1 teaspoon baking soda
½ teaspoon salt

2 eggs, lightly beaten
1 cup Libby's® Solid Pack Pumpkin
½ cup vegetable oil
2 cups peeled, finely chopped apples
Streusel Topping (see below)

Preheat oven to 350°F. In large bowl, combine flour, sugar, pumpkin pie spice, baking soda, and salt; set aside. In medium bowl, combine eggs, pumpkin, and oil. Add liquid ingredients to dry ingredients; stir just until moistened. Stir in apples. Spoon batter into greased or paper-lined muffin-pan cups, filling three-fourths full. Sprinkle Streusel Topping over batter. Bake 35 to 40 minutes, or until toothpick comes out clean.

STREUSEL TOPPING

2 tablespoons all-purpose flour
¼ cup sugar

½ teaspoon ground cinnamon
4 teaspoons butter

In small bowl, combine flour, sugar, and cinnamon. Cut in butter until mixture is crumbly.

VARIATION

For 6 giant muffins, follow directions above, increasing baking time to 40 to 45 minutes.

APPLE-RAISIN BRAN MUFFINS

NABISCO FOODS GROUP

Makes 12 muffins

2 cups Nabisco® 100% Bran
1¼ cups skim milk
1 cup all-purpose flour
⅓ cup firmly packed light brown sugar
2 teaspoons Davis® Baking Powder

½ teaspoon baking soda
¼ cup Fleischmann's® Margarine, melted
½ cup Egg Beaters® 99% Real Egg
   Product
½ cup chopped apple
½ cup seedless raisins

Preheat oven to 400°F. Mix bran and milk; let stand 5 minutes. Blend flour, sugar, baking powder, and baking soda; set aside. Mix margarine and egg product into bran mixture. Stir in flour mixture just until blended. Stir in apple and raisins. Spoon batter into 12 greased 2½-inch muffin-pan cups. Bake 18 to 20 minutes. Serve warm.

To microwave: Prepare batter as above. Fill 6 paper-lined 2½-inch microwave-safe muffin-pan cups two-thirds full. Microwave at HIGH 2 to 2½ minutes or until toothpick inserted comes out clean, rotating pan after 1 minute. Remove from pan; repeat with remaining batter. Serve warm.

APPLESAUCE CHEDDAR MUFFINS

SARGENTO CHEESE COMPANY, INC.

Makes 12 muffins

2 cups baking powder biscuit mix
¼ cup sugar
1 teaspoon cinnamon
1 egg, well beaten
½ cup unsweetened applesauce
¼ cup skim milk

2 tablespoons oil
1 cup (4 ounces) Sargento® Preferred
   Light® Fancy Shredded Cheddar
   Cheese
1 tablespoon light margarine
2 tablespoons sugar

Preheat oven to 400°F. Combine biscuit mix, ¼ cup sugar, and cinnamon. In separate bowl, combine egg, applesauce, milk, oil, and cheese. Add to dry ingredients and mix lightly. Coat muffin-pan cups with a nonstick vegetable spray or paper liners. Fill each cup two-thirds full. Bake 20 minutes. Remove muffins from pan and brush tops lightly with melted margarine, roll in 2 tablespoons sugar.

PINEAPPLE CARROT RAISIN MUFFINS

DOLE FOOD COMPANY

Makes 12 muffins

2 cups all-purpose flour
1 cup sugar
2 teaspoons baking powder
½ teaspoon ground cinnamon
¼ teaspoon ground ginger
½ cup shredded Dole® Carrots

½ cup Dole® Raisins
½ cup chopped walnuts
1 can (8 ounces) Dole® Crushed
  Pineapple
2 eggs
½ cup margarine, melted
1 teaspoon vanilla extract

Preheat over to 375°F. Combine flour, sugar, baking powder, cinnamon, and ginger. Stir in carrots, raisins, and nuts. Separately, combine undrained pineapple, eggs, margarine, and vanilla. Stir into dry ingredients until just blended. Spoon batter into greased muffin-pan cups. Bake 20 to 25 minutes. Turn out onto wire rack to cool.

LEMON POPPY SEED MUFFINS

BORDEN INC.

Makes 12 to 15 muffins

2 cups unsifted flour
½ teaspoon baking soda
½ teaspoon salt
¼ teaspoon baking powder
4 teaspoons poppy seeds
2 tablespoons grated lemon rind
¾ cup sugar

½ cup Borden® Country Store® or
  Meadow Gold® Butter, softened
2 eggs
1 cup Borden® or Meadow Gold®
  Buttermilk
1 teaspoon vanilla extract

Preheat oven to 400°F. Combine flour, baking soda, salt, baking powder, poppy seeds, and lemon rind. In large mixer bowl, beat sugar and butter until fluffy; beat in eggs until smooth. Add buttermilk and vanilla; mix well. Stir in flour mixture just until moistened. Fill paper-lined or greased muffin-pan cups three-fourths full. Bake 20 minutes or until golden. Serve warm.

BANANA MUFFINS

KELLOGG COMPANY

Makes 12 muffins

1¼ cups all-purpose flour
1 tablespoon baking powder
½ teaspoon salt
½ teaspoon ground cinnamon
¼ teaspoon ground nutmeg
½ cup firmly packed brown sugar

2 cups KELLOGG'S CORN FLAKES®
   cereal, slightly crushed
1 egg
⅓ cup milk
¼ cup vegetable oil
1 cup mashed fully ripe bananas

Preheat oven to 400°F. Stir together flour, baking powder, salt, cinnamon, nutmeg brown sugar, and crushed cereal. Set aside. Combine egg, milk, and oil. Stir in bananas. Add flour mixture, stirring only until combined. Portion batter evenly into 12 greased 2½-inch muffin-pan cups. Bake 20 to 25 minutes or until lightly browned. Serve warm.

PEACHY BRAN MUFFINS

KELLOGG COMPANY

Makes 12 muffins

1¼ cups all-purpose flour
1 tablespoon baking powder
½ teaspoon salt
¼ cup firmly packed brown sugar
½ teaspoon ground cinnamon
1 egg

1 cup canned peaches, drained and
   chopped
1 cup KELLOGG'S® ALL-BRAN® cereal
⅓ cup milk
¼ cup vegetable oil

Preheat oven to 400°F. Stir together flour, baking powder, salt, brown sugar, and cinnamon; set aside. In large mixing bowl, beat egg slightly. Stir in peaches, cereal, milk, and oil. Let stand about 1 to 2 minutes or until cereal is softened. Stir again. Add flour mixture, stirring only until combined. Portion batter evenly into 12 greased 2½-inch muffin-pan cups. Bake 18 to 20 minutes or until done.

PEANUT BUTTER CEREAL MUFFINS

BEST FOODS, A DIVISION OF CPC INTERNATIONAL INC.

Makes 12 muffins

1¼ cups unsifted flour
⅓ cup sugar
1 tablespoon baking powder
½ teaspoon salt
2 cups whole bran cereal, corn flakes, or
   whole wheat flakes

1¼ cups skim milk
½ cup Skippy® Creamy or Super Chunk®
   Peanut Butter
1 egg, slightly beaten
½ cup raisins

Preheat oven to 400°F. Grease twelve 2½-by-1¼-inch muffin-pan cups. In small bowl, stir flour, sugar, baking powder, and salt. In medium bowl, combine cereal and milk. Let stand 1 to 2 minutes or until cereal is softened. Stir in peanut butter and egg until well mixed. Add raisins. Stir in flour mixture just until mixed. Divide among prepared muffin-pan cups, nearly filling. Bake 25 to 30 minutes or until golden brown. Immediately remove muffins from pan. Cool on wire rack or serve warm.

ORANGE BRAN MUFFINS

BEST FOODS, A DIVISION OF CPC INTERNATIONAL INC.

Makes 12 muffins

Mazola® No Stick™ Corn Oil Cooking
   Spray
1¼ cups whole-bran cereal
1 cup orange juice
2 eggs, slightly beaten
⅓ cup Mazola® Corn Oil
1½ to 2 teaspoons grated orange peel

1 teaspoon vanilla
1¼ cups flour
½ cup quick oats
⅓ cup firmly packed brown sugar
¼ cup wheat germ
1 tablespoon baking powder
¼ teaspoon cinnamon

Preheat oven to 350°F. Coat twelve 2½-by-1¼-inch muffin-pan cups with cooking spray. In medium bowl, combine cereal, orange juice, eggs, corn oil, orange peel, and vanilla. Let stand 2 minutes. In large bowl, combine flour, oats, brown sugar, wheat germ, baking powder, and cinnamon. Add cereal mixture to flour mixture all at once, stirring just until moistened. Spoon into prepared muffin-pan cups. Bake 20 minutes or until lightly browned and firm to the touch. Cool in pan on wire rack about 5 minutes.

BRAN BATTER ROLLS

KELLOGG COMPANY

Makes 16 rolls

1 cup KELLOGG'S® ALL-BRAN® cereal	1 cup milk
2½ to 3 cups all-purpose flour	½ cup water
2 tablespoons sugar	2 tablespoons margarine *or* butter
1½ teaspoons salt	1 egg, slightly beaten
1 package active dry yeast	Poppy seed *or* sesame seed (optional)

Preheat oven to 400°F. In large bowl of electric mixer, stir together cereal, 1 cup flour, sugar, salt, and yeast; set aside. In small saucepan, heat milk, water, and margarine until warm (115°F to 120°F). Add to cereal mixture. Reserve 1 tablespoon of egg. Add remaining egg to cereal mixture. Beat 30 seconds at low speed of electric mixer, scraping bowl constantly. Beat 3 minutes at high speed. By hand, stir in enough remaining flour to make a stiff batter. Cover loosely. Let rise in warm place until double in volume. Stir down batter. Portion batter evenly into 16 greased 2½-inch muffin-pan cups. Brush tops of rolls with reserved egg. Sprinkle with poppy or sesame seed, if desired. Bake 18 to 20 minutes or until golden brown. Serve warm.

VARIATION

For lighter texture: After portioning dough into muffin pan cups, let rise in warm place until almost double in volume. Do not cover. Bake at 400°F. about 15 minutes or until golden brown.

SOUPS & STEWS

PEAR-RASPBERRY SOUP
McCormick & Company, Inc.
65

"SHOW STOPPER" SOUP
McCormick & Company, Inc.
66

SWEET POTATO SOUP WITH SCALLOPS
McCormick & Company, Inc.
66

THAI CHICKEN AND RICE SOUP
JFC International, Inc.
67

CHICKEN VEGETABLE SOUP,
HONG KONG STYLE
JFC International, Inc.
68

BRUNSWICK STEW
Campbell Soup Company
69

CARIBBEAN PORK STEW
Durkee-French Foods
70

MEXICAN VEGETABLE BEEF SOUP
Lawry's Foods, Inc.
70

TORTILLA SOUP
McCormick & Company, Inc.
71

CREAM OF JALAPEÑO SOUP
Sargento Cheese Company, Inc.
72

NEW ENGLAND CLAM CHOWDER
Borden, Inc.
72

CREAMY BROCCOLI SOUP
Kraft General Foods, Inc.
73

QUICK COUNTRY MINESTRONE
Thomas J. Lipton Co.
74

PIZZA SOUP
Thomas J. Lipton Co.
75

GRANDMA'S TURKEY STEW
Oscar Mayer Foods Corporation
75

PEAR-RASPBERRY SOUP

MCCORMICK & COMPANY, INC.

Makes 4 cups

6 large ripe pears
¾ cup water
½ cup sugar
¾ cup extra dry vermouth
6 McCormick/Schilling® Cardamom
   Seeds

1 2-inch piece McCormick/Schilling
   Vanilla Bean
1 2-inch piece McCormick/Schilling Stick
   Cinnamon
8 McCormick/Schilling Whole Allspice
1 tablespoon Red Raspberry Purée (see
   below)

Peel pears and cut into small pieces. In large saucepan, combine pears and next 7 ingredients. Bring to a boil. Reduce heat and simmer 10 minutes. Cool slightly. Remove whole spices. Purée pear mixture in food processor. Add 1 tablespoon raspberry purée. Mix well. Chill. To serve, ladle pear mixture into individual serving dishes. Dip the tip of a teaspoon into Raspberry Purée and draw a spiral on the surface of soup. Draw the tip of the spoon across the spiral to form a design.

RASPBERRY PUREE

Makes ½ cup

1 package (10 ounces) frozen red
   raspberries in heavy syrup
1 tablespoon sugar

4 McCormick/Schilling® Whole Cloves
1 teaspoon minced McCormick/Schilling
   Crystalized Ginger

Combine ingredients in a saucepan. Bring to a boil. Reduce heat and simmer 10 minutes. Strain and chill.

"SHOW STOPPER" SOUP

MCCORMICK & COMPANY, INC.

Makes 6 servings, 1 cup each

I package (10 ounces) frozen chopped spinach

3½ cups milk

½ cup drained oysters

¼ cup butter

¼ cup flour

¼ teaspoon McCormick/Schilling® ground Nutmeg

½ teaspoon McCormick/Schilling ground White Pepper

2 teaspoons McCormick/Schilling Instant Minced Onion

I teaspoon McCormick/Schilling Chicken Flavor Base

¾ teaspoon McCormick/Schilling Bon Appétit®

I cup whipping cream

Whipping cream for garnish

Crushed McCormick/Schilling Red Pepper for garnish

Thaw spinach; drain excess liquid. Pour 1½ cups milk into blender jar. Gradually add spinach, blending until smooth after each addition. Pour into a bowl. Puree oysters in blender. Add to spinach mixture. Set aside. Melt butter in large saucepan. Stir in next 6 ingredients. Cook over medium heat until bubbly. Stir in spinach mixture. Add remaining 2 cups milk and 1 cup whipping cream. Cook, stirring constantly, over medium heat, until mixture begins to boil. Reduce heat and simmer 2 minutes. Garnish with dollops of unsweetened whipped cream topped with crushed red pepper.

SWEET POTATO SOUP WITH SCALLOPS

MCCORMICK & COMPANY, INC.

Makes 5 servings, 1 cup each

4 teaspoons McCormick/Schilling® Chicken Flavor Base

I quart water

I cup mashed cooked sweet potatoes

I teaspoon McCormick/Schilling Instant Minced Onion

¾ teaspoon McCormick/Schilling Bon Appétit®

⅛ teaspoon McCormick/Schilling ground Black Pepper

I cup diced (½-inch) cooked sweet potatoes

I cup finely chopped scallops

In 4-quart saucepan, combine first 6 ingredients. Heat to a boil. Reduce heat. Add diced sweet potatoes and scallops. Simmer 15 minutes.

THAI CHICKEN AND RICE SOUP

JFC INTERNATIONAL, INC.

Makes about 6 cups

1 tablespoon Dynasty® Chinese Stir-Fry Oil

1 whole chicken breast, skinned, boned, and cut into small bite-size pieces

1 small onion, chopped

1 can (14½ ounces) Dynasty® Chicken Stock

1 can (14 ounces) coconut milk*

1 cup fresh *or* frozen (thawed) whole kernel corn

1 cup cooked rice

2 tablespoons Dynasty® Oyster-Flavored Sauce

2 tablespoons rice vinegar

1 tablespoon minced fresh coriander (cilantro) *or* parsley

1 to 2 teaspoons Dynasty® Hot Chili Oil

Heat medium saucepan over high heat. Add oil; coat pan. Add chicken and onion; sauté 4 to 5 minutes, or until chicken is lightly browned and onion is translucent. Add chicken stock, coconut milk, corn, rice, oyster sauce, and rice vinegar. Cook and stir until mixture boils. Remove from heat; stir in coriander and chili oil. Serve while hot.

*Note: If coconut milk is unavailable, combine 1¼ cups shredded unsweetened coconut and 2 cups hot water in electric blender container. Whir on high speed 1 minute; strain milk and use as directed above.

To microwave: Combine oil, chicken, and onion in 3-quart microwave-safe dish. Cover with lid or plastic wrap, venting corner. Microwave on HIGH 3 to 4 minutes, or until chicken is cooked and onion is translucent, stirring halfway through cooking. Stir in remaining ingredients. Cover and microwave on HIGH 6 to 8 minutes, or until heated through, stirring halfway through cooking.

CHICKEN VEGETABLE SOUP, HONG KONG STYLE

JFC INTERNATIONAL, INC.

Makes 4 to 5 servings, about 10 cups total

1 package (5.29 ounces) Dynasty® Saifun

4 Dynasty® Shiitake

1 package (10.5 ounces) tofu, drained well

3 to 4 cups vegetable oil

¼ pound lean, ground chicken, turkey, or pork

4 cans (14½ ounces each) Dynasty® Chicken Stock

1 medium zucchini, halved lengthwise and cut crosswise into ½-inch lengths

1 carrot, halved lengthwise and cut crosswise into ¼-inch lengths

3 green onions and tops, halved lengthwise and cut crosswise into ½-inch lengths

1 teaspoon Dynasty® Sesame Oil (optional)

Soak 1 bundle saifun in hot water 20 minutes. Save remaining saifun for use some other time. Drain saifun; coarsely chop. Set aside. Cover shiitake with hot water; let stand 20 minutes. Drain shiitake. Remove and discard shiitake stems; thinly slice shitake. Blot tofu with paper towel to dry; cut into ¾- to 1-inch cubes. Heat oil in medium saucepan to 350°F. Add tofu cubes to hot oil, a few at a time; cook 2 to 3 minutes, or until lightly browned. Remove with slotted spoon; drain on paper towel. Heat large saucepan over high heat. Add chicken; stir-fry 2 to 3 minutes, or until browned. Stir in chicken stock, zucchini, carrot, and shiitake. Bring to a boil. Reduce heat; cover and simmer 5 minutes, or until vegetables are tender. Stir in tofu, saifun, and green onions; heat through. Remove from heat; stir in sesame oil. Salt to taste and serve.

VARIATION

Substitute with ½ package (3½ ounce size) Dynasty® Saifun/Harusame. Soak 25 minutes; continue as directed.

BRUNSWICK STEW

CAMPBELL SOUP COMPANY

Makes 12 servings, 1 cup each.

5-pound stewing chicken, cut up
6 cups water
2 bay leaves
2 teaspoons salt
½ teaspoon pepper
4 slices bacon, cut into ½-inch pieces
2 medium onions, sliced and separated into rings
2 medium potatoes, peeled and cubed

1 can (16 ounces) whole tomatoes, undrained, cut up
1 can (8 ounces) whole-kernel golden corn, drained
1 cup frozen lima beans
1 tablespoon Worcestershire sauce
1 can (20¾ ounces) Campbell's® Pork & Beans in Tomato Sauce
2 tablespoons chopped fresh parsley (optional)

In 6-quart Dutch oven, combine chicken, water, bay leaves, salt and pepper. Heat to boil. Reduce heat; simmer, covered, 2½ hours or until tender. Strain broth; skim fat. Reserve 4 cups broth (add water to equal 4 cups). Discard bay leaves. When cool, remove chicken from bones; cut up. In same Dutch oven, cook bacon until crisp. Drain on paper towels. Spoon off all but 2 tablespoons drippings. Add onions; cook until tender, stirring often. Stir in potatoes, tomatoes, corn, lima beans, Worcestershire sauce, reserved broth, and chicken. Heat to boiling. Reduce heat; simmer, uncovered, 30 minutes. Stir in pork and beans. Simmer, uncovered, 30 minutes longer. Stir in bacon. Add parsley, if desired.

CARIBBEAN PORK STEW
DURKEE-FRENCH FOODS

Makes 6 servings

2 tablespoons vegetable oil
1½ pounds boneless pork loin (rib end),
   cubed
1 can (13¾ ounces) chicken broth
1 can (8 ounces) tomato sauce
1 pound sweet potatoes, peeled and cut
   in 1-inch cubes
2 teaspoons Durkee® Onion Powder
2 teaspoons Durkee® Garlic Powder

½ teaspoon Durkee® Ground Cinnamon
½ teaspoon Durkee® Ground Cumin
⅛ teaspoon Durkee® Crushed Red
   Pepper
1 red pepper, cut in strips
1 green pepper, cut in strips
⅓ cup orange juice
1 cup sliced green onions

Heat oil in Dutch oven over high; cook pork until evenly browned, about 5 minutes; drain. Add broth, tomato sauce, potatoes, and seasonings. Bring to a boil; simmer, covered, 25 minutes. Add peppers, orange juice and green onions. Simmer, covered, 5 minutes. Serve with cooked rice.

MEXICAN VEGETABLE BEEF SOUP
LAWRY'S FOODS, INC.

Makes 6 servings

1 pound lean ground beef
½ cup chopped onions
1 package (1.25 ounces) Lawry's® Taco
   Spices and Seasonings
1 can (28 ounces) whole tomatoes,
   cut up

1 package (16 ounces) frozen mixed
   vegetables, thawed
1 can (15¼ ounces) kidney beans,
   undrained
1 can (14½ ounces) beef broth
Cilantro, chopped (optional)

In Dutch oven, brown ground beef and onions, stirring, until beef is cooked through; drain fat. Add taco spices and seasonings, tomatoes, vegetables, beans, and broth. Bring to a boil; reduce heat and simmer, uncovered, 5 minutes, stirring occasionally. For extra flavor, add chopped cilantro.

Top each serving with corn chips and grated Cheddar cheese.

TORTILLA SOUP

MCCORMICK & COMPANY, INC.

Makes 7 cups broth

1 cup tomato juice
2 tablespoons McCormick/Schilling® Beef Flavor Base
7 cups hot water
2 McCormick/Schilling Whole Black Peppercorns
1 McCormick/Schilling Bay Leaf
2 tablespoons McCormick/Schilling Instant Minced Onion

¼ teaspoon McCormick/Schilling Garlic Powder
½ cup coarsely chopped celery
½ cup thinly sliced carrots
1 can (4 ounces) mild green chilies, drained and cut in strips
2 whole hot chilies
Meatballs (see below)
Tortilla chips
Monterey Jack cheese, shredded

Place first 11 ingredients in large saucepan. Bring to a boil. Reduce heat and simmer 25 minutes. Remove bay leaf and hot chilies. To serve, place a few meatballs in soup plate. Ladle broth over meatballs. Add a few tortilla chips and sprinkle with shredded cheese.

MEATBALLS

Makes 22 to 23 meatballs

1 tablespoon McCormick/Schilling® Instant Minced Onion
¼ cup dry breadcrumbs
¼ cup milk
1 egg, beaten
½ pound ground beef
½ pound ground pork
½ cup chopped blanched almonds
⅛ teaspoon McCormick/Schilling ground Black Pepper

⅛ teaspoon McCormick/Schilling ground Oregano
⅛ teaspoon McCormick/Schilling ground Cumin
1 teaspoon McCormick/Schilling Chervil Leaves
½ teaspoon McCormick/Schilling Shredded Green Onion
¾ teaspoon McCormick/Schilling Bon Appétit®
1 tablespoon peanut oil

In large bowl, mix onion, breadcrumbs, milk, and egg. Add all other ingredients except peanut oil and mix well. Shape into 1¼-inch meatballs. Heat peanut oil in skillet. Cook meatballs 4 minutes, turning to brown on all sides. Add small amount of oil if necessary.

CREAM OF JALAPEÑO SOUP

SARGENTO CHEESE COMPANY, INC.

Makes 6 cups

4 tablespoons butter *or* margarine
I large onion, chopped
I large carrot, peeled and finely chopped
I large green pepper, seeded and finely chopped
3 jalapeño peppers, seeded and finely chopped

3 tablespoons flour
3 cups chicken broth
2 cups whipping cream
I cup (4 ounces) Sargento® Fancy Shredded Swiss Cheese
I cup (4 ounces) Sargento® Shredded *or* Fancy Shredded Cheddar Cheese

In large saucepan, melt 2 tablespoons butter and cook onion, carrot, and green pepper over low heat, stirring occasionally until tender, about 8 minutes. Stir in jalapeño peppers. Remove from saucepan. Melt remaining 2 tablespoons butter in separate saucepan. Stir in flour and cook, stirring constantly, 2 minutes. Gradually stir in broth and cream. Increase heat and bring to a boil, stirring constantly. Reduce heat and simmer until thickened, about 10 minutes. Stir in both cheeses; stir in vegetables.

NEW ENGLAND CLAM CHOWDER

BORDEN, INC.

Makes about 5 cups

3 tablespoons diced salt pork *or* 3 slices bacon
¼ cup finely chopped onion
2 cups pared, diced potatoes
I bottle (8 ounces) Doxsee® or Snow's® Clam Juice

2 cans (6½ ounces each) Doxsee® or Snow's® Chopped Clams, drained, with liquid reserved
⅛ teaspoon thyme leaves
1½ cups Borden® or Meadow Gold® Half-and-Half

In medium saucepan, brown pork. Add onion; cook until tender. Add potatoes, clam juice, reserved clam liquid, and thyme. Cover; simmer 10 to 15 minutes or until potatoes are tender. Add clams and half-and-half; heat through. *Do not boil.* Refrigerate leftovers.

CREAMY BROCCOLI SOUP

KRAFT GENERAL FOODS INC.

Makes 5 servings, 1 cup each

¼ cup chopped onion
1 tablespoon Parkay® Margarine
2 cups milk
1 package (8 ounces) Philadelphia® Brand
  Cream Cheese, cubed
¾ pound Velveeta® Pasteurized Process
  Cheese Spread, cubed

1 package (10 ounces) Birds Eye®
  Chopped Broccoli, cooked and
  drained
¼ teaspoon ground nutmeg
Dash of pepper

In 2-quart saucepan, cook onion in margarine until tender. Reduce heat to medium. Add milk and cream cheese, stir until cream cheese is melted. Add remaining ingredients; heat thoroughly, stirring occasionally.

To microwave: Microwave onion and margarine in microwave-safe 2-quart bowl on HIGH 30 seconds or until onions are tender. Add milk; microwave on HIGH 3 to 4 minutes, stirring every 2 minutes. Stir in cream cheese; microwave on HIGH 4 to 6 minutes or until cream cheese is melted, stirring every 2 minutes. Stir in remaining igredients; microwave on HIGH 30 seconds or until thoroughly heated.

VARIATIONS

Substitute Birds Eye® Chopped Spinach for broccoli.
Substitute Birds Eye® Cauliflower, chopped, for broccoli.
Substitute Birds Eye® Asparagus Spears, chopped, for broccoli.

Preparation time: 15 minutes   *Cooking time:* 15 minutes

QUICK COUNTRY MINESTRONE

THOMAS J. LIPTON CO.

Makes about 4 servings

2 tablespoons olive *or* vegetable oil
½ cup chopped onion
1 tablespoon finely chopped garlic
5 cups water
1 package Lipton® Pasta & Sauce—Herb Tomato
1 package (10 ounces) frozen cut green beans, thawed

½ teaspoon salt
⅛ teaspoon pepper
1 cup red kidney beans, rinsed and drained
Parmesan cheese (optional)
Fresh basil leaves for garnish (optional)

In 3-quart saucepan, heat oil and cook onion with garlic over medium heat, stirring occasionally, until onion is tender. Add water and bring to a boil. Stir in Pasta & Herb Tomato Sauce, green beans, salt, and pepper. Reduce heat and simmer, stirring occasionally, 7 minutes or until pasta is tender. Stir in kidney beans and heat through. Serve, if desired, with grated Parmesan cheese. Garnish, if desired, with fresh basil leaves.

To microwave: Decrease water to 4½ cups. In 3-quart microwave-safe round casserole, microwave oil, onion, and garlic, uncovered at HIGH (100% Power) 2 minutes or until onion is tender. Add water and microwave 6 minutes or until boiling. Stir in Pasta & Herb Tomato Sauce, green beans, salt, and pepper, and microwave 13 minutes or until pasta is tender, stirring once. Stir in kidney beans; let stand, covered, 5 minutes. Serve as above.

PIZZA SOUP

THOMAS J. LIPTON CO.

Makes about 3½ cups

1 medium onion, chopped

2 ounces pepperoni or salami, cut into small pieces

½ teaspoon Lawry's® Garlic Powder with Parsley

½ teaspoon oregano leaves

1 envelope Lipton® Noodle Soup Mix with Real Chicken Broth

3 cups water

2 tablespoons tomato paste

½ cup (about 1½ ounces) shredded mozzarella cheese

In medium saucepan, cook onion, pepperoni, garlic powder, and oregano over medium-high heat, stirring frequently, 3 minutes or until onion is tender. Stir in remaining ingredients except cheese. Bring to a boil; then simmer, stirring occasionally, 5 minutes. To serve, sprinkle with cheese.

To microwave: In 2-quart microwave-safe casserole, microwave onion, pepperoni, garlic powder, and oregano at HIGH (100% Power) 2 minutes. Stir in remaining ingredients except cheese. Microwave, uncovered, 10 minutes, stirring once. To serve, sprinkle with cheese.

VARIATION

Omit pepperoni *or* salami. Add 1 tablespoon oil.

GRANDMA'S TURKEY STEW

OSCAR MAYER FOODS CORPORATION

Makes 4 servings

1 package Louis Rich® Fresh Turkey Wings or Drumsticks

3 tablespoons cornstarch

2 teaspoons instant chicken bouillon

½ teaspoon poultry seasoning

1 package (16 ounces) frozen mixed vegetables

1 cup buttermilk baking mix

⅓ cup milk

Rinse turkey. Place in skillet with 1 cup water. Bring to a boil; turn down heat. Cover. Simmer 2 hours. Remove turkey. Measure liquid; add water to make 2 cups. Return liquid to skillet; stir in cornstarch, bouillon, and poultry seasoning. Add vegetables. Bring to a boil; turn down heat. Cover. Simmer 5 minutes. Remove turkey from bones. Add turkey to skillet. Separately, combine baking mix and milk to make dumplings; drop in 4 spoonfuls onto simmering stew. Cook, uncovered, 5 minutes. Cover. Cook 5 minutes more.

SALADS &
SALAD DRESSINGS

Fruit Salad Delights

CATALINA SALAD
McCormick & Company, Inc.
80

CITRUS TOSS
Sargento Cheese Company, Inc.
80

POPPY FRUIT SALAD
Sargento Cheese Company, Inc.
81

LANAI FRUIT SALAD
Dole Food Company
81

FESTIVE CRANBERRY MOLD
Dole Food Company
82

SPARKLING BERRY SALAD
Thomas J. Lipton Co.
82

THE JELL-O WAY
The Story of Jell-O
83

UNDER-THE-SEA SALAD
Kraft General Foods, Inc.
85

FIVE-CUP SALAD
Kraft General Foods, Inc.
85

Robust Vegetable Salads

GREEK SALAD
Lindsay International, Inc.
86

SWISS SALAD MEDLEY
Beatrice Cheese, Inc.
86

SEVEN-LAYER SALAD
Kraft General Foods, Inc.
87

**NATURALLY CHEESY
LAYERED LETTUCE BOWL**
Beatrice Cheese, Inc.
87

BAKED GERMAN POTATO SALAD
Kraft General Foods, Inc.
88

GREAT AMERICAN POTATO SALAD
Kraft General Foods, Inc.
89

CATALINA SALAD

MCCORMICK & COMPANY, INC.

Makes 6 individual salads; 1½ cups salad dressing

2 pink grapefruit
2 ripe avocados
2 Granny Smith apples
Salad greens
1 cup mayonnaise
½ cup orange juice
¼ teaspoon McCormick/Schilling®
  ground Mustard

½ teaspoon McCormick/Schilling
  Dill Weed
½ teaspoon McCormick/Schilling
  Instant Minced Onion
⅛ teaspoon McCormick/Schilling
  ground White Pepper
¼ teaspoon McCormick/Schilling
  Bon Appétit®

Peel and section grapefruit. Peel and slice avocados. Core and slice apples or cut apples into thin spirals as follows: Cut a thin slice from the blossom end, then use a potato peeler to cut the apple in continuous spirals. Wash and dry salad greens. Combine mayonnaise with remaining ingredients. Mix well. Chill. Arrange a bed of salad greens on each of 6 salad plates. Arrange grapefruit, avocado, and apple slices or spirals on greens. Spoon dressing over each salad.

CITRUS TOSS

SARGENTO CHEESE COMPANY, INC.

Makes 4 servings

2 tablespoons lemon juice
2 teaspoons sugar
¼ cup hazelnut *or* vegetable oil
3 cups torn salad greens
1¼ cups (5 ounces) Sargento® Fancy
  Shredded Cheddar Cheese
½ cup (1½ ounces) Sargento® Fancy
  Shredded Parmesan Cheese

1½ cups orange sections
1 cup grapefruit sections
1 cup seedless green grapes
1 can (8 ounces) sliced water chestnuts,
  well drained
⅓ cup coarsely chopped hazelnuts, toasted

To make dressing, combine lemon juice and sugar in small bowl. Gradually add oil, whisking until smooth and thickened; reserve.

Place salad greens, cheeses, orange and grapefruit sections, grapes and water chestnuts in large bowl. Add dressing; toss gently. Sprinkle with hazelnuts. Serve immediately.

POPPY FRUIT SALAD

SARGENTO CHEESE COMPANY, INC.

Makes 4 servings

2 tablespoons cider vinegar
2 tablespoons honey
½ teaspoon dry mustard
⅓ cup vegetable oil
1½ teaspoons poppy seeds
2 medium pears, sliced
⅔ cup seedless red grapes, cut in half

⅔ cup seedless green grapes, cut in half
1½ cups (6 ounces) Sargento® Fancy
   Shredded Sharp Cheddar Cheese
½ cup coarsely chopped walnuts *or*
   pecans, toasted
Lettuce leaves (optional)

Combine vinegar, honey, and mustard in small bowl. Gradually add oil, whisking until smooth and thickened. Stir in poppy seeds; set aside.

Combine pears, grapes, and cheese in large bowl. Add dressing. Toss gently to coat thoroughly. Sprinkle with walnuts. Serve on lettuce-lined plates, if desired.

LANAI FRUIT SALAD

DOLE FOOD COMPANY

Makes 12 servings

1 can (20 ounces) Dole® Pineapple
   Chunks
4 Dole® Oranges, peeled and chunked
4 apples, seeded and chunked
3 Dole® Bananas, peeled and sliced
2 baskets strawberries

2 cups assorted seedless grapes
1 carton (8 ounces) vanilla yogurt
1 tablespoon lime juice
½ teaspoon grated lime peel
1 teaspoon honey

Drain pineapple; reserve juice for beverage. Toss together all fruit. To make dressing, stir together yogurt, lime juice and peel, and honey. Serve dressing with salad.

FESTIVE CRANBERRY MOLD

DOLE FOOD COMPANY

Makes 8 servings

1 can (8¼ ounces) Dole® Crushed Pineapple
1 envelope unflavored gelatin
1 tablespoon sugar
¾ cup port wine
1 medium red apple, cored and diced

1 can (8 ounces) whole-berry cranberry sauce
⅓ cup chopped pecans *or* walnuts
Zest from ½ Dole® Orange
¼ teaspoon ground cardamon
Dole® salad greens

Drain pineapple well; reserve syrup. In medium saucepan, combine gelatin and sugar. Stir in reserved syrup and port. Heat mixture until gelatin dissolves. Chill until slightly thickened. Fold in pineapple, apple, cranberry sauce, nuts, 1 teaspoon orange zest, and cardamon. Pour into 1-quart mold. Refrigerate until set. Unmold on serving plate lined with salad greens.

SPARKLING BERRY SALAD

THOMAS J. LIPTON CO.

Makes about 12 servings, ½ cup each

2 envelopes Knox® Unflavored Gelatine
2 cups cranberry-raspberry juice
⅓ cup sugar
1 cup club soda
¼ cup creme de cassis (black-currant-flavored liqueur; optional)

1 teaspoon lemon juice
1 teaspoon fresh grated orange peel (optional)
3 cups assorted blueberries, raspberries, or strawberries
Sour cream (optional)

In medium saucepan, sprinkle unflavored gelatine over 1 cup cranberry-raspberry juice; let stand 1 minute. Stir over low heat until gelatine is completely dissolved, about 5 minutes. Stir in sugar until dissolved.

In large bowl, blend remaining 1 cup cranberry-raspberry juice, soda, gelatine mixture, liqueur, lemon juice, and, if desired, orange peel.Chill, stirring occasionally, until mixture is consistency of unbeaten egg whites, about 60 minutes. Fold in berries. Pour into 6-cup mold or bowl; chill until firm, about 3 hours. Unmold and serve, with sour cream, if desired.

VARIATION

Use 2 cups cranberry juice cocktail instead of cranberry-raspberry juice and increase sugar to ½ cup.

THE JELL-O WAY
The Story of Jell-O

In 1845 Peter Cooper, designer of the first American steam locomotive, popularly known as the Tom Thumb, created an entirely new dessert made of gelatin. He obtained a patent and described his creation as "a transparent, concentrated substance containing all the ingredients fitting it for table use in a portable form, and requiring only the addition of hot water to dissolve it, so that it may be poured into moulds and when cold will be fit for use." Like most great thinkers, however, Cooper had many exciting and profitable inventions, plans, and ideas to keep him busy. He put his gelatin on the shelf, and there it sat for the next fifty years.

Then along came Pearl B. Wait, a carpenter by trade who had been dabbling in the business of manufacturing cough medicine and laxative tea in his home in the 1890s. Wait was interested in making his mark in the new packaged-foods industry. He and his wife, May, experimented in their kitchen and he enhanced Cooper's invention by adding fruit flavors to it. His wife excitedly proclaimed the product name should be Jell-O and told Wait to sell the creation door-to-door to housewives by demonstrating the simplicity of using it to create delicious desserts. But Wait lacked the sales skills and marketing know-how to get his fledgling company off the ground, and he grew discouraged. He was happy to get $450 for the Jell-O rights from his next-door neighbor, Orator Frank Woodward.

Overwhelming with magnetism and boundless energy in traditional Horatio Alger fashion, Woodward had quit school at age twelve and started his first company eight years later. In 1899, after great success selling Raccoon Corn Plasters, Sherman's Headache Remedy, and other curatives of the day, he was enthusiastically promoting Grain-O, a roasted-cereal beverage for people who couldn't drink coffee or tea. Woodward decided Jell-O would be a good addition to his already-successful company.

When Woodward's salesmen showed up at church socials, picnics, fairs, and dances to demonstrate the easy creation of spectacular Jell-O desserts, they usually became the highlight of the event. Woodward gave away samples and fancy tin molds. He offered Jell-O discounts to his employees so they could advertise the product personally by selling it to family and friends.

But converting the housewife to this light and fruity dessert wasn't easy in an era of rich cakes and pies. One day when Woodward was touring his factory plant with his plant superintendent, the two stood silently before countless cases of piled-up Jell-O. Glumly, Woodward asked his companion, "Will you buy all this Jell-O and the whole Jell-O business for $35?" His manager quickly refused. Then, suddenly, the advertising campaign started producing results. People were becoming captivated by the shimmering desserts. By 1902, sales hit $250,000. Fashionable women with wavy curls and bun hairdos, wearing white aprons, smiled triumphantly from the Ladies Home Journal to proclaim Jell-O as "America's Most Famous Dessert". It could be topped with whipped cream or thin custard, and for "something very fancy, there are hundreds of delightful combinations that can be quickly prepared." Four years later sales zoomed to $1 million annually.

In 1925, with an exchange of stocks, the Postum Cereal Company of Battle Creek, Michigan, purchased and merged with the Jell-O Company. These products formed the core of the great General Foods Corporation. The $450 formula was now worth $67 million as a business. Whenever Woodward thought of the prompt rejection of his rash offer, he exhaled a sigh of relief.

Ethel Barrymore, Jack Benny, and other celebrities of the day were interviewed for their favorite Jell-O recipes. The brilliant artist Rose O'Neill, who, along with Norman Rockwell and other notable artists, illustrated Jell-O recipe booklets, was asked her opinion of the dessert. "When I tell you I haven't time to be a housewife and have never in my life made up anything edible except Jell-O, you will know I must appreciate the advantages offered by the 'easy Jell-O way.'"

The advertising agency assigned to the Jell-O account decided a child model would make a perfect trademark for Jell-O, showing how appealing the dessert is for children and how easy it is to prepare. Franklin King, the artist assigned to design the trademark, interviewed hundreds of models without finding the right image. Finally, as he watched his four-year-old daughter, Elizabeth, playing in the nursery, inspiration struck. He took some pictures and showed them to the agency. Elizabeth King became the Jell-O Girl. Every month for the next four years, new pictures were taken of Elizabeth to be used in all print ads and store displays. Since 1973, Bill Cosby has contributed to the ad campaign with his charismatic and successful Jell-O pudding television commercials geared toward children. The dessert has become one of the most popular and successful specialty grocery items of the twentieth century.

UNDER-THE-SEA SALAD

KRAFT GENERAL FOODS, INC.

Makes 6 servings, about 3½ cups total

1 can (16 ounces) pear halves in syrup
1 package (4-serving size) Jell-O® Brand
  Lime-Flavor Gelatin
¼ teaspoon salt (optional)
1 cup boiling water
1 tablespoon lemon juice

2 packages (3 ounces each) Philadelphia®
  Brand Cream Cheese, softened
⅛ teaspoon ground cinnamon (optional)
Salad greens (optional)
Mayonnaise (optional)
Pear halves, drained and diced (optional)

Drain pears, reserving ¾ cup of the syrup. Dice pears and set aside. Dissolve gelatin and salt in boiling water. Add reserved syrup and lemon juice to gelatin. Pour 1¼ cups into an 8-by-4-inch loaf pan or 4-cup mold. Chill until set but not firm, about 1 hour. Very slowly blend remaining gelatin into cream cheese, beating until smooth. Add cinnamon and pears and spoon over clear gelatin in pan. Chill until firm, about 4 hours. Unmold. Garnish with crisp salad greens, mayonnaise, and additional pears, if desired.

Note: Recipe may be doubled, using a 9-by-5-inch loaf pan.

FIVE-CUP SALAD

KRAFT GENERAL FOODS, INC.

Makes 4 to 6 servings

1 cup Kraft® Miniature Marshmallows
1 cup Breakstone's® Sour Cream
1 cup orange sections

1 cup grapes
1 cup Bakers® Angel Flake® Coconut

In large bowl, mix together ingredients. Chill.

VARIATIONS

Substitute 1 cup peach slices for orange sections.

Substitute 1 can (11 ounces) mandarin orange segments, drained, for orange sections.

Add 1 can (8 ounces) pineapple chunks, drained.

Preparation time: 10 minutes, plus chilling

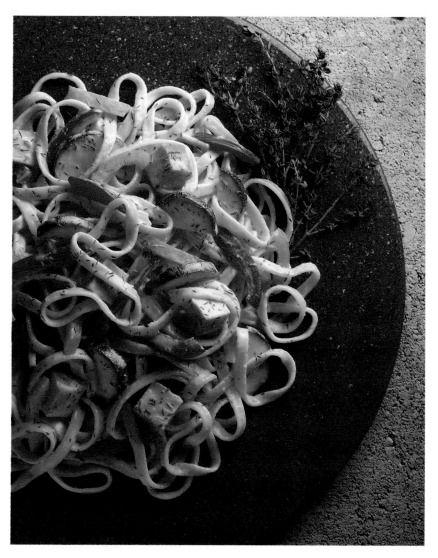

Smoked Turkey and Pepper
Pasta Salad

COURTESY OF KRAFT GENERAL FOODS, INC.

Sizzling Steak Fajitas
COURTESY OF NABISCO FOODS GROUP

Crunchy Corn Relish
COURTESY OF DURKEE-FRENCH FOODS

GREEK SALAD

LINDSAY INTERNATIONAL, INC.

Makes 8 servings

⅓ cup olive *or* salad oil
¼ cup lemon juice
¾ teaspoon dried oregano, crushed
½ teaspoon salt
¼ teaspoon pepper
8 cups torn mixed greens
2 cups cherry tomatoes, halved

1 can (6 ounces, 1½ cups) Lindsay® Large Pitted Ripe Olives, drained
1 medium cucumber, sliced
1 cup sliced radishes
½ cup sliced green onions
¼ cup snipped parsley
2 cups (8 ounces) crumbled feta cheese

For dressing, in a screw-top jar shake together oil, lemon juice, oregano, salt, and pepper. Cover and chill. In a salad bowl, combine torn greens, tomatoes, olives, cucumber, radishes, onions, and parsley over greens; top with feta cheese. Shake chilled dressing and drizzle over salad; toss gently.

SWISS SALAD MEDLEY

BEATRICE CHEESE, INC.

Makes 8 servings

1 can (16 ounces) peas, drained
1 can (16 ounces) kidney beans, drained
1 can (6 ounces) black olives, drained and sliced
⅓ cup chopped green onions
½ large green pepper, chopped
3 stalks celery, chopped

10 ounces (2½ cups) County Line® Swiss Cheese, grated
4 eggs, hard cooked and chopped
¾ cup bread and butter pickles, chopped
1 cup mayonnaise
2 tablespoons horseradish sauce
½ teaspoon salt
¼ cup slivered almonds, toasted

In large mixing bowl, combine peas, kidney beans, olives, green onions, green pepper, celery, cheese, eggs, and pickles. In small bowl, mix mayonnaise, horseradish sauce, and salt; add to other ingredients along with toasted almonds. Chill and serve.

To toast almonds: Preheat oven to 350°F.

Place almonds in a shallow pan and bake for 10 minutes. Toasting time will vary depending on the size of the almonds.

SEVEN-LAYER SALAD

KRAFT GENERAL FOODS, INC.

Makes 8 servings

1½ quarts shredded lettuce
2 cups chopped tomatoes
2 cups mushroom slices
1 package (10 ounces) Birds Eye® Green Peas, thawed and drained
4 ounces Kraft® Natural Mild Cheddar Cheese, cubed

1 cup red onion rings
2 cups Miracle Whip® Light Reduced Calorie Salad Dressing
Oscar Mayer® Bacon slices (optional)
Kraft® Natural Mild Cheddar Cheese, shredded (optional)

In 2-quart serving bowl, layer lettuce, tomatoes, mushrooms, peas, cubed cheese, and onions. Spread salad dressing over onions, sealing to edge of bowl; cover. Chill several hours or overnight. Garnish with crisply cooked bacon slices, crumbled, and shredded Cheddar cheese, if desired.

Preparation time: 15 minutes, plus chilling

NATURALLY CHEESY LAYERED LETTUCE BOWL

BEATRICE CHEESE, INC.

Makes 4 servings

1 cup shredded County Line® Sharp Cheddar Cheese
1 cup plain yogurt *or* sour cream
1 large head iceberg lettuce
1½ cups shredded County Line® Old World Swiss Cheese
¾ cup fresh spinach, torn into bite-size pieces

¾ cup cooked brown *or* white rice, chilled
1 can (11 ounces) Mandarin orange segments
¾ cup chopped pecans
Dollop of plain yogurt *or* sour cream for garnish

Stir together Cheddar cheese and 1 cup yogurt; set aside. Remove inside portion of head lettuce. Spread *½ cup* of Cheddar cheese mixture inside shell. Layer with *¾ cup* Swiss cheese, spinach, rice, *½ cup* cheese mixture, orange segments, *¾ cup* Swiss cheese, remaining cheese mixture, and pecans. Refrigerate 3 hours or until ready to serve. Cut into wedges. Garnish with dollop of yogurt or sour cream.

BAKED GERMAN POTATO SALAD

KRAFT GENERAL FOODS, INC.

Makes 6 to 8 servings

6 slices Oscar Mayer® Bacon, chopped
3½ cups cooked new potatoes, quartered
¾ cup chopped celery
¾ cup chopped green bell pepper
¾ cup chopped onion
½ cup Miracle Whip® Salad Dressing

1 tablespoon Kraft® Pure Prepared
  Mustard
1 teaspoon celery seed
Salt
Pepper

Preheat oven to 400°F. Cook bacon until crisp; remove bacon, reserving 2 table-spoons fat. Combine reserved fat, bacon, potatoes, celery, green bell peppers, and onions. Add combined salad dressing, mustard, and seasonings; mix lightly. Spoon into 2-quart casserole. Bake 20 minutes.

VARIATIONS

Substitute 2 tablespoons Dijon mustard for prepared mustard.

Substitute cooked red potatoes, cut into 1-inch cubes, for quartered new potatoes.

Preparation time: 20 minutes   *Cooking time:* 20 minutes

GREAT AMERICAN POTATO SALAD

KRAFT GENERAL FOODS, INC.

Makes 6 servings

1 cup Miracle Whip® Salad Dressing
1 teaspoon Kraft® Pure Prepared
  Mustard
½ teaspoon celery seed
½ teaspoon salt
⅛ teaspoon pepper

4 cups cubed cooked potatoes
2 hard-cooked eggs, chopped
½ cup chopped onion
½ cup celery slices
½ cup chopped sweet pickle

Stir together salad dressing, mustard, celery seed, salt, and pepper. Add remaining ingredients; mix lightly. Chill.

VARIATIONS

Substitute Miracle Whip® Light Reduced Calorie Salad Dressing for regular salad dressing.

Omit celery and pickle. Add 1½ cups chopped ham and ½ cup chopped green bell pepper.

Omit celery seed, celery, and pickle. Add 1 cup chopped cucumber and ½ teaspoon dill weed.

Omit mustard, celery seed and pickle. Add 3 tablespoons Sauceworks® Horseradish Sauce and 1½ cups cubed roast beef.

Preparation time: 30 minutes, plus chilling

MOZZARELLA, TOMATO, AND BASIL SALAD

BEATRICE CHEESE, INC.

Makes 6 servings

4 cups halved cherry tomatoes, sliced
  plum tomatoes, *or* diced and seeded
  garden tomatoes
¼ cup chopped red *or* white onion
¼ cup minced fresh parsley
3 tablespoons vegetable *or* olive oil
1 tablespoon red wine vinegar

½ teaspoon dried basil *or* 2 tablespoons
  chopped fresh basil leaves
Freshly ground black pepper to taste
2 cups (8 ounces) County Line®
  Shredded Reduced Fat/Sodium
  Mozzarella Cheese
Salad greens

In a salad bowl, combine all ingredients except cheese and greens. Let tomatoes marinate 30 to 60 minutes. Stir in cheese and serve on a bed of salad greens.

MARKET SALAD

SARGENTO CHEESE COMPANY, INC.

Makes 8 servings

2 cups small cauliflower florets

2 cups small broccoli florets

2 medium carrots, cut into short, thin strips

1 can (16 ounces) garbanzo beans, well drained

¾ cup chopped red bell pepper *or* pimiento

2 cups (8 ounces) Sargento® Fancy Shredded Low-Moisture Part-Skim Mozzarella Cheese

⅓ cup white wine vinegar

1 teaspoon dried oregano leaves, crushed

2 cloves garlic, minced

¼ teaspoon salt

½ cup vegetable oil

2 teaspoons capers (optional)

Combine cauliflower, broccoli, carrots, beans, bell pepper, and cheese in large bowl; set aside. Combine vinegar, oregano, garlic, and salt in small bowl. Gradually add oil, whisking until smooth and thickened. Stir in capers. Add to vegetable and cheese mixture. Toss gently. Cover; chill thoroughly. Stir several times during chilling.

ROBUST VEGETABLE SALADS

GARDEN GAZPACHO SALAD

THOMAS J. LIPTON CO.

Makes about 8 side-dish servings

1 cup (8 ounces) Wish-Bone® Robusto Italian Dressing
¼ cup tomato juice
6 dashes hot pepper sauce (optional)
2 medium cucumbers, chopped

2 medium tomatoes, chopped
2 medium green peppers, chopped
1 medium onion, chopped
1 loaf unsliced round bread (about 9-inch diameter)
Lettuce leaves

In large bowl, blend dressing, tomato juice, and pepper sauce. Stir in vegetables. Cover and marinate in refrigerator, stirring occasionally, at least 2 hours. Cut lengthwise slice off top of bread. Hollow out center, leaving ½-inch shell. Just before serving, line bread shell with lettuce and fill with vegetable mixture. To serve, spoon out vegetable mixture, then cut bread shell into wedges.

VARIATIONS

Substitute Wish-Bone® Italian, Lite Italian, *or* Blended Italian Dressing for Robusto Italian Dressing.

FOUR-BEAN SALAD

CAMPBELL SOUP COMPANY

Makes 16 servings, ½ cup each

¾ cup wine vinegar
¼ cup vegetable oil
1 tablespoon sugar
¼ teaspoon pepper
1 can (20¾ ounces) Campbell's® Pork and Beans in Tomato Sauce

1 can (16 ounces) black beans, drained
1 can (16 ounces) red kidney beans, drained
1½ cups cut green beans, cooked
1 medium red onion, halved lengthwise and sliced
Cucumber slices for garnish

In large bowl, combine vinegar, oil, sugar, and pepper. Add beans and onion; toss gently to coat. Cover; refrigerate until serving time, at least 4 hours. Serve in cucumber-lined salad bowl.

MARINATED PEPPER SALAD

CAMPBELL SOUP COMPANY

Makes 6 servings, 4½ cups total

⅓ cup olive oil
¼ cup lime juice
2 tablespoons chopped fresh cilantro
2 tablespoons Vlasic® Sweet Banana Pepper Juice
½ teaspoon dried oregano leaves, crushed
½ teaspoon garlic powder
¼ teaspoon salt
¼ teaspoon ground red pepper
2 cups sliced Campbell's® Fresh Mushrooms

1 cup Vlasic® Sweet Banana Pepper Rings, drained
1 medium avocado, seeded, peeled, and sliced crosswise
1 Campbell's® Fresh Tomato, chopped
1 Campbell's® Fresh Tomato, sliced, for garnish
Curly endive for garnish
Vlasic® Mild Banana Peppers for garnish

To make dressing, in a small bowl combine oil, lime juice, cilantro, pepper juice, oregano, garlic, salt, and red pepper. In medium bowl, combine mushrooms, pepper rings, avocado, and chopped tomato. Add dressing; toss gently to coat. Cover; refrigerate until serving time, at least 2 hours. To serve, line plate with tomato slices and endive. With slotted spoon, place salad on plate. Top with whole peppers.

GARDEN SALAD WITH WARM BACON VINAIGRETTE DRESSING

OSCAR MAYER FOODS CORPORATION

Makes 4 servings

10 slices Oscar Mayer® Thick Sliced Bacon, cut into quarters
1 medium onion, coarsely chopped
¼ cup water
¼ cup vinegar
2 tablespoons sugar

⅛ teaspoon black pepper
8 cups (about 10 ounces) fresh spinach leaves *or* leaf lettuce, cleaned and torn into bite-size pieces
1 medium tomato, cut into ½-inch chunks

Place salad greens and chopped tomato in large serving bowl; set aside. Cook bacon and onion in large skillet over medium heat until bacon is crisp. Drain. Add remaining dressing ingredients to bacon and onions and cook over medium heat 3 minutes. Pour hot dressing over salad greens and toss. Serve immediately.

LAYERED TACO SALAD

KRAFT GENERAL FOODS, INC.

Makes 8 servings

1 tablespoon oil
4 boneless skinless chicken breast halves
   (approximately 1¼ pounds), cubed
¾ cup salsa
1 quart torn lettuce
3 cups coarsely broken tortilla chips
1 can (15 ounces) kidney beans, rinsed
   and drained

¼ cup green onion slices
Guacamole (see below)
1 cup (4 ounces) Kraft® Natural
   Shredded Sharp Cheddar Cheese
2 slices Oscar Mayer® Bacon, crisply
   cooked, crumbled

Heat oil in wok or 10-inch skillet over medium-high; add chicken. Stir-fry 4 to 5 minutes or until tender. Reduce heat to medium. Stir in salsa; cover. Simmer 5 minutes. In 3- to 4-quart serving bowl, layer lettuce, chips, beans, onions, and chicken mixture. Cover with Guacamole, spreading to edges of bowl to seal. Sprinkle with cheese. Cover; chill. Add bacon; toss lightly just before serving.

To microwave: Omit oil. To cook chicken, place in 1½-quart casserole; cover. Microwave on HIGH 4 to 5 minutes or until tender, stirring every 2 minutes. Drain; stir in salsa. Microwave on HIGH 1 minute. Continue as directed.

GUACAMOLE

1 ripe avocado, peeled and mashed
½ cup Miracle Whip® Salad Dressing

½ cup salsa
¼ cup milk

Mix all ingredients until well blended.

Preparation time: 20 minutes, plus chilling

SOUTHWEST PASTA SALAD

BEST FOODS, A DIVISION OF CPC INTERNATIONAL INC.

Makes 6 servings

½ cup Mazola® Corn Oil
⅓ cup lime juice
⅓ cup chopped cilantro
2 tablespoons pickled jalapeño peppers, seeded and chopped
2 cloves garlic, minced
¾ teaspoon ground cumin
¾ teaspoon salt

6 ounces Mueller's® Pasta Ruffles, cooked, rinsed with cold water, and drained
1 can (16 ounces) black beans, rinsed and drained
¾ cup diced red onion
¾ cup diced red pepper
¾ cup diced yellow pepper

In small bowl, stir corn oil, lime juice, cilantro, jalapeño peppers, garlic, cumin, and salt until blended. In large bowl, combine pasta, beans, red onion, and peppers. Add dressing; toss to coat. Cover; chill 1 hour.

CURRIED PINEAPPLE PASTA SALAD

DOLE FOOD COMPANY

Makes 8 servings

1 can (20 ounces) Dole® Pineapple Chunks
3 chicken breast halves (2 cups), cooked and shredded
8 ounces macaroni (or small pasta), cooked
2 cups sliced Dole® Celery
½ cup sliced Dole® Green Onions

½ cup Dole® Red Bell Pepper, seeded and slivered
½ cup sliced ripe olives
¾ cup mayonnaise
⅓ cup chopped chutney
¼ cup dairy sour cream
2 teaspoons curry powder
1 teaspoon salt

Drain pineapple. In salad bowl, combine pineapple, chicken, pasta, celery, onion, red pepper, and olives. For dressing, blend remaining ingredients. Toss salad with dressing. Cover and refrigerate until chilled.

BOW TIE SALAD
DOLE FOOD COMPANY

Makes 10 servings

1 package (10 ounces) bow tie pasta
1 Dole® Red Bell Pepper, seeded and slivered
2 cups Dole® Broccoli florets
1 cup Dole® Cauliflower florets
1 clove garlic, pressed

½ cup rice vinegar
¼ cup vegetable oil
2 tablespoons teriyaki sauce
1 tablespoon sesame seeds, toasted
2 teaspoons sesame oil
¼ teaspoon red pepper flakes

Cook pasta according to package directions. Combine with remaining ingredients. Refrigerate overnight.

PARTY PASTA SALAD
DOLE FOOD COMPANY

Makes 12 to 15 servings

1 package (12 ounces) twistee egg noodles
1 clove garlic, pressed
1 cup vegetable oil
½ cup distilled white vinegar
¼ cup lemon juice
1 tablespoon Dijon mustard
1 tablespoon Worcestershire sauce

Salt to taste
Pepper to taste
1 red bell pepper, seeded and chunked
3 cups Dole® Broccoli florets
3 cups Dole® Cauliflower florets
1½ cups Dole® Pitted Dates, halved
1 cup Dole® Whole Natural Almonds, toasted

Cook noodles according to package directions. For dressing, combine next 8 ingredients. In large bowl, toss hot noodles and dressing. Add remaining ingredients except almonds. Refrigerate 2 hours or overnight. Toss in almonds just before servings.

To toast almonds: Preheat oven to 350°F. Place almonds in a shallow pan and bake for 10 minutes. Toasting time will vary depending on the size of the almonds.

PICNIC-PERFECT PASTA SALAD
DOLE FOOD COMPANY

Makes 4 servings

1 can (8 ounces) Dole® Pineapple Chunks in Juice
2 tablespoons sesame oil
1 tablespoon honey
1 tablespoon soy sauce
1 tablespoon minced crystalized ginger
1 large clove garlic, pressed

2 cups cooked spiral pasta
1 cup cooked chunked chicken *or* deli chicken
2 tablespoons sliced Dole® Green Onion
2 cups cooked Dole® Broccoli florets
⅓ cup Dole® Red Bell Pepper strips
1 tablespoon sesame seed, toasted

Drain pineapple; reserve ⅓ cup juice. For salad dressing, in screw-top jar combine reserved juice, sesame oil, honey, soy sauce, ginger, and garlic. In large bowl, combine pineapple, pasta, chicken, and onion. Toss with dressing. Cover; refrigerate 2 hours or longer. Add broccoli and bell pepper. Toss well, sprinkle with sesame seeds.

PASTA DEL SOL
DOLE FOOD COMPANY

Makes 6 to 8 servings

1 can (20 ounces) Dole® Pineapple Chunks
8 ounces spiral pasta
1 small Dole® Red Bell Pepper, chunked
1½ cups slivered ham *or* Cheddar cheese
1 cup sliced Dole® Carrots
1 cup frozen peas, thawed

Zest and juice from 1 Dole® Orange
½ cup vegetable oil
1 tablespoon sugar
1 tablespoon sweet basil, crumbled
¼ teaspoon black pepper
Dash nutmeg

Drain pineapple; reserve ½ cup juice. Cook pasta according to package directions. Combine pineapple, pasta, bell pepper, ham, carrots, and peas in large bowl. For dressing, combine reserved *½ cup* pineapple juice with *1 tablespoon* orange zest, *½ cup* orange juice, and remaining ingredients. Pour over salad. Toss well. Cover; refrigerate at least 1 hour or overnight.

PASTA SALAD NIÇOISE

LINDSAY INTERNATIONAL, INC.

Makes 8 servings

⅓ cup salad oil
3 tablespoons lemon juice
2 tablespoons vinegar
½ teaspoon dry mustard
½ teaspoon paprika
½ teaspoon dried basil, crushed
8 ounces linguine, broken in half
1 cup cherry tomatoes, halved

1 package (9 ounces) frozen French-style green beans, cooked, drained, and chilled
1 can (12 ounces) tuna, drained and flaked
4 eggs (hard cooked and sliced)
½ cup Lindsay® Small Pitted Ripe Olives, drained

For salad dressing, in a screw-top jar shake together salad oil, lemon juice, vinegar, dry mustard, paprika, and basil.

Cook linguine in boiling salted water until tender. Immediately drain in colander. Rinse with cold water; drain. In salad bowl, combine linguine, cherry-tomato halves, and green beans. Pour dressing over mixture. Toss gently to mix.

Break the tuna into bite-size chunks; mound tuna atop linguine mixture. Arrange sliced eggs and olives around tuna. Cover and chill several hours. Toss gently before serving.

SAVORY SHELL SALAD

SARGENTO CHEESE COMPANY, INC.

Makes 8 servings

2 cups uncooked salad *or* medium pasta shells
2 medium tomatoes, seeded and diced
2 green onions, thinly sliced
¼ cup white wine vinegar
½ teaspoon oregano

2 cloves garlic, minced
¼ teaspoon sugar
⅓ cup olive oil
1¼ cups (5 ounces) Sargento® Fancy Shredded Cheddar Cheese

Cook pasta according to package directions; cool. In large bowl, toss together pasta, tomatoes, and onions. In small bowl, stir together vinegar, oregano, garlic, and sugar. Gradually add oil, whisking until smooth and thickened. Add to pasta. Toss to coat thoroughly. Stir in cheese. Cover and refrigerate until chilled. Toss before serving.

TORTELLINI ASPARAGUS SALAD

LAWRY'S FOODS, INC.

Makes 4 servings

1 pound fresh asparagus, cut into ½-inch
pieces
2 cups tightly packed fresh spinach
leaves, torn into bite-size pieces
1 cup diced red bell pepper
2 packages (9 ounces each) small cheese-
filled tortellini, cooked and drained

¼ cup red wine vinegar
2 tablespoons olive *or* vegetable oil
1½ teaspoons lemon juice
1 teaspoon sugar
1 teaspoon Lawry's® Garlic Salt

Place asparagus on steamer rack; place in deep pot with 1 inch of boiling water.
Cover and steam 10 minutes. Remove and set aside. Steam spinach in same pot
about 45 seconds or until just wilted. In large bowl, combine asparagus, spinach,
bell pepper, and tortellini; blend well. In small bowl, combine vinegar, oil, lemon
juice, sugar, and garlic salt; blend well. Pour over tortellini mixture; toss well.

Serve with fresh bread.

VARIATIONS

Substitute 1½ cups broccoli florets for asparagus.
Substitute chopped pimientos for red bell pepper.

To microwave: Place asparagus and spinach in microwave-safe bowl; sprinkle with
water. Cover with plastic wrap, venting 1 corner, and microwave on HIGH 2 minutes to steam. In large bowl, combine asparagus, spinach, bell pepper, and tortellini; blend well. In small bowl, combine vinegar, oil, lemon juice, sugar, and garlic
salt; blend well. Pour over tortellini mixture; toss well.

THAI SALAD

BEST FOODS, A DIVISION OF CPC INTERNATIONAL INC.

Makes 4 servings

⅓ cup Mazola® Corn Oil
⅓ cup lime juice
2 tablespoons chopped fresh mint leaves
2 tablespoons chopped cilantro
2 tablespoons pickled jalapeño peppers, chopped and seeded
½ teaspoon salt
½ teaspoon sugar

6 ounces Mueller's® Twist Trio®, cooked, rinsed with cold water, and drained
½ cup chopped red onion
1 large cucumber, sliced
12 ounces medium shrimp, shelled and cooked
Lettuce leaves

In small bowl, stir corn oil, lime juice, mint, cilantro, jalapeño peppers, salt, and sugar until blended, to make dressing. In medium bowl, combine pasta and red onion. Toss with half the dressing. Arrange on lettuce-lined platter with cucumber and shrimp; drizzle with remaining dressing.

GARDEN PASTA TOSS

KRAFT GENERAL FOODS, INC.

Makes 6 to 8 servings

2 cups (5½ ounces) rotini, cooked and drained
2 cups zucchini slices, halved
½ cup chopped red bell pepper
8 slices Oscar Mayer® Bacon, crisply cooked, crumbled
2 eggs, hard cooked and coarsely chopped
1 teaspoon dried oregano leaves, crushed

½ teaspoon onion powder
½ teaspoon pepper
¾ pound Velveeta® Pasteurized Process Cheese Spread, cubed
¾ cup Kraft® Real Mayonnaise
3 tablespoons milk
2 teaspoons Kraft® Pure Prepared Mustard
Lettuce (optional)

Mix rotini, zucchini, red bell pepper, bacon, eggs, and seasonings in large bowl. Heat pasteurized process cheese spread, mayonnaise, milk, and mustard in saucepan over low heat, stirring until pasteurized process cheese spread is melted. Pour over rotini mixture; mix lightly. Chill. Mix lightly just before serving. Serve on lettuce-covered platter, if desired.

Preparation time: 20 minutes, plus chilling

ARTICHOKE PASTA SALAD

PET INCORPORATED

Makes 4 servings, 1½ cups each

2 jars (6 ounces each) Progresso®
Marinated Artichoke Hearts,
undrained
½ pound fusille, cooked and drained
¼ cup Progresso® Grated Parmesan
Cheese
½ cup Progresso® Italian Style Bread
Crumbs

1 tablespoon Progresso® Red Wine
Vinegar
⅓ cup chopped celery
⅓ cup chopped green bell pepper
1 medium tomato, diced
¼ cup chopped red onion

In large bowl, combine all ingredients; toss gently. Serve chilled, if desired.

PASTA, CHICKEN AND BROCCOLI PESTO TOSS

SARGENTO CHEESE COMPANY, INC.

Makes 8 servings

4 ounces (about 2 cups) vegetable spiral
pasta
2 cups cubed, cooked chicken *or* turkey
breast
2 cups small broccoli florets, cooked
crisp-tender and cooled
1½ cups (6 ounces) Sargento® Fancy
Shredded Low-Moisture Part-Skim
Mozzarella Cheese

⅔ cup lightly packed fresh basil leaves
2 cloves garlic
1 cup mayonnaise
1 tablespoon lemon juice
½ teaspoon salt
½ cup (1½ ounces) Sargento® Fancy
Shredded Parmesan Cheese
½ cup pine nuts *or* coarsely chopped
walnuts, toasted

Cook pasta according to package directions until tender; drain and cool. Combine
pasta, chicken, broccoli, and mozzarella cheese in large bowl. Process basil and
garlic in food processor or blender until finely chopped. Add mayonnaise, lemon
juice, and salt. Process to combine thoroughly. Stir in Parmesan cheese. Add to
pasta mixture and toss to coat all ingredients. Stir in pine nuts. Serve immediately
or cover and refrigerate. For maximum flavor, remove from refrigerator and toss
gently 30 minutes before serving.

HOT AND COLD VEAL SALAD

MCCORMICK & COMPANY, INC.

Makes 4 individual salads; 1 cup sauce

½ pound thin veal cutlets
½ pound veal sweetbreads
½ cup butter
1 tablespoon flour
½ cup malt vinegar
⅔ cup water
¼ teaspoon McCormick/Schilling® ground Mustard
¼ teaspoon McCormick/Schilling Paprika

⅛ teaspoon McCormick/Schilling Thyme Leaves
⅛ teaspoon McCormick/Schilling Tarragon Leaves
¼ teaspoon McCormick/Schilling ground Black Pepper
¼ teaspoon McCormick/Schilling Instant Minced Onion
Salad greens

Cut veal in small pieces, about 2-by-2-by-¼ inches. Parboil sweetbreads. Cool. Remove membrane and cut meat in small pieces, about 2-by-2-by-½ inches. Sauté veal and sweetbreads in butter until lightly browned. Remove meat and keep warm. Sprinkle flour over butter in skillet. Stir and cook over low heat 1 minute. Add vinegar, water, and next 6 ingredients. Cook, stirring and scraping pan 1 minute. Pour into heatproof bowl and keep warm. Arrange 4 plates of salad greens. Place meat, alternating slices of veal and sweetbreads, over center of greens. Pour ¼ *cup* of sauce over meat. Serve immediately.

MARINATED BEEF SALAD

NABISCO FOODS GROUP

Makes 8 servings

1 pound thinly sliced roast beef, cut into julienne strips
¾ cup chopped onion
¾ cup chopped tomato
1 cup Ortega® Mild, Medium *or* Hot Thick and Chunky Salsa

½ cup Regina® Red Wine Vinegar
¼ cup vegetable oil
8 cups clean, torn lettuce
1 cup (4 ounces) shredded Cheddar cheese
Tortilla chips (optional)

In small bowl, combine roast beef, onion, tomato, salsa, vinegar, and oil; chill until serving time.

Place 1 cup lettuce on each of 8 plates. Top with about ½ *cup* beef mixture and *2 tablespoons* cheese. Serve with tortilla chips, if desired.

TURKEY WALDORF SALAD

BEST FOODS, A DIVISION OF CPC INTERNATIONAL INC.

Makes about 5 cups

⅔ cup Hellmann's® *or* Best Foods®
   Mayonnaise
2 tablespoons lemon juice
½ teaspoon salt
¼ teaspoon pepper

2 cups diced cooked turkey *or* chicken
2 apples, cored and chopped
⅔ cup sliced celery
½ cup chopped walnuts

In large bowl, stir mayonnaise, lemon juice, salt, and pepper until smooth. Add turkey, apples, celery, and walnuts; toss to coat well. Cover and refrigerate.

SMOKED TURKEY AND PEPPER PASTA SALAD

KRAFT GENERAL FOODS, INC.

Makes 5 to 6 servings

¾ cup Miracle Whip® Salad Dressing
1 tablespoon Dijon mustard
½ teaspoon dried thyme leaves
8 ounces fettuccine, cooked and drained
1 cup (8 ounces) diced Louis Rich®
   Smoked Boneless Turkey Breast

¾ cup zucchini slices, halved
½ cup red bell pepper strips
½ cup yellow bell pepper strips
Salt
Pepper

Mix salad dressing, mustard, and thyme until well blended. Add pasta, turkey, and vegetables; mix lightly. Season with salt and pepper to taste. Chill. Add additional dressing before serving, if desired.

VARIATIONS

Substitute Miracle Whip® Light Reduced Calorie Salad Dressing for regular salad dressing.

Substitute rotini, shell, or elbow macaroni for fettucine.

Substitute ⅓ cup red bell pepper, ⅓ cup yellow bell pepper, and ⅓ cup green bell pepper for red and yellow peppers.

Preparation time: 15 minutes, plus chilling

HUMANKIND'S EARLIEST PROCESSED FOOD
The Story of Hot Dogs

Sausages, the earliest known processed food, are first mentioned in history in in Homer's *Odyssey*. The Gauls and ancient Romans enjoyed spiced ground meat held together with outer casings as one of their dietary mainstays.

In 1987 the Germans of Frankfurt celebrated the five hundredth anniversary of the invention of the modern frankfurter which, they claim, predates the discovery of the New World by five years. The origin of the modern frankfurter, has been disputed, however. Also called the wiener, the sausage, some say, was actually first processed in Vienna, (Wien), Austria. To further complicate things, Frankfurters tend to call the sausage a wiener, and Viennese like to call it a frankfurter. Still others believe that today's frankfurter—or wiener—may have originated in neither city but rather may be a blend of sausages brought to the United States by butchers of several nationalities. A German immigrant selling hot dogs with milk rolls and sauerkraut from his pushcart in New York City's Bowery in the 1860s may have been the first to put the hot dog on a roll. Around the turn of the century, a German butcher, Charles Feltman, brought the frankfurter from his homeland and sold 3,684 "dachshund sausages" from his Coney Island stand during his first year in business. Throngs of visitors to the Chicago Colombian Exposition consumed an enormous quantity of the easy-to-eat dachshund sausages in 1893, the same year that St. Louis bar owner Chris Von de Ahe, also owner of the St. Louis Browns major league baseball team, began the great U.S. tradition of hot dogs at ball games.

The first hot dog bun was probably created for the visitors of the St. Louis Louisiana Purchase Exposition in 1904. A hot dog concessionaire, Anton Feucht-wanger, had run low on the white cotton gloves he loaned to customers to protect their fingers from the hot sausages. He sought help from his brother-in-law, a baker, who solved the problem by creating the first hot dog-size buns.

The frankfurter received its current nickname one cold April day in 1906. Concessionaire Harry Stevens, whose company is still the major concessionaire in New York and Florida ballparks and other sports stadiums, was losing money trying to sell ice cream and ice-cold sodas at the New York Polo Grounds. He sent his salesmen out to round up all the sausages and buns they could locate. Within an hour, they were promoting hot sausages, freshly retrieved from portable tanks of hot water, by hawking, "Red hots! Get your dachshund sausages while they're hot!" A sports cartoonist, Tad Dorgan, desperate for an idea before his press deadline, heard the vendors' cries and quickly drew a caricature of barking dachshund sausages snuggled in cozy buns. He couldn't spell dachshund, so he simply wrote "hot dog!"

Hot dogs have been fare fitting for royalty on occasion: In 1939, Franklin D. Roosevelt entertained King George VI of England with a hot dog and beer feast; in 1957, Queen Elizabeth II served the American Bar Association a royal hot dog banquet.

But hot dogs are truly a food for every day. Chicago's O'Hare International Airport sells more of them than anyplace else in the world, ringing up more than 2 million annually at its restaurants and snack bars. Throughout the United States, 95 percent of all homes serve the country's favorite sausage. During peak outdoor cookery months—Memorial Day to Labor Day—the country consumes more than 5 billion hot dogs, according to the Oscar Mayer Company. Laid end to end, that's enough hot dogs to circle the globe more than fifteen times.

WIENER SAUERKRAUT SALAD
OSCAR MAYER FOODS CORPORATION

Makes 6 servings

1 package (16 ounces) Oscar Mayer® Wieners	¼ cup chopped green pepper
2 cups sauerkraut, drained	½ cup sour cream
1 cup thinly sliced radishes	½ cup mayonnaise
	Lettuce leaves

Cut unheated wieners into ½-inch pieces. Combine with sauerkraut, radishes, and green pepper in large bowl. Cover; let sit 1 hour. Mix sour cream and mayonnaise in small bowl. Toss with sauerkraut; refrigerate before serving. Serve on lettuce leaves.

SCARBOROUGH FAIR SALAD

OSCAR MAYER FOODS CORPORATION

Makes 4 servings

1 pound Louis Rich® Breast of Turkey
1 package (2 ounces) slivered almonds
1 tart green apple
1 tablespoon lemon juice
2 stalks celery, chopped
2 green onions with tops, chopped
1 tablespoon chopped fresh parsley

½ cup mayonnaise
¼ teaspoon ground thyme
⅛ teaspoon garlic powder
⅛ teaspoon oregano leaves
⅛ teaspoon pepper
⅛ teaspoon rosemary leaves
⅛ teaspoon sage

Preheat oven to 350°F. Cut turkey into ½-inch cubes, set aside. Toast almonds on shallow baking sheet for 8 minutes or until lightly browned; cool. Cut apple into chunks and toss with lemon juice in large bowl. Add turkey, almonds, celery, onion, and parsley. In small bowl, combine mayonnaise, thyme, garlic powder, oregano leaves, pepper, rosemary leaves, and sage to make dressing. Add to turkey mixture and toss. Cover and chill thoroughly before serving.

TURKEY IN AVOCADOS

LINDSAY INTERNATIONAL, INC.

Makes 6 servings

⅓ cup plain yogurt
¼ cup mayonnaise *or* salad dressing
1 teaspoon lemon juice
¼ teaspoon dill weed
⅛ teaspoon salt
Dash pepper
1½ cups cubed cooked turkey *or* chicken

1 small tomato, seeded and chopped
½ cup Lindsay® Colossal Pitted Ripe
    Olives, drained and halved
3 tablespoons sliced green onion
3 avocados
Lemon juice

Stir together yogurt, mayonnaise, 1 teaspoon lemon juice, dill weed, ⅛ teaspoon salt, and dash pepper. Stir in turkey or chicken, tomato, olives, and green onion. Cover and chill thoroughly. To serve, halve and seed avocados; brush lightly with lemon juice. Spoon about *½ cup* mixture into each half.

CHUNKY CHICKEN SALAD
OR SANDWICH SPREAD

THOMAS J. LIPTON CO.

Makes about 6 servings

1 cup Lipton® California Dip
  (see below)
2 cups cut-up cooked chicken

1 cup sliced celery
¼ cup sliced sweet gherkins
¼ cup sliced pitted ripe olives

In large bowl, toss California Dip with chicken, celery, gherkins, and olives.

CALIFORNIA DIP

Makes about 2 cups

1 envelope Lipton® Onion Recipe
  Soup Mix

1 container (16 ounces) sour cream

Blend together and chill.

LUNCH BOX SANDWICH

Slices of bread *or* rolls

Thin slices of boiled *or* baked ham

Lightly butter slices of bread or rolls. Arrange 1 or 2 slices of ham on bread. Top with 2 to 3 tablespoons Chunky Chicken Salad. Cover with second slice of bread.

CHEDDAR CHICKEN AND APPLE SALAD

BEATRICE CHEESE, INC.

Makes 6 servings

¼ cup no-cholesterol mayonnaise
2 tablespoons skim milk
2 to 3 teaspoons snipped fresh dill *or* ½
  teaspoon dill
2 cups cooked cubed chicken *or* turkey
  breast
1 cup diced celery

1 Granny Smith apple, cored and diced
1 Red Delicious apple, cored and diced
4 green onions with tops, thinly sliced
2 cups (8 ounces) County Line®
  Shredded Reduced-Fat/Sodium
  Cheddar Cheese
Freshly ground pepper to taste

In small bowl, combine mayonnaise, milk, and dill to make dressing. In salad bowl, combine all remaining ingredients. Toss with dressing to coat.

Serve on lettuce or stuff into pita-bread halves.

GRILLED CHICKEN SALAD VINAIGRETTE

RAGU FOODS CO.

Makes 6 to 8 servings

1 package Adolph's® Marinade in
   Minutes—Garlic Dijon Flavor
½ cup wine vinegar
¼ cup water
2 pounds boneless chicken breasts
1 cup thinly sliced celery
1 medium onion, sliced
1 jar (7 ounces) roasted peppers,
   drained and sliced

1 jar (6 ounces) marinated artichoke
   hearts, drained and sliced
1 can (2¼ ounces) sliced ripe olives,
   drained
⅓ cup olive oil
3 tablespoons wine vinegar
1 teaspoon Dijon mustard
Salt to taste
Pepper to taste
Leaf lettuce

Preheat grill or broiler. In medium bowl, thoroughly combine contents of marinade package with *½ cup* vinegar and *¼ cup* water. Place chicken in marinade; pierce deeply with a fork: Marinate 15 minutes, turning chicken occasionally. Remove chicken from marinade. Grill or broil chicken 5 to 6 inches from heat, 5 to 7 minutes per side or until thoroughly cooked. Thinly slice chicken; let cool. Combine sliced chicken with celery, onion, roasted peppers, artichoke hearts, olives, olive oil, vinegar, mustard, salt, and pepper. Stir to combine thoroughly. Serve chilled over leaf lettuce.

SOUTHWEST CHICKEN SALAD

LINDSAY INTERNATIONAL, INC.

Makes 4 servings

¼ cup salad oil
2 tablespoons white wine vinegar
2 tablespoon lime juice
½ teaspoon chili powder
¼ teaspoon dry mustard
Several drops bottled hot pepper sauce
¼ teaspoon salt
4 ounces medium shell macaroni,
   cooked, drained, and rinsed with cold
   water
1 can (6 ounces; 1⅔ cup) Lindsay®
   Medium Pitted Ripe Olives, drained

1 can (8¾ ounces) whole-kernel corn,
   drained
1 cup chopped cooked chicken
4 ounces Monterey Jack cheese, cubed
½ medium avocado, seeded, peeled, and
   cut into bite-size chunks
2 canned jalapeño peppers, rinsed,
   seeded, and chopped
2 tablespoons sliced green onion
1 jar (2 ounces) diced pimiento, drained

In a screw-top jar, shake together oil, vinegar, lime juice, chili powder, dry mustard, pepper sauce, and salt. Pour over macaroni; stir to coat. Stir in remaining ingredients; cover and chill.

POPPY-SEED DIJON DRESSING
NABISCO FOODS GROUP

Makes 1¾ cups

1 cup vegetable oil
¼ cup Regina® Red Wine Vinegar
¼ cup honey

2 tablespoons Grey Poupon® Dijon *or*
  Country Dijon Mustard
1 tablespoon minced onion
1 tablespoon poppy seed

In bowl, whisk oil, vinegar, honey, and mustard; blend in onion and poppy seed. Serve with tossed salad.

Store, covered, in refrigerator up to 1 week. Bring to room temperature and mix thoroughly before serving.

LAST-MINUTE DRESSING
LAWRY'S FOODS, INC.

Makes 1 cup

⅔ cup vegetable oil
¼ cup white wine vinegar
1½ tablespoons Dijon mustard
1 tablespoon water

2 teaspoons sugar
1 teaspoon Lawry's® Seasoned Salt
½ teaspoon Lawry's® Lemon Pepper
  Seasoning

In medium bowl or food processor, combine all ingredients. Blend well with wire whisk or process 15 seconds.

Use on any green salad or pour over grilled chicken or beef entree.

DRESSED-UP SALAD DRESSING

LAWRY'S FOODS, INC.

Makes about 2 cups

1 bottle (8 ounces) Wish-Bone® Italian Salad Dressing
1 tablespoon Dijon mustard
1 tablespoon Parmesan cheese
½ teaspoon Lawry's® Garlic Powder with Parsley
1 egg white, hard cooked and finely chopped

¼ cup finely chopped green bell pepper
¼ cup finely chopped red bell pepper
¼ cup finely chopped yellow bell pepper
1 tablespoon chopped almonds
Tossed greens
Tomato wedges

In food processor or blender, combine dressing, mustard, cheese, and garlic powder with parsley; process 15 seconds to blend well. In medium bowl, combine remaining ingredients; pour dressing mixture over pepper mixture. Serve over tossed greens and tomato wedges. Add any remaining bell pepper to salad for extra color.

(Note: To save time, chop egg white, peppers, and almonds in the food processor; add dressing, mustard, cheese, and garlic powder. Process to desired texture.)

SAY CHEESE
The Story of Cheese

Legend has it that somewhere in an Asian desert more than four thousand years ago an Arab trader tried to take a gulp of milk stored in a pouch he had made from a calf's stomach. Attached to his camel's hump during the undulating ride through the desert, the pouch had absorbed the full blast of the sun. The milk had curdled. The Arab was too hungry to care. He poured out the clear liquid and ate the precipitate. Not a bad taste, thought the nomad. He had discovered a new way of storing milk and from that moment on cheese became a delicious and important part of the diets of most primitive and many civilized people of the world. The nomad didn't know that the acid that transformed his milk was rennet, found in the gastric juices of the fourth stomach of young milk-drinking animals. For today's cheese making, rennin, the milk-coagulating enzyme, is extracted from the lining of calves' stomachs and commercially processed. Plant-juice agents such as thistle juice and safflower juice are also used to curdle milk into cheese. These different fermenting agents produce different kinds of cheeses.

Bacteria, present in all milk, will act to sour milk and cause the solid, protein part of the milk to separate from the liquids, or the curds to separate from the whey. Hence, what Miss Muffet ate was an early stage of cottage cheese. This manner of making cheese was probably discovered independently in different parts of the world when milk accidently soured. The ancient method is still used to make cottage cheese, now usually with the addition of rennin.

The amount of water left in cheese and the ripening method used to make the product determine its hardness or softness. Hard cheeses are used for grating; best known of these, the hardest of all, is Parmesan, named for the Italian town of Parma. According to sales in the United States, our favorite hard cheese is Cheddar, originally made in Cheddar, England. Made from whole milk it contains a small amount of fat. Our most popular soft cheese is cottage cheese, manufactured from skim milk and with very little fat content.

Cheese, like wine, develops its unique flavor from the characteristics of its region of origin. The breed of cattle or goat, the kinds of grasses or flowers the animals ate, the happenstance of any of millions of microorganisms settling out of the air: All act to produce the distinctive cheese flavors associated with different regions. New York Cheddar cheese, for example, tastes very different from Wisconsin Cheddar.

The final step of making cheese, the process of aging with natural enzymes and molds, defines the singular flavor and makes the cheese a gastronomic delicacy. Blue-mold cheese, among the most robust, include the famous Roquefort, from the French town of the same name, a semisoft cheese made from rich sheep's milk and aged in ancient caves.

The best-selling blue cheese in the United States is Beatrice Cheese, Inc.'s Treasure Cave® brand, made from whole milk. Ripened in the traditional manner, Treasure Cave® is cured for one hundred days and nights in a massive labyrinth of whitewashed sandstone caves along the Straight River in Faribault, Minnesota. The temperature of the caves is a constant 54° Fahrenheit, the same as well water, perfect for aging a rich, full-flavored blue.

SUPER DRESSING

BEATRICE CHEESE, INC.

Makes 2 cups

Salad greens
Cucumbers
Tomatoes
1 package (4 ounces) Treasure Cave®
  Blue Cheese, crumbled
1 cup mayonnaise

⅓ cup milk
¼ teaspoon celery salt
⅛ teaspoon garlic salt
⅛ teaspoon onion salt
Dash pepper

Prepare greens, cucumbers, and tomatoes for salad. Combine all remaining ingredients in medium-size bowl. Serve with salad. If dressing thickens on standing, add more milk.

CREAMY DRESSING

BEATRICE CHEESE, INC.

Makes 2 cups

1 package (4 ounces) Treasure Cave®
  Blue Cheese
3 ounces cream cheese
½ cup milk

½ cup sour cream
2 tablespoons lemon juice
Mixed salad greens *or* cabbage

Blend two-thirds of the package of blue cheese with all of the cream cheese. Gradually add milk. Blend in sour cream and lemon juice. Spoon onto mixed salad greens or mix with shredded cabbage for salad. Crumble remaining cheese over salad.

SWEET-SOUR DRESSING

BEATRICE CHEESE, INC.

Makes 2½ cups

2 package (4 ounces) Treasure Cave®
  Blue Cheese, crumbled
¼ cup sugar

1 teaspoon salt
⅓ cup vinegar
1 cup sour cream

Combine all ingredients. Cover and refrigerate for at least 30 minutes before serving.

SCENE-STEALING
SIDE DISHES

CUCUMBER SAUTÉ
MCCORMICK & COMPANY, INC.

Makes 4 individual salads, 3 cups total

4 slices bacon
2 cucumbers
1 medium red bell pepper
1 small yellow onion
⅛ teaspoon McCormick/Schilling® ground White Pepper
¼ teaspoon McCormick/Schilling Celery Seed
¼ teaspoon McCormick/Schilling Seasoning Salt
¼ teaspoon McCormick/Schilling Parsley Flakes
¼ teaspoon sugar
3 tablespoons water
2 tablespoons red wine vinegar
½ teaspoon cornstarch
Additional bacon for garnish (optional)
Fresh parsley for garnish (optional)

Fry bacon. Drain. Reserve 2 tablespoons bacon fat. Set aside. Peel, quarter, and seed cucumbers. Cut into julienne strips. Seed red pepper. Cut into thin bite-size strips.

Peel onion and cut into ⅛-inch slices. Separate onion into rings. Heat bacon fat in skillet over medium-high heat. Add cucumbers, red peppers, and onion. Stir-fry 3 minutes.

Remove vegetables from skillet. Combine remaining 8 ingredients. Mix well. Add to skillet, stirring constantly, until mixture thickens. Add vegetables and heat through. Arrange cucumbers, peppers, and onions on 4 salad plates. Crumble bacon. Garnish each serving with bacon and fresh parsley, if desired.

CORNFLAKE-TOPPED CAULIFLOWER ESCALLOP

KELLOGG COMPANY

Makes 8 servings

2 tablespoons margarine *or* butter, melted

⅛ teaspoon garlic powder

1½ cups KELLOGG'S CORN FLAKES® cereal, crushed to ¾ cup

4 cups sliced cauliflower (1 medium-size head)

1 chicken bouillon cube

¾ cup hot water

¼ cup margarine *or* butter

¼ cup all-purpose flour

⅛ teaspoon white pepper

1 cup half-and-half

2 tablespoons chopped pimiento

1 cup sliced green onions

Preheat oven to 350°F. Combine melted margarine with garlic powder and crushed cereal. Set aside for topping. Cook cauliflower in small amount of water until almost tender, about 10 minutes. Drain well. Set aside. Dissolve bouillon cube in ¾ cup hot water. Set aside. Melt margarine in large saucepan over low heat. Stir in flour and pepper. Add bouillon and half-and-half gradually, stirring until smooth. Increase heat to medium and cook until bubbly and thickened, stirring constantly. Remove from heat. Stir in pimiento, green onions, and cauliflower. Spoon mixture into 10-by-6-by-2-inch (1½ quart) glass baking dish. Sprinkle cereal mixture evenly over top. Bake about 20 minutes or until thoroughly heated.

DREAMS COMING TRUE
The Story of Lawry's®

In the twenties, thirties, and forties, Los Angeles was a land of dreams and Hollywood fantasies. Even the restaurants and bakeries were designed to look like something more than just buildings where food was sold. People talked business deals at lunch inside a massive brown derby, bought tasty hot dogs in a building that looked like a giant hot dog, and selected baked goods in the whimsical blue-and-white windmills of the Van de Kamp bakeries dotting the dreamscape. The Dutch were known for cleanliness, Frank Lawrence had reasoned: It made sense to dramatize that theme in the bakeries he owned with his brother-in-law, Theodore Van de Kamp.

Lawrence next used his charm and showmanship at the Tam O'Shanter, a restaurant-turned-inn that transported guests right to Normandy, France, inside and out. People were enchanted. The famous restaurant, the oldest in Los Angeles, still exists in its original location.

Then Lawrence decided to create a restaurant where prime rib would be carved and served right at the table, as it was in a place he had heard about in London, the acclaimed Simpson's-in-the-Strand. Other restaurateurs considered this a foolhardy scheme. But Lawrence chose a site in the former swampland between Santa Monica and Los Angeles, where two other restaurants sat placidly amid wild mustard on the otherwise vacant land. Today, Lawry's® The Prime Rib is the premier restaurant in its original location, now the world-famous La Cienaga Restaurant Row with thirty-five restaurants.

In his restaurant, Lawrence blended art deco and stylized Old English decor. He wanted to call the place Larry's but decided on Lawry's because it sounded more English. From the day in 1938 when the first prime ribs were wheeled on a cart to table side, the place was a success.

Lawry's brought many firsts to the United States' restaurant scene. Valets first parked cars there. At a time when the usual restaurant salad presentation was cottage cheese, fruit, or gelatin, Lawry's began tossing salad greens tableside to serve before the main course, thus opening a whole new market for salad dressings and toppings. As far as can be determined, Lawry's was the first restaurant to feature a baked potato topped with butter and chives as an elegant side dish. The unforgettable Lawry's creamed spinach (recipe to follow) was presented with every beef dinner.

One morning, Frank Lawrence's son tasted a salt blend that he particularly liked on his eggs at his aunt's house. "If you like it so much, take it home with you," Aunt Tessie said. The blend, created by the chef of the El Paseo restaurant, intrigued Frank Lawrence. With some improvement, it might taste good on roast beef, he decided. He proceeded to turn his home kitchen into a lab for nearly a year. The final blend of seventeen herbs and spices sat on every table in his restaurant. Customers were so taken with the seasoning that they kept pilfering the bottles. Even so, it didn't occur to Lawrence that the salt seasoning might be an important product idea.

The food broker wasn't certain when a visionary family member, Walter Van de Kamp, presented the seasoning to him for possible sale through Ralph's grocery chain. "I like your restaurant, Walter, and I like the product, but I doubt if it will sell," the broker said. But he agreed to show the product to Ralph's buyer. The buyer was also doubtful about its salability but agreed to try ten cases anyway.

From this tiny beginning in the land of fantasies, Lawry's® Seasoned Salt has become the world's largest-selling spice blend. In 1979 Lawry's® became a member of the Thomas J. Lipton family of companies, and it now manufactures and markets 250 products for international consumer and food service use.

CREAMED SPINACH À LA LAWRY'S

LAWRY'S FOODS, INC.

Makes 8 servings

4 bacon slices, finely chopped
1 cup finely chopped onion
¼ cup all-purpose flour
2 teaspoons Lawry's® Seasoned Salt
½ teaspoon Lawry's® Seasoned Pepper
½ teaspoon Lawry's Garlic Powder with
  Parsley

1½ to 2 cups milk
2 packages (10 ounces each) frozen
  spinach, cooked and drained
Fresh basil for garnish
Additional cooked bacon for garnish

In medium skillet, cook bacon until almost crisp. Add onion to bacon and cook until onion is tender, about 10 minutes. Remove from heat. Add flour, seasoned salt, seasoned pepper, and garlic powder with parsley; blend well. Gradually stir in milk, starting with 1½ cups; cook and stir over low heat until thickened. Add spinach and mix thoroughly. If too thick, add additional milk. Garnish with fresh basil and additional cooked bacon.

Excellent with prime ribs of beef.

SNAPPY PODS AMANDINE

LAWRY'S FOOD, INC.

Makes 4 servings

½ cup cold water
1 tablespoon soy sauce
2 teaspoons cornstarch
1 teaspoon instant chicken bouillon granules
½ teaspoon Lawry's® Seasoned Pepper
½ teaspoon Lawry's® Garlic Salt

1 tablespoon vegetable oil
1 package (6 ounces) frozen Chinese pea pods, thawed
½ cup sliced fresh mushrooms *or* 1 can (4 ounces) sliced mushrooms, drained
2 tablespoons toasted, slivered almonds

In small bowl, combine water, soy sauce, cornstarch, bouillon granules, seasoned pepper, and garlic salt; blend well and set aside. In large skillet, heat oil and stir-fry pea pods 2 minutes. Stir in mushrooms. Add cornstarch mixture; cook and stir until thickened and glazed. Sprinkle with almonds.

Serve with other Chinese dishes or grilled steak or fish.

To toast almonds: Preheat oven to 350°F. Place almonds in a shallow pan and bake for 10 minutes. Toasting time will vary depending on size of the almonds.

GOURMET VEG-KABOBS

LAWRY'S FOODS, INC.

Makes 4 to 6 servings

½ cup salad oil
⅓ cup lemon juice
3 tablespoons red wine
1 tablespoon Lawry's® Lemon Pepper
   Seasoning
2 teaspoons crushed red pepper flakes
1 teaspoon Lawry's® Seasoned Salt

2 yellow *or* green medium zucchini, cut
   into chunks
2 small onion, cut into wedges
16 medium mushroom caps
Cherry tomatoes
6 to 8 (6-inch) skewers
3 tablespoons grated Parmesan cheese

In medium bowl, mix together first 6 ingredients; blend well. Add vegetables; cover and refrigerate 30 minutes or overnight. Thread zucchini, onion, mushrooms, and tomatoes on skewers. Broil skewers 6 inches from heat 12 to 15 minutes; brush often with reserved marinade. Sprinkle on cheese and broil until lightly browned.

   Goes well with steamed rice and oven-baked chicken.

VARIATION

Add chunked chicken *or* cubed beef onto skewers before broiling.

LIGHT BATTER-FRIED VEGETABLES

BEST FOODS, A DIVISION OF CPC INTERNATIONAL INC.

Makes 4 cups

¾ cup Argo® or Kingsford's® Corn Starch
¼ cup unsifted flour
1 teaspoon baking powder
½ teaspoon salt
¼ teaspoon pepper
½ cup water

1 egg, slightly beaten
1 quart (about) Mazola® Corn Oil
4 cups cut-up vegetables, such as
    zucchini, carrots, onion, and
    mushrooms

In medium bowl, stir together corn starch, flour, baking powder, salt, and pepper. Add water and egg; stir until mixture is smooth. Pour corn oil into large skillet, filling not more than one-third full. Heat corn oil over medium heat to 375°F. Dip vegetables into batter, stirring batter occasionally. Fry a few vegetables at a time, turning once, 2 to 3 minutes or until golden brown and crisp. Drain on paper towels.

VARIATIONS

Herb Batter: Add 1 teaspoon dried basil leaves and 1 clove garlic, minced or pressed.
Beer Batter: Omit water. Add ⅓ cup cold beer.

HOMESTYLE ZUCCHINI AND TOMATOES
THOMAS J. LIPTON CO.

Makes about 4 servings

2 tablespoons oil
1 medium clove garlic, finely chopped, *or*
 ¼ teaspoon garlic powder
3 medium zucchini, thinly sliced (about 4½
 cups)

1 can (14½ ounces) whole peeled
 tomatoes, drained and chopped, with
 liquid reserved
1 envelope Lipton® Golden Onion
 Recipe Soup Mix
½ teaspoon basil leaves

In large skillet, heat oil and cook garlic with zucchini over medium-high 3 minutes. Stir in tomatoes, then soup mix thoroughly blended with reserved liquid and basil. Bring to a boil; simmer, stirring occasionally, 10 minutes or until zucchini is tender and sauce is slightly thickened.

To microwave: In 2-quart casserole, combine zucchini with tomatoes. Stir in soup mix thoroughly blended with reserved liquid, garlic, and basil. Microwave, covered, at HIGH (100% Power) 5 minutes, stirring once. Remove cover and microwave 4 minutes or until zucchini is tender, stirring once. Let stand, covered, 2 minutes.

VARIATION
Substitute Lipton® Onion Recipe Soup Mix for Lipton® Golden Onion Recipe Soup Mix.

ZUCCHINI WAFFLES
BEATRICE CHEESE, INC.

Makes three 9-inch waffles

3 cups grated zucchini
2 eggs
1½ cups buttermilk baking mix
1 cup shredded County Line® Cheddar
 Cheese

1 small onion, diced
Salt to taste
pepper to taste

Mix all ingredients well and let set overnight. Bake on preheated greased waffle baker. Serve with meat, in place of potatoes, with beef-mushroom gravy.

PROVOLONE-STUFFED ZUCCHINI

LINDSAY INTERNATIONAL, INC.

Makes 4 servings

2 large zucchini, halved lengthwise
2 tablespoons chopped onion
1 tablespoon butter *or* margarine
½ teaspoon cornstarch
1 tablespoon dairy sour cream
¾ cup (3 ounces) shredded provolone cheese

½ cup Lindsay® Small Pitted Ripe Olives, drained and sliced
½ cup shredded carrot
2 tablespoons grated Parmesan cheese
½ teaspoon dried basil, crushed

Preheat oven to 350°F. Cut off ends of zucchini. Cook zucchini, covered, in boiling water about 7 minutes or until crisp-tender; drain. Scoop out and reserve the pulp, leaving a ¼-inch shell.

Cook onion in butter until tender. Combine cornstarch and sour cream; stir in provolone cheese, olives, carrot, Parmesan cheese, basil, reserved pulp, and cooked onion.

Spoon into zucchini shells; arrange in a 12-by-7½-by-2-inch baking dish. Bake, uncovered, 20 to 25 minutes or until heated through.

CHEESY STUFFED MUSHROOMS

SARGENTO CHEESE COMPANY, INC.

Makes 6 servings

12 large mushrooms
½ cup finely chopped onion
1 tablespoon olive oil
1 tablespoon minced parsley
½ teaspoon basil

⅓ cup dry white wine
1 cup (4 ounces) Sargento® Shredded *or* Fancy Shredded Mozzarella Cheese
¼ cup (1 ounce) Sargento® Grated Parmesan Cheese

Preheat oven to 350°F. Remove stems from mushrooms; reserve caps. Coarsely chop stems and sauté with onions in oil over medium-low heat until tender, about 5 minutes. Stir in parsley, basil, and wine. Simmer 10 minutes or until wine is absorbed; remove from heat. Cool about 5 minutes. Stir in cheeses. Fill mushroom caps with cheese mixture. Place in 9-by-9-inch baking dish. Bake, uncovered, 12 to 15 minutes.

TEXAS SPAGHETTI SQUASH

BEATRICE CHEESE, INC.

Makes 8 to 10 servings

2 cups pinto beans, cooked
1 teaspoon ground coriander
1 teaspoon cumin
1/8 teaspoon cayenne pepper
1/2 cup water
1 spaghetti squash (1 1/2 to 2 pounds)
1 cup brown rice
1 1/2 cups chopped green onions

1 clove garlic, minced
1 egg, beaten
1 1/2 cups grated County Line® Monterey Jack Cheese
1 cup plain yogurt
1 1/2 cups grated County Line® Cheddar Cheese
Tomatoes, chopped, for garnish

Preheat oven to 350°F. In small saucepan, combine pinto beans, coriander, cumin, pepper, and water. Simmer. Cut squash in half lengthwise. Remove seed and membrane. In large dutch oven, cook water until tender, about 35 minutes. Cool. Using a fork, scrape out squash to form spaghetti. In small saucepan, cook rice (according to package directions). Cool. Add 1/2 cup onions, garlic, egg, and yogurt. Stir.

In a 13-by-9 baking dish, layer as follows: squash, beans, Monterey Jack cheese, rice mixture, 1 cup green onions, and Cheddar cheese. Bake 30 minutes. Garnish with chopped tomatoes.

CARROTS AU GRATIN
KELLOGG COMPANY

Makes 8 servings

5 tablespoons margarine, divided
1½ cups KELLOGG'S CORN FLAKES®
  cereal, crushed to ¾ cup
⅓ cup chopped onion
3 tablespoons all-purpose flour
1 teaspoon salt (optional)

⅛ teaspoon pepper
1½ cups skim milk
1 cup (4 ounces) shredded American
  cheese
4 cups sliced carrots (about 1½ pounds)
  cooked and drained
1 tablespoon dried parsley flakes

Preheat oven to 350°F. Melt *2 tablespoons* margarine. Combine with crushed cereal. Set aside for topping. Melt remaining *3 tablespoons* margarine in large saucepan over low heat. Add onion. Cook, stirring frequently, until onion is softened but not browned. Stir in flour, salt, and pepper. Add milk gradually, stirring until smooth. Increase heat to medium and cook until bubbly and thickened, stirring constantly. Add cheese, stirring until melted. Remove from heat. Stir in carrots and parsley flakes. Spread mixture in 10-by-6-by-2-inch (1½ quart) glass baking dish coated with cooking spray. Sprinkle cereal mixture evenly over top. Bake about 20 minutes or until thoroughly heated and bubbly. Remove from oven. Let stand about 5 minutes before serving.

SCALLOPED CORN
KELLOGG COMPANY

Makes 8 servings

1 can (12 ounces) cream-style corn
1 package (10 ounces) frozen corn,
  thawed
1 egg, well beaten
⅔ cup milk
¼ teaspoon salt

½ teaspoon dry mustard
¼ teaspoon paprika
⅓ cup chopped green pepper
3 cups KELLOGG'S CORN FLAKES®
  cereal, crushed to 1½ cups
2 tablespoons margarine *or* butter,
  melted

Preheat oven to 350°F. Combine cream-style corn, thawed corn, egg, milk, salt, mustard, paprika, green pepper, and *½ cup* crushed cereal. Pour into lightly greased 10-by-6-by-2-inch (1½-quart) glass baking dish. Combine remaining cereal with margarine. Sprinkle over top. Bake 35 to 40 minutes or until set.

GREEN BEAN AND ONION MEDLEY

LAWRY'S FOODS, INC.

Makes 6 servings

1 pound fresh green peas, stems and
  strings removed
½ pound pearl onions, peeled
1 tablespoon olive *or* vegetable oil

2 teaspoons white wine vinegar
½ teaspoon Lawry's® Seasoned Salt
½ teaspoon Lawry's® Seasoned Pepper
Romano cheese, grated (optional)

In large pot, bring 2 quarts water to a boil. Add green beans and onions. Reduce heat and simmer, partially covered, 20 minutes or until beans and onions are crisp-tender; drain and remove to medium bowl. Stir in remaining ingredients; toss well. Sprinkle with freshly grated Romano cheese, if desired. Serve immediately.

To microwave: In 2-quart microwave-safe casserole, combine green beans, onions, and ⅓ cup water. Cover with plastic wrap, venting corner, and microwave on HIGH 8 to 10 minutes; drain liquid. Stir in remaining ingredients. Cover and microwave 2 minutes. Serve immediately.

CHEDDAR BROCCOLI CORN BAKE

KELLOGG COMPANY

Makes 8 servings

¼ cup margarine *or* butter
2 tablespoons all-purpose flour
¼ teaspoon salt
1½ cups milk
1½ cups (6 ounces) shredded Cheddar
  cheese

2 cups KELLOGG'S CORN FLAKES®
  cereal, crushed to 1 cup
1 can (12 ounces) whole-kernel corn,
  drained
2 packages (10 ounces each) frozen
  broccoli spears, cooked and drained

Preheat oven to 350°F. Melt *2 tablespoons* margarine in large saucepan over low heat. Stir in flour and salt. Add milk gradually, stirring until smooth, increase heat to medium and cook until bubbly and thickened, stirring constantly. Add cheese, stirring until melted. Stir in *¼ cup* crushed cereal and corn and remove from heat. Arrange broccoli in 12-by-7½-by-2-inch (2 quart) glass baking dish. Pour cheese sauce over broccoli. Melt remaining margarine in small saucepan. Stir in remaining cereal. Sprinkle over casserole. Bake about 30 minutes or until thoroughly heated.

SWEET POTATOES ANNA

DURKEE-FRENCH FOODS

Makes 6 servings

2 pounds sweet potatoes, peeled and
  thinly sliced
¼ cup melted butter
1 tablespoon sugar
1½ teaspoons Durkee® Ground Cinnamon
¾ teaspoon Durkee® Ground Ginger

¾ teaspoon salt
¼ teaspoon Durkee® Ground Nutmeg
¼ teaspoon Durkee® Ground Black
  Pepper
1 cup (4 ounces) shredded Swiss cheese

Preheat oven to 425°F. Toss potatoes with butter, sugar, and seasonings; mix well.
In foil-lined 9-inch cake pan, arrange a layer of potatoes, closely overlapping slices.
Sprinkle with cheese; layer remaining potatoes on top. Loosely cover pan. Bake 60
minutes or until fork-tender. Remove foil; invert onto serving plate.

BUTTERSCOTCH YAMS

BEST FOODS, A DIVISION OF CPC INTERNATIONAL INC.

Makes 6 servings

6 medium yams
½ cup Karo® Light *or* Dark Corn Syrup
½ cup firmly packed brown sugar
¼ cup heavy *or* light cream *or* half-and-half

2 tablespoons Mazola® Margarine
½ teaspoon ground cinnamon
½ teaspoon salt

Pierce yams with fork several times. Microwave on HIGH (100% Power) 12 to 14
minutes or until tender. Let stand 10 minutes. Peel yams and cut into quarters. In
3-quart microwavable baking dish, combine corn syrup, brown sugar, cream, margarine, cinnamon, and salt. Microwave on HIGH (100% Power) 3 to 4 minutes,
stirring once. Add yams; toss to coat well. Microwave on HIGH (100% Power) 6
minutes or until glazed, spooning sauce over yams after 3 minutes.

ROAST POTATOES POUPON
NABISCO FOODS GROUP

Makes 6 servings

12 small red-skin potatoes, quartered
2 cloves garlic, peeled
⅓ cup Grey Poupon® Dijon *or* Country
   Dijon Mustard

⅓ cup Blue Bonnet® Margarine, melted
2 tablespoons chopped parsley

In large, heavy pot with tight-fitting lid, place potatoes and garlic in a single layer. Cook, covered, over very low heat 45 to 60 minutes or until done, stirring occasionally.

   Mix mustard, margarine, and parsley; toss with hot potatoes. Serve immediately.

GERMAN POTATO BAKE
KRAFT GENERAL FOODS, INC.

Makes 6 servings

4 cups cubed hot cooked potatoes
½ pound Velveeta® Pasteurized Process
   Cheese Spread, cubed
2 tablespoons Parkay® Margarine
¾ cup Miracle Whip® Salad Dressing
¼ cup sour cream

5 slices Oscar Mayer® Bacon, crisply
   cooked, crumbled
¼ cup green onion slices
1 jar (2 ounces) chopped pimiento,
   drained
¼ teaspoon pepper
¼ teaspoon paprika

Preheat oven to 350°F. Combine potatoes, *¼ pound* pasteurized process cheese spread, and margarine; stir over low heat until pasteurized process cheese spread is melted. Add salad dressing, sour cream, *2 tablespoons* bacon, *2 tablespoons* onion, pimiento, and pepper; mix well. Spoon into 1½-quart casserole. Top with remaining pasteurized process cheese spread, bacon, and onion. Sprinkle with paprika. Bake 20 to 25 minutes or until thoroughly heated.

VARIATION

Substitute ¼ cup chopped red bell pepper for pimiento.

Preparation time: 30 minutes

Cooking time: 25 minutes

WESTERN BEAN BAKE
CAMPBELL SOUP COMPANY

Makes 15 servings, ½ cup each

2 cans (16 ounces each) Campbell's®
    Pork & Beans in Tomato Sauce *or* 2
    cans (15½ ounces each) Campbell's®
    Ranchero Beans
1 can (16 ounces) pinto beans, drained
1 can (16 ounces) black beans, drained
1 can (4 ounces) chopped green chilies,
    drained

½ cup thinly sliced onion, separated into
    rings
1 tablespoon chopped fresh cilantro
1 tablespoon lime juice
Lime twist for garnish
Fresh cilantro for garnish
Sour cream (optional)

Preheat oven to 350°F. In 2-quart casserole, combine beans, chilies, onions, chopped cilantro, and juice. Bake, uncovered 1 hour or until hot and bubbly. Stir before serving. Garnish with lime twist and cilantro. Serve with sour cream if desired.

CAJUN-STYLE BEANS
CAMPBELL SOUP COMPANY

Makes 6 servings, ½ cup each

1 tablespoon butter *or* margarine
½ cup diced cooked ham
½ cup chopped onion
1 stalk celery, chopped
1 medium green pepper, chopped
1 large clove garlic, minced

1 can (16 ounces) Campbell's® Pork and
    Beans in Tomato Sauce
2 tablespoons chopped pimiento
¼ teaspoon black pepper
⅛ teaspoon ground red pepper

In 10-inch skillet over medium heat, in hot butter, cook ham, onion, celery, green pepper, and garlic until vegetables are tender, stirring often. Stir in beans, pimiento, black pepper, and red pepper. Heat to boiling. Reduce heat; simmer, uncovered, 5 minutes, stirring occasionally.

ARTICHOKE RICE BAKE

LAWRY'S FOODS, INC.

Makes 4 servings

2 tablespoons Imperial® Margarine
8 ounces fresh mushrooms, sliced
I small onion, chopped
I½ teaspoons Lawry's® Garlic Salt
½ teaspoon Lawry's® Seasoned Pepper
2 cups chicken broth

I cup long-grain rice
2 medium tomatoes, chopped
2 cans (7 ounces each) artichoke hearts, drained and quartered
Chopped parsley for garnish

In large skillet, melt margarine and sauté mushrooms, onion, garlic salt, and seasoned pepper until tender. Add broth and rice. Bring to a boil; reduce heat, cover, and simmer 25 minutes or until liquid is absorbed. Stir in tomatoes and artichoke hearts; let stand 2 minutes. Garnish with chopped parsley.

VARIATION

For a Cajun-style main dish, stir in 1 cup of cooked shrimp, chicken, or pork and ½ teaspoon hot pepper sauce.

SPANISH MILLET (OR RICE)

BEATRICE CHEESE, INC.

Makes 6 servings

2 cups cooked millet *or* brown rice
I cup cooked lentils
I cup tomatoes, chopped and drained
½ can tomato paste
¼ cup chopped green pepper

½ cup minced onion
½ teaspoon black pepper
I½ teaspoons garlic powder
I teaspoon sugar
I¾ cup County Line® Sharp Colby Cheese, shredded

Preheat oven to 375°F. Mix together all ingredients except cheese. Place half of mixture in greased 2-quart baking dish. Sprinkle *1¼ cups* shredded cheese over top. Add remaining mixture. Bake 30 minutes. Remove from oven and sprinkle remaining shredded cheese on top; return to oven until cheese is melted, about 10 minutes.

ALMOND WILD RICE BAKE

DOLE FOOD COMPANY

Makes 6 to 8 servings

1 cup raw wild rice
2¼ cups water, divided
½ teaspoon salt
4 cups sliced fresh mushrooms
1 small onion, chopped
½ cup sliced Dole® Celery
¼ cup margarine
1 pound lean ground beef

1 cup light sour cream
1 cup Dole® Whole Natural Almonds, toasted
¼ cup teriyaki sauce
¼ teaspoon cracked black pepper
1 cup Dole® Raisins
Chopped parsley for garnish (optional)

Preheat oven to 350°F. Simmer rice, covered, in *2 cups* water with salt 45 minutes. In large ovenproof skillet, sauté mushrooms, onion, and celery in margarine until onion is soft. Push to sides of skillet. Add beef. Cook until redness disappears. Stir and combine with sautéed vegetables in skillet. Add rice, remaining *¼ cup* water, sour cream, almonds, teriyaki sauce, and black pepper to skillet. Bake, uncovered, 40 minutes. Stir several times. Stir in raisins. Garnish with chopped parsley, if desired.

PARMESAN RICE

LINDSAY INTERNATIONAL, INC.

Makes 8 servings

½ cup chopped onion
2 tablespoons butter *or* margarine
1 can (28 ounces) tomatoes, cut up, undrained
1 cup water
¾ cup long-grain rice
½ cup dry white wine

2 teaspoons instant chicken bouillon granules
Several dashes bottle hot pepper sauce
Dash pepper
⅓ cup grated Parmesan cheese
½ cup Lindsay® Small Pitted Ripe Olives, drained

In a 3-quart saucepan cook onion in butter or margarine until tender but not brown. Stir in undrained tomatoes, water, rice, wine, bouillon granules, pepper sauce, and pepper. Cover; simmer about 30 minutes or until rice is done and most of liquid is absorbed. Reserve *2 tablespoons* Parmesan cheese. Stir olives and remaining Parmesan cheese into rice mixture; heat through. Sprinkle with reserved Parmesan before serving.

PASTA MAIN DISHES

SPICY SHRIMP WITH FUSILLE
Ragú Foods Co.
137

PENNE WITH MUSHROOM CLAM
SAUCE AND CHEESES
Beatrice Cheese, Inc.
137

PASTA WITH FISH SAUCE
Lindsay International, Inc.
138

PASTA PRIMAVERA
Dole Food Company
138

SPRINGTIME NOODLES ALFREDO
Thomas J. Lipton Co.
139

PEPPERONI PASTA RUFFLES
Ragú Foods Co.
140

STUFFED SHELLS PRIMAVERA
Ragú Foods Co.
140

GARDEN CHEESE SHELLS
Borden, Inc.
141

FLORENTINE STUFFED SHELLS
Sargento Cheese Company, Inc.
141

SINGAPORE SPICY NOODLES
Lawry's Foods, Inc.
142

PASTA CINTORO
Lawry's Foods, Inc.
143

VEAL SAUCE LUCIA
Lawry's Foods, Inc.
143

WINE-CHEESE SAUCED PASTA
Lindsay International, Inc.
144

FETTUCCINE WITH
HERBED CHEESE SAUCE
Sargento Cheese Company, Inc.
144

HEARTY MANICOTTI
Sargento Cheese Company, Inc.
145

TANGY ASPARAGUS LINGUINE
Sargento Cheese Company, Inc.
146

VEGETABLE 'N CHICKEN ALFREDO
Sargento Cheese Company, Inc.
147

SPICY SHRIMP WITH FUSILLE

RAGÚ FOODS CO.

Makes 4 servings

1 pound medium shrimp, peeled and
  deveined
2 tablespoons butter
1 jar (28 ounces) Ragú® Fino Italian
  Brand Pasta Sauce
Tabasco sauce to taste

Salt to taste
Pepper to taste
¾ package (16-ounce size) fusille, cooked
  and drained
1 tablespoon chopped fresh parsley

In large skillet, lightly sauté shrimp in butter. Add pasta sauce, Tabasco sauce, salt, and pepper. Simmer, covered, until shrimp are cooked. Spoon sauce over hot cooked pasta; toss to coat well. Top pasta with shrimp; sprinkle with parsley.

PENNE WITH MUSHROOM
CLAM SAUCE AND CHEESES

BEATRICE CHEESE, INC.

Makes 4 to 6 servings

2 tablespoons butter *or* margarine
2 tablespoons olive oil
1 small white onion, chopped
½ pound mushrooms, cleaned and sliced
1 teaspoon garlic powder
½ cup Marsala wine
1 can (8 ounces) clams, chopped, with
  juice
1 pound penne (or other tubular pasta)

¾ cup whipping cream
½ cup shredded County Line® Mozzarella
  Cheese
½ cup shredded County Line® Swiss
  Cheese
½ cup crumbled blue cheese
6 sprigs parsley, chopped
Fresh ground pepper

Melt butter in 12-inch skillet. Add olive oil, onion, and mushrooms; sauté until tender. Add ½ *teaspoon* garlic powder and wine. Bring to a boil; reduce heat, add clams, and cook until thickened. Cook pasta according to package instructions; drain. Meanwhile, in double boiler, mix together cream, ½ *teaspoon* garlic powder, and cheeses. Stir until melted. Keep warm.

   In a large bowl, mix together pasta, cheese mixture, clam/mushroom mixture, and parsley. Serve immediately with fresh ground pepper.

PASTA WITH FISH SAUCE

LINDSAY INTERNATIONAL, INC.

Makes 6 servings

1 large onion, chopped
1 clove garlic, minced
2 tablespoons butter *or* margarine
1 can (28 ounces) tomatoes, cut up, undrained
½ teaspoon dried oregano, crushed
¼ teaspoon dried basil, crushed
⅛ teaspoon pepper

1 can (7½) ounces minced clams
1 package (16 ounces) frozen fish fillets, partially thawed and cut into 1-inch cubes
½ cup Lindsay® Small Pitted Ripe Olives, drained
Hot cooked linguine *or* spaghetti

In Dutch oven, cook onion and garlic in butter until tender. Stir in *undrained* tomatoes, oregano, basil, and pepper. Drain clams, adding liquid to tomato mixture. Simmer, uncovered, about 30 minutes, stirring occasionally. Add fish, olives, and clams to sauce. Simmer, covered, 5 minutes, stirring once. Serve over pasta.

PASTA PRIMAVERA

DOLE FOOD COMPANY

Makes 8 servings

1 package (8 ounces) pasta
1 clove garlic, pressed
1 Dole® Red Bell Pepper, slivered
½ pound snow peas
3 cups Dole® Broccoli florets
1 cup diced Dole® Green Onions

¼ cup chopped parsley
2 tablespoons olive oil
1 tablespoon sweet basil, crumbled
Black pepper (optional)
¼ cup grated Parmesan cheese

Cook pasta according to package directions. Meanwhile, in 12-inch skillet, sauté garlic with all remaining vegetables in oil 1 minute. Cover and steam 5 minutes. Shake skillet occasionally. Add basil and cooked pasta. Toss well until pasta is heated through. Turn onto serving platter. Sprinkle generously with black pepper, if desired, and Parmesan cheese.

SPRINGTIME NOODLES ALFREDO

THOMAS J. LIPTON CO.

Makes about 4 servings

2 tablespoons butter *or* margarine
2 medium carrots, sliced
1 medium zucchini *or* yellow squash,
  thinly sliced
1 medium clove garlic, finely chopped
1⅓ cups water
1 cup milk
1 package Lipton® Noodles & Sauce—
  Alfredo

1 tablespoon snipped fresh dill *or* ½
  teaspoon dried dill weed
½ cup frozen peas, thawed (optional)
Pepper to taste
Parmesan cheese, grated (optional)
Carrot for garnish
Dill for garnish

In large skillet, melt butter and cook carrots, zucchini, and garlic over medium-high heat, stirring occasionally, 3 minutes or until vegetables are tender; remove and set aside. Into skillet, add water and milk and bring to the boiling point. Stir in noodles and sauce and dill and continue boiling over medium heat, stirring occasionally, 7 minutes or until noodles are tender. Stir in vegetables, peas, if desired, and pepper; heat through. Sprinkle, if desired, with grated Parmesan cheese. Garnish with carrot and dill.

To microwave: In 1½-quart microwave-safe casserole, microwave butter, carrots, zucchini, and garlic, uncovered, at HIGH (100% Power) 6 minutes or until vegetables are tender, stirring once; remove and set aside. In casserole, stir in water, milk, and Noodles & Sauce. Microwave 11 minutes or until noodles are tender. Stir in vegetables, dill, peas, and pepper; cover and let stand 2 minutes. Serve as above.

PEPPERONI PASTA RUFFLES

RAGÚ FOODS CO.

Makes 4 to 6 servings

1 small green pepper, diced
1 small red pepper, diced
1 tablespoon olive oil
1 jar (30¾ ounces) Ragú® Thick and
Hearty Spaghetti Sauce
1 package (3½ ounces) sliced pepperoni,
halved

8 ounces mozzarella cheese, diced
1 package (14 ounces) pasta ruffles,
cooked and drained
Salt to taste
Pepper to taste

In large skillet, sauté green and red peppers in hot olive oil until tender. Add spaghetti sauce and simmer over low heat, stirring occasionally, about 10 minutes or until heated through. Spoon sauce, pepperoni, and cheese over hot pasta; toss to coat well. Season to taste with salt and pepper.

STUFFED SHELLS PRIMAVERA

RAGÚ FOODS CO.

Makes 6 servings

2 cups chopped fresh broccoli
2 medium zucchini, shredded
1 cup chopped fresh mushrooms
1 small onion, chopped
½ cup finely chopped carrots
2 tablespoons butter
Pinch nutmeg
Salt to taste
Pepper to taste
1 pound ricotta cheese

2 cups (8 ounces) shredded mozzarella
cheese
1 egg, lightly beaten
¼ cup grated Parmesan cheese
3 tablespoons chopped fresh basil
1 package (12 ounces) jumbo pasta shells
for stuffing, cooked and drained
1 jar (30 ounces) Ragú® Chunky
Gardenstyle Spaghetti Sauce

Preheat oven to 350°F. In large skillet, sauté broccoli, zucchini, mushrooms, onion, and carrots in butter until vegetables are tender. Season with nutmeg, salt, and pepper. In large bowl, thoroughly combine ricotta cheese, mozzarella cheese, egg, Parmesan cheese, and basil. Add sautéed vegetables; stir to mix well. Spoon *1 cup* spaghetti sauce evenly in a 13-by-9-inch baking dish. Fill shells with vegetable/ cheese mixture. Arrange in baking dish. Spoon remaining sauce over shells. Bake, covered, 45 minutes. Uncover and bake 10 minutes or until bubbly.

GARDEN CHEESE SHELLS
BORDEN, INC.

Makes 4 servings

2 cups chopped fresh broccoli
I cup shredded carrots
½ cup chopped onion
I clove garlic, finely chopped
2 tablespoons vegetable oil
I tablespoon flour
½ cup Borden® Lite-line® *or* Viva®
   Protein-Fortified Skim Milk

I ½ cups Borden® Lite-line® *or* Viva®
   Cottage Cheese
¼ cup grated Parmesan cheese
Salt to taste
Pepper to taste
8 to 10 Creamette® Jumbo Shells,
   cooked as package directs

Preheat oven to 325°F. In skillet, cook vegetables in oil until tender-crisp. Stir in flour, then milk; cook and stir until thickened. Remove from heat; add cottage cheese, *2 tablespoons* Parmesan cheese, salt, and pepper. Stuff shells; place in shallow baking dish. Top with remaining Parmesan cheese. Bake, covered, 25 minutes. Refrigerate leftovers.

FLORENTINE STUFFED SHELLS
SARGENTO CHEESE COMPANY, INC.

Makes 8 servings

24 uncooked jumbo pasta shells for filling
I package (10 ounces) frozen chopped
   spinach, thawed
I egg, beaten
2 cups (15 ounces) Sargento® Ricotta
   Cheese
I ½ cups (6 ounces) Sargento® Shredded
   or Fancy Shredded Mozzarella Cheese

⅓ cup finely chopped onion
2 cloves garlic, minced
¼ teaspoon salt
⅛ teaspoon ground nutmeg
2 cups meatless spaghetti sauce
½ cup (2 ounces) Sargento® Grated
   Parmesan Cheese

Preheat oven to 350°F. Cook pasta shells according to package directions. Squeeze spinach to remove as much moisture as possible. Combine spinach, egg, ricotta and mozzarella cheeses, onion, garlic, salt, and nutmeg; stir to blend well. Stuff shells with ricotta mixture, using about *2 tablespoons* for each shell. Arrange in lightly greased 13-by-9-inch baking dish. Pour spaghetti sauce over shells. Sprinkle with grated cheese. Bake, covered, 30 to 40 minutes.

SINGAPORE SPICY NOODLES

LAWRY'S FOODS, INC.

Makes 4 servings

1¼ cups water
2 tablespoons ketchup
2½ teaspoons packed brown sugar
1½ teaspoons chopped cilantro
1 teaspoon cornstarch
¾ teaspoon Lawry's® Seasoned Salt
¾ teaspoon Lawry's® Garlic Powder
   with Parsley

¼ teaspoon crushed red pepper
2½ tablespoons chunky peanut butter
¼ cup sliced green onions
8 ounces linguine, cooked and drained
1 cup shredded red cabbage
Green onion curls for garnish

In medium saucepan, combine water, ketchup, sugar, cilantro, cornstarch, and seasonings. Bring to a boil. Reduce heat; simmer, uncovered, 5 minutes. Cool 10 minutes; blend in peanut butter and green onions. Toss sauce with hot linguine and red cabbage. Garnish with green onion curls.

Serve with a marinated cucumber salad.

VARIATION

For a heartier entrée, add cooked shredded chicken or pork.

PASTA CINTORO

LAWRY'S FOODS, INC.

Makes 4 servings

2 tablespoons Imperial® Margarine
2 tablespoons olive *or* vegetable oil
1 teaspoon dried basil, crushed
¾ teaspoon Lawry's® Garlic Powder with Parsley
½ teaspoon Lawry's® Lemon Pepper Seasoning
½ cup chopped red bell pepper

1 medium zucchini, cut into 1-inch julienne strips
1 cup thinly sliced mushrooms
2 medium tomatoes, chopped
¼ to ½ cup chicken broth
8 ounces angel hair pasta, cooked
Parmesan cheese

In large skillet, melt margarine. Add olive oil, basil, garlic powder with parsley, and lemon pepper seasoning; blend well. Add vegetables and lightly sauté. Add chicken broth and heat 1 minute. Add pasta and toss to coat with vegetable mixture.

Serve with a light sprinkling of Parmesan cheese.

VEAL SAUCE LUCIA

LAWRY'S FOODS, INC.

Makes 4 servings

2 tablespoons vegetable oil
1½ pounds veal stew meat, cut into bite-size cubes
1 medium onion, chopped
1 medium carrot, grated
¾ teaspoon dried basil, crushed
¾ teaspoon Lawry's® Garlic Powder with Parsley

1 package (1.5 ounces) Lawry's® Extra Rich and Thick Spaghetti Sauce Spices and Seasonings
1¾ cups water
1 can (6 ounces) tomato paste
½ cup frozen peas
8 ounces linguine *or* other pasta of your choice, cooked and drained

In Dutch oven, heat oil and brown veal; drain fat. Add onion, carrot, basil and garlic powder with parsley; sauté 5 minutes. Add spaghetti sauce spices and seasonings, water, and tomato paste; blend well. Bring to a boil; reduce heat and simmer, covered, 30 minutes. Add peas and heat 5 minutes. Ladle sauce over hot pasta.

Serve with Caesar salad and garlic bread.

WINE-CHEESE SAUCED PASTA

LINDSAY INTERNATIONAL, INC.

Makes 8 servings

¼ cup chopped onion
3 tablespoons butter *or* margarine
¼ cup all-purpose flour
1 teaspoon instant chicken bouillon granules
¼ teaspoon white pepper
2⅓ cups milk
½ cup dry white wine

2½ cups (10 ounces) shredded Monterey Jack cheese
1½ cups (6 ounces) shredded Gruyère cheese
1 cup Lindsay® Extra Large Pitted Ripe Olives, drained
2 tablespoons chopped pimiento
Hot cooked spinach fettuccine *or* other pasta

In saucepan, cook onion in butter until tender. Stir in flour, bouillon granules, and white pepper. Add milk all at once. Cook and stir until thickened and bubbly. Add wine. Gradually stir in cheeses just until melted. Stir in olives and pimiento. Serve atop fettuccine.

FETTUCCINE WITH HERBED CHEESE SAUCE

SARGENTO CHEESE COMPANY, INC.

Makes 6 servings

3 tablespoons butter *or* margarine
⅓ cup sliced green onion
1 clove garlic, minced
1 tablespoon flour
½ teaspoon salt
½ teaspoon basil
½ teaspoon oregano

¼ teaspoon pepper
1¾ cups milk
1 cup (4 ounces) Sargento® Shredded *or* Fancy Shredded Mozzarella Cheese
1 cup (8 ounces) Sargento® Ricotta Cheese
3 tablespoons chopped parsley
10 ounces fettuccine *or* spaghetti

In medium saucepan, melt butter. Add onion and garlic. Cook until tender, about 5 minutes. Stir in flour, salt, basil, oregano, and pepper. Gradually stir in milk. Cook and stir until thick and bubbly. Remove from heat. Add cheeses; stir until melted and thoroughly combined. Stir in parsley; keep warm. Meanwhile, cook fettuccine according to package directions. Toss immediately with cheese sauce.

HEARTY MANICOTTI

SARGENTO CHEESE COMPANY, INC.

Makes 6 servings

1¼ cups water, divided
1 pound Italian sweet sausage links
1 pound ground beef
1 medium onion, chopped
1 can (15 ounces) tomato puree
1 can (6 ounces) tomato paste
1 teaspoon sugar
½ teaspoon black pepper
1¾ teaspoons basil, divided

1½ teaspoons salt, divided
1 package (12 ounces) manicotti shells
2 cups (15 ounces) Sargento® Ricotta Cheese
2 cups (8 ounces) Sargento® Shredded Low-Moisture Part-Skim Mozzarella Cheese, divided
2 tablespoons chopped parsley
Sargento® Grated Parmesan Cheese (optional)

Preheat oven to 375°F. In 5-quart covered Dutch oven, combine ¼ *cup* water and sausage; cook over medium heat 5 minutes. Uncover and allow sausage to brown well; drain sausage on paper towels.

Brown beef and onion in Dutch oven over medium heat; drain. Stir in tomato purée, tomato paste, sugar, pepper, *1 teaspoon* basil, *1 teaspoon* salt, and *1 cup* water; simmer, covered, 45 minutes.

Cut sausage into bite-size pieces; add to beef mixture. Simmer 15 minutes, stirring occasionally.

Meanwhile, cook manicotti shells according to package directions; rinse and drain well.

In large bowl, combine ricotta and *1 cup* mozzarella cheese, parsley, ¾ *teaspoon* basil, and ½ *teaspoon* salt. Spoon into shells and set aside.

Spoon half of meat sauce into large, shallow baking dish. Arrange cheese-stuffed shells over sauce. Spoon remaining sauce over shells. Sprinkle with remaining mozzarella cheese. Bake 30 minutes. Serve with grated cheese, if desired.

TANGY ASPARAGUS LINGUINE

SARGENTO CHEESE COMPANY, INC.

Makes 4 servings

5 ounces linguine
2 tablespoons light margarine
¼ cup finely chopped onion
3 cloves garlic, minced
8 ounces fresh asparagus, peeled and
  sliced diagonally into ½-inch pieces
2 tablespoons dry white wine

2 tablespoons fresh lemon juice
Freshly ground black pepper
¼ cup (1 ounce) Sargento® Grated
  Parmesan
¾ cup (3 ounces) Sargento® Preferred
  Light® Fancy Shredded Mozzarella
  Cheese
Strips of lemon zest (optional)

Chop and measure all ingredients before beginning. Bring water to a boil and cook linguine to al dente (firm to the bite). Drain. Meanwhile, melt margarine over medium heat in a large skillet. Sauté onions and garlic until onions are soft. Add asparagus and continue to sauté for 2 minutes. Add wine and lemon juice and cook an additional minute. Season with pepper to taste. Remove from the heat. Toss with hot pasta and Parmesan cheese. Remove to serving platter and top with mozzarella cheese. Garnish with strips of lemon zest, if desired. Serve immediately.

VEGETABLE 'N CHICKEN ALFREDO

SARGENTO CHEESE COMPANY, INC.

Makes 4 servings

4 tablespoons butter *or* margarine, divided
3 tablespoons flour
3 cups milk
¾ cup (3 ounces) Sargento® Grated Parmesan Cheese
½ teaspoon basil
¼ teaspoon salt
¼ teaspoon pepper
1 tablespoon vegetable oil

3 chicken-breast halves, boned, skinned, and cut into thin strips
¼ cup thinly sliced green onions
4 cups sliced fresh vegetables (broccoli, mushrooms, green or red bell peppers, celery, green beans, carrots, zucchini)
½ pound pasta, cooked and drained
Additional Sargento® Grated Parmesan Cheese

In medium saucepan, melt 2 tablespoons butter. Add flour and cook over low heat 2 minutes, stirring occasionally. Whisk in milk. Bring to a simmer and cook over medium heat until thickened, stirring constantly. Stir in *¾ cup* grated cheese, basil, salt, and pepper. Set aside; keep warm.

Heat remaining butter and oil in large frying pan. Add chicken and cook over medium heat, stirring constantly until cooked through. Remove chicken from pan; set aside.

In same pan, cook green onions and other vegetables until crisp-tender, about 5 minutes. Toss vegetables with hot pasta and chicken. Serve with sauce and additional grated cheese.

GARDEN VEGETABLE SPAGHETTI SAUCE

CONTADINA FOODS, INC., NESTLÉ FOOD COMPANY

Makes 8 servings, about 7 cups total

3 tablespoons olive oil
1 cup julienne-cut green pepper
1 cup sliced mushrooms
1 cup julienne-cut carrots
1 cup chopped onion
1 cup halved and sliced zucchini
½ cup broccoli florets
2 large cloves garlic, minced
1¾ cups (14½-ounce can) Contadina®
  Whole Peeled Tomatoes and juice,
  cut up

1⅓ cups (12-ounce can) Contadina®
  Tomato Paste
2 cups water
¼ cup red wine *or* beef broth
1 tablespoon capers, rinsed (optional)
1 teaspoon dried basil leaves, crushed
1 teaspoon dried oregano leaves,
  crushed
¾ teaspoon salt
¼ teaspoon pepper
1 pound (16 ounces) dry spaghetti,
  cooked and drained

In large saucepan, heat oil; sauté pepper, mushrooms, carrots, onion, zucchini, broccoli, and garlic for 2 to 3 minutes or until onion is translucent. Stir in tomatoes and juice, tomato paste, water, wine, capers (if desired), basil, oregano, salt, and pepper. Bring to a boil; reduce heat and simmer for 20 to 30 minutes, stirring occasionally. Serve over hot spaghetti.

HOME-STYLE LASAGNA ROLLS

RAGÚ FOODS CO.

Makes 6 servings

1½ pounds ground beef
1 cup chopped fresh mushrooms
1 medium onion, finely chopped
1 small carrot, minced
1 clove garlic, minced
¼ cup dry red wine
⅛ teaspoon nutmeg
⅛ teaspoon cayenne pepper
Salt to taste

Pepper to taste
2 cups (8 ounces) shredded mozzarella cheese
1 egg, lightly beaten
¼ cup grated Parmesan cheese
1 jar (28 ounces) Ragú® Slow-Cooked Homestyle Spaghetti Sauce
¾ package (16-ounce size) lasagna noodles, cooked and drained

Preheat oven to 350°F. In large skillet, thoroughly brown ground beef; drain fat. Add mushrooms, onion, carrot, and garlic; sauté until vegetables are tender. Add wine, nutmeg, cayenne pepper, salt, and pepper; cook until wine is almost evaporated. Remove from heat; allow to cool 10 to 15 minutes. In medium bowl, thoroughly combine meat mixture, mozzarella cheese, egg, and *1 tablespoon* Parmesan cheese. Pour *½ jar* spaghetti sauce in a 13-by-9-inch baking dish. Evenly spread *⅓ cup* meat filling over length of each lasagna noodle. Carefully roll up noodle. Place seam side down in baking dish. Repeat with remaining noodles. Evenly spread remaining sauce over lasagna rolls. Bake, covered, 40 minutes. Uncover; sprinkle with *3 tablespoons* Parmesan cheese. Bake 5 minutes or until bubbly.

CLASSIC LASAGNA

BEST FOODS, A DIVISION OF CPC INTERNATIONAL INC.

Makes 12 servings

I container (15 ounces) ricotta cheese *or*
   I pound cream-style cottage cheese
I egg, beaten slightly
I cup grated Parmesan cheese

Meat Sauce (see below)
I pound Mueller's® Lasagne, cooked, as
   package directs, and drained
12 ounces mozzarella cheese

In bowl stir together ricotta cheese, egg, and ¾ cup Parmesan cheese. In 13-by-9-by-2-inch baking dish spread 1½ cups Meat Sauce. Layer ⅓ cup cooked lasagne noodles, *2 cups* sauce, one half of ricotta cheese mixture, and one third of mozzarella cheese. Repeat. Top with remaining noodles, sauce, and cheeses. Bake at 350°F for 50 minutes or until bubbly.

MEAT SAUCE

Makes 7½ cups

I pound ground beef
I chopped onion
2 tablespoons Mazola® Corn Oil
2 cans (28 ounces *each*) tomatoes
I can (6 ounces) tomato paste
3 cloves garlic, minced

½ cup chopped parsley
2 teaspoons sugar
1½ teaspoons salt
2 teaspoons dried basil
I teaspoon dried oregano
¼ teaspoon pepper

In 5-quart Dutch oven heat corn oil over medium heat. Add ground beef, onion, garlic, and parsley. Sitrring frequently, cook about 10 minutes or until beef is browned. Place tomatoes in blender container; cover. Blend on high speed 30 seconds or until finely chopped. Add to beef mixture. Stir in tomato paste, sugar, basil, salt, oregano, and pepper. Bring to a boil. Reduce heat and simmer, stirring occasionally, 45 minutes.

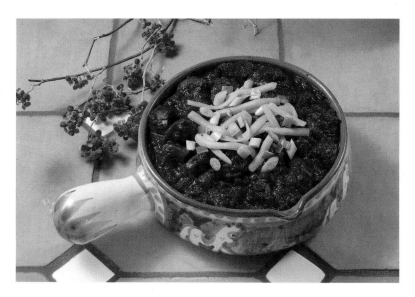

A.1.® *Texas Chili*
COURTESY OF NABISCO FOODS GROUP

Quick and Easy Tamale Pie
COURTESY OF THOMAS J. LIPTON CO.

Caribbean Chicken

COURTESY OF KELLOGG COMPANY

Teriyaki Chicken,
Oven-Roast Pork Hawaiian

COURTESY OF DOLE FOOD COMPANY

FAST 'N FUN PASTA PIZZA

DURKEE-FRENCH FOODS

Makes 4 to 6 servings

1 pound ground beef
1 jar (15½ ounces) spaghetti sauce
3 cups fusilli *or* elbow macaroni, cooked in unsalted water and drained
2 eggs, slightly beaten
1 can (2.8 ounces) Durkee® French-Fried Onions

⅓ cup (about 1½ ounces) grated Parmesan cheese
Assorted toppings: chopped green pepper, sliced mushrooms, olives
1 cup (4 ounces) shredded mozzarella cheese

Preheat oven to 375°F. In medium skillet, brown ground beef; drain. Stir in spaghetti sauce; reduce heat and simmer, uncovered, 5 minutes. In medium bowl, combine hot pasta, eggs, ½ *can* onions, and Parmesan cheese. Spread pasta mixture over greased 12-inch pizza pan. Top with ground-beef mixture and desired toppings. Bake, covered, 25 minutes or until heated through. Top with mozzarella cheese and remaining onions; bake, uncovered, 3 minutes or until onions are golden brown. Cut into wedges to serve.

Preparation time: 15 minutes

IRRESTIBLE PIÈCES
DE RÉSISTANCE

TRADITIONAL MEAT LOAF

BORDEN, INC.

Makes 4 to 6 servings

1½ pounds lean ground beef
1½ cups fresh bread crumbs
  (3 slices bread)
⅔ cup ketchup
¼ cup chopped onion
1 egg, beaten

2 teaspoons dry mustard
1½ teaspoons Wyler's® *or* Steero®
  Beef-Flavor Instant Bouillon
¼ teaspoon pepper
1 tablespoon brown sugar

Preheat oven to 350°F. In large bowl, combine meat, crumbs, *⅓ cup* ketchup, onion, egg, *1 teaspoon* mustard, bouillon, and pepper; mix well. In shallow baking dish, shape into loaf. Bake 1 hour. In small bowl, combine remaining *⅓ cup* ketchup, *1 teaspoon* mustard, and brown sugar. Pour over loaf; bake 10 minutes. Garnish as desired. Refrigerate leftovers.

To microwave: Prepare loaf as above; cover with waxed paper. Cook on HIGH 13 to 15 minutes, rotating dish after 8 minutes. Top with sauce; cook on HIGH 3 minutes or until center of loaf is firm. Cover; let stand 5 minutes. (Note: Microwave ovens vary in wattage and power output; cooking times may need to be adjusted).

SOUPERIOR MEAT LOAF

THOMAS J. LIPTON CO.

Makes about 8 servings

1 envelope Lipton® Onion Recipe
   Soup Mix
2 pounds ground beef
1½ cups fresh bread crumbs

2 eggs
¾ cup water
⅓ cup ketchup

Preheat oven to 350°F. In large bowl, combine all ingredients. In large baking pan, shape into loaf. Bake 1 hour or until done.

To microwave: Combine as above. In 2-quart oblong baking dish, shape into loaf. Microwave, uncovered, at HIGH (100% Power), turning dish occasionally, 25 minutes or until done; drain. Let stand, covered, 5 minutes.

VARIATIONS

Substitute Lipton® Beefy Onion, Onion-Mushroom, *or* Beefy Mushroom Recipe Soup Mix for Lipton® Onion Recipe Soup Mix.

APPLE-GLAZED HAM LOAF

KELLOGG COMPANY

Makes 10 to 12 servings

1 jar (10 ounce) apple jelly
¼ cup firmly packed brown sugar
3 tablespoons lemon juice
½ teaspoon dry mustard
2 eggs
3 cups KELLOGG'S CORN FLAKES®
   cereal, crushed to ¾ cup

¼ cup firmly packed brown sugar
¾ cup milk
⅓ cup finely chopped onion
⅛ teaspoon pepper
1½ teaspoons dry mustard
1 pound ground cooked ham
1 pound ground pork

Preheat oven to 350°F. For glaze, stir together first 4 ingredients in small saucepan. Cook over low heat, stirring frequently, until jelly melts. Bring to a boil. Boil 1 minute, stirring constantly. Remove from heat. Cool to room temperature. In large mixing bowl, beat eggs slightly. Add crushed cereal, *¼ cup* brown sugar, milk, onion, pepper, and *1½ teaspoons* dry mustard. Beat well. Add ham and pork. Mix until combined. Shape into loaf. Place in greased or foil-lined shallow baking pan. Bake about 1 hour and 15 minutes or until well browned. Brush loaf with glaze several times during last 30 minutes of baking. Serve with remaining glaze.

ITALIAN STUFFED PEPPERS

CAMPBELL SOUP COMPANY

Makes 8 servings

5 large green *or* sweet red peppers
1 pound ground beef
½ pound sweet Italian sausage, casing
 removed
½ cup chopped onion
2 large cloves garlic, minced
1 teaspoon dried oregano leaves,
 crushed

1 can (10¼ ounces) Franco-American®
 Beef Gravy
2 tablespoons tomato paste
½ cup diced mozzarella cheese
¼ cup grated Parmesan cheese (or more,
 if desired)
Hot cooked rice

Preheat oven to 350°F. Cut *4* peppers in half lengthwise; discard seed and membranes. Chop remaining pepper; reserve. In 10-inch skillet in ¾ inch boiling water, place pepper halves, cut side down, overlapping to fit. Reduce heat to low. Cover; simmer 5 minutes. Remove from heat. Drain peppers on paper towels. Empty water from skillet; dry skillet. In same skillet, over medium-high heat, cook beef, sausage, reserved chopped pepper, and onion with garlic and oregano until meat is browned and vegetables are tender, stirring to separate meat. Spoon off fat. Stir in gravy and tomato paste. Heat to boiling. Reduce heat to low; simmer 5 minutes. Remove from heat. Stir in cheeses. Spoon meat mixture into pepper shells. In 13-by-9-inch baking dish, arrange stuffed peppers. Cover with foil. Bake 25 minutes or until hot. Serve over rice with additional Parmesan cheese, if desired.

TANGY TUNA AND RICE LOAF

BEATRICE CHEESE, INC.

Makes 4 to 6 serving

2 envelopes unflavored gelatin
½ cup cold water
I can (8 ounces) tomato sauce
I cup cooked rice
¼ cup chopped green pepper
I cup grated County Line® Medium
    Sharp Cheddar Cheese

½ cup sour cream
Few drops hot pepper sauce
½ teaspoon salt
½ teaspoon onion salt
I teaspoon Worcestershire sauce
I can (6½ ounces) flaked tuna

Soften gelatin in cold water. In saucepan, heat tomato sauce; add gelatin and stir until dissolved. Add remaining ingredients. Blend well, and pour into greased 9-by-5-inch loaf pan. Chill until set. Unmold and slice. Garnish with egg slices and fresh parsley.

TUNA CRUZ MELT

LAWRY'S FOODS, INC.

Makes 4 servings

I can (12½ ounces) water-packed white
    tuna, drained
I can (4 ounces) diced green chilies,
    drained
I can (2.2 ounces) sliced pitted ripe
    olives, drained

¼ cup mayonnaise
½ teaspoon Lawry's® Seasoned Salt
4 flour tortillas
I cup (4 ounces) grated Cheddar cheese
I green onion with top, chopped
Parsley for garnish

In medium bowl, flake tuna. Add chilies, olives, mayonnaise, and seasoned salt; blend well. Spoon ¼ of mixture onto each tortilla. Top with equal portions of Cheddar cheese. Place on broiler pan and broil, 4 inches from heat, until cheese is hot and bubbly. Sprinkle each tortilla with green onion. Garnish each serving with parsley. Serve open-faced, or fold over soft-taco style.

CHICKEN TOSTADAS

LINDSAY INTERNATIONAL, INC.

Makes 6 servings

6 (6-inch) tortillas
Cooking oil
2 whole medium chicken breasts,
    skinned, boned, and cut into thin
    strips
¼ cup sliced green onions
2 tablespoons butter *or* margarine
1 can (8 ounces) tomato sauce

½ teaspoon garlic salt
¼ teaspoon ground cumin
2 cups shredded lettuce
1 cup (4 ounces) shredded Monterey
    Jack cheese
1 large avocado, seeded, peeled, and
    sliced
½ cup Lindsay® Jumbo Pitted Ripe Olives,
    drained and sliced

Preheat oven to 250°F. In small skillet, cook tortillas one at a time, in ¼ inch hot oil for 20 to 40 seconds on each side, until crisp and golden. Drain on paper towels; keep warm in foil in oven. In medium skillet, cook chicken and onion in butter until chicken is done and onion is tender. Add tomato sauce, garlic salt, and cumin. Reduce heat; simmer, covered, about 15 minutes. Atop each tortilla, layer lettuce, chicken, cheese, avocado, and olives.

CORNFLAKE ENCHILADAS

KELLOGG COMPANY

Makes 6 servings

1½ cups tomato paste
4 cups water
I teaspoon salt
4 teaspoons chili powder
½ teaspoon ground cumin
2 garlic cloves, finely chopped
I pound ground beef

I medium-size onion, finely chopped
2 cups (8 ounces) shredded Cheddar
   cheese
I cup KELLOGG'S CORN FLAKES®
   cereal, crushed to ½ cup
½ cup sliced ripe olives
12 tortillas

Preheat oven to 350°F. In medium-size saucepan, stir together tomato paste, water, salt, chili powder, cumin, and garlic. Bring to a boil. Reduce heat and simmer, uncovered, 20 minutes. Remove from heat. In large saucepan, brown ground beef with onion. Drain. Stir in *1 cup* tomato mixture, *1 cup* cheese, crushed cereal, and olives. Pour remaining tomato mixture into 13-by-9-by-2-inch baking pan. Spoon 2 measuring-tablespoons of beef mixture onto center of each tortilla. Roll up tortilla and place in pan, seam side down. Top filled tortillas with remaining beef mixture. Bake 15 minutes. Sprinkle remaining cheese over top. Bake about 5 minutes longer or until cheese melts and enchiladas are thoroughly heated.

THE MAGIC OF CALIFORNIA DIP
The Story of Lipton Dip

In 1954, the Lipton company noticed a dramatic surge in Los Angeles sales of its onion soup mix. After investigating, marketing personnel determined the reason: A food writer had raved about a housewife's amazing new recipe for a party dip. The recipe called for only two ingredients: Lipton® Onion Recipe Soup Mix and sour cream.

Some testing in The Lipton Kitchens was necessary to find the best proportions of the ingredients before the company would widely publicize the popular dip. At first the recipe called for one cup of Lipton mix to one cup of sour cream, "enough to blow your head off," as the home economist in The Lipton Kitchens put it. The many months of experiments created an onion and sour-cream shortage in the New Jersey area of Englewood Cliffs, home of Lipton's headquarters. In the end, Lipton, decided on one envelope of Lipton Onion Soup Mix to one sixteen-ounce container of sour cream. The final recipe, and others created with California Dip, as the blend came to be called, quickly changed the party scene. Tiny tidbits on limp toast triangles and other drooping canapés were replaced throughout the social scene, from intimate gatherings to major charity balls, with potato chips and California Dip.

Until the dip was introduced, sour cream had been little known, used mostly by people of middle European descent; now it enjoyed an explosion in popularity.

People discovered other uses for California Dip as well, like atop baked potatoes. Potato chips also enjoyed an unprecedented increase in sales.

California Dip established a completely new cooking concept, the use of dried soup mixes as ingredients in all types of recipes. A year after the introduction of the new dip, head of The Lipton Kitchens Dorothy Ebbott bundled up in thermal containers a pot roast, veal, birds in sauce, fish fillets, and a vegetable casserole, all prepared with onion soup mix. She took them to one of the most influential food writers in the country, Clementine Paddleford of the *New York Herald-Tribune*. Paddleford extolled the virtues of cooking with soup mixes, the ease of preparation, the good taste, and the uniqueness of the recipes.

The large volume of Lipton Onion Soup Mix sold throughout the country has made Lipton one of the biggest users of onions in the United States. This tremendous demand encouraged California growers to develop a special onion hybrid containing a higher content of solids and less water than in other onions. *The Lipton cut* a precise manner of cutting, was developed for the special blend of white and toasted sliced onions. Mature onions are harvested for the soup mix because younger onions have a higher sugar content; sugar caramelizes and causes burning.

Today this simple dip ranks as one of the most famous recipes of the twentieth century. Everybody knows about the Lipton California Dip, including those who will never learn to use another recipe.

CALIFORNIA ENCHILADAS

THOMAS J. LIPTON CO.

Makes 6 servings

1 can (15 ounces) tomato sauce
1½ teaspoons hot pepper sauce
½ teaspoon garlic powder
2 cups (about 6 ounces) shredded
   Monterey Jack *or* Muenster cheese
1½ cups cut-up cooked chicken

1 cup Lipton® California Dip (see below)
1 can (4 ounces) chopped green chilies,
   drained
12 corn tortillas, softened
1 large green pepper, cut into 12 thin
   strips

Preheat oven to 375°F. In small saucepan, combine tomato sauce, *½ teaspoon* pepper sauce, and garlic powder. Simmer, stirring occasionally, 15 minutes.

In medium bowl, combine *1½ cups* cheese, chicken, California Dip, chilies, and remaining pepper sauce. Spread *2½ tablespoons* mixture on each tortilla; roll up and place seam side down in lightly greased 2-quart oblong baking dish. Top each tortilla with *1 tablespoon* prepared sauce, remaining cheese, and green-pepper strip. Bake 15 minutes or until cheese is melted. Serve with remaining heated sauce.

LIPTON® CALIFORNIA DIP

Makes about 2 cups

1 envelope Lipton® Onion Recipe
   Soup Mix

1 container (16 ounces) sour cream

Blend together and chill.

QUICK AND EASY TAMALE PIE

THOMAS J. LIPTON CO.

Makes 2 main-dish or 4 snack-size portions

½ pound ground beef
2 envelopes Lipton® Tomato Cup•a•Soup® Instant Soup
½ cup water
1 can (7 ounces) whole kernel corn, drained
¼ cup sliced green onions
2 tablespoons chopped pitted ripe olives (optional)

¼ teaspoon chili powder
3 slices (¾ ounces each) American cheese, halved
2 corn muffins, cut in ½-inch cubes
Fresh coriander (optional)
Pitted ripe olives, sliced (optional)
Jalapeño peppers (optional)
Mexican Sour Cream Topping (see below)

In medium skillet, brown ground beef. Stir in soup mix, water, corn, green onions, olives (if desired), and chili powder until well blended. Top with cheese; then evenly spread muffin cubes over cheese. Cook 5 minutes or until heated through and cheese is melted. Garnish, if desired, with fresh coriander, olives, and jalapeño peppers. Serve with Mexican Sour Cream Topping.

To microwave: Reduce water to ¼ cup. In shallow microwave-safe 1-quart casserole, microwave ground beef with green onions at HIGH (100% Power) 2½ minutes or until beef is no longer pink, stirring once. Stir in soup mix, water, corn, olives (if desired), and chili powder until well blended. Top with cheese; then evenly spread muffin cubes over cheese. Microwave 5 minutes or until heated through and cheese is melted, turning casserole once. Garnish as above.

To double recipe: Prepare in 2-quart microwave-safe shallow casserole and microwave ground beef 6 minutes or until no longer pink, stirring twice. Increase final cooking time to 8 minutes or until heated through and cheese is melted.

MEXICAN SOUR CREAM TOPPING

½ cup sour cream
2 tablespoons chopped jalapeño peppers

1 teaspoon lime juice

Blend together.

TAOS TACOS

LAWRY'S FOODS, INC.

Makes 6 servings

1 pound lean ground beef
1 package (1.25 ounces) Lawry's® Taco
   Spices and Seasonings
½ cup beer
¼ cup water
1 can (15¼ ounces) kidney beans, drained
1 medium tomato, chopped
¼ cup thinly sliced green onions

1 tablespoon chopped cilantro *or* parsley
Flour tortillas, taco shells, or pita breads
Grated Cheddar *or* Monterey Jack cheese
   for garnish
Guacamole for garnish
Salsa for garnish
Dairy sour cream for garnish

In large skillet, brown ground beef, stirring until cooked through; drain fat. Add taco spices and seasonings, beer, and water; blend well. Bring to a boil; reduce heat and simmer, uncovered, 10 minutes. Add kidney beans, tomato, green onions, and cilantro; blend well. Simmer 5 minutes. Serve in tortillas, taco shells, or pita breads. Garnish each serving with your choice of grated Cheddar or Monterey Jack cheese, guacamole, salsa, and dairy sour cream.

VARIATION

Use ¾ cup water instead of ½ cup beer and ¼ cup water.

TEMPTING TACO BURGERS

THOMAS J. LIPTON CO.

Makes about 4 servings

1 envelope Lipton® Onion-Mushroom
   Recipe Soup Mix
1 pound ground beef
½ cup chopped tomato
¼ cup finely chopped green pepper

1 teaspoon chili powder
¼ cup water
Hamburger rolls (optional)
Shredded lettuce (optional)
Cheddar cheese (optional)

In large bowl, combine first 6 ingredients; shape into 4 patties. Grill or broil until done. Serve, if desired, on hamburger rolls, and top with shredded lettuce and Cheddar cheese.

To microwave: Prepare patties as above. In oblong baking dish, arrange patties and microwave, uncovered, at HIGH (100% Power) 10 minutes, turning patties once. Let stand, covered 5 minutes. Serve as above.

VARIATIONS

Substitute Lipton® Onion, Beefy Onion, *or* Beefy Mushroom Recipe Soup Mix for Lipton® Onion-Mushroom Recipe Soup Mix.

POCKET BURGERS

DURKEE-FRENCH FOODS

Makes 4 servings

1 pound lean ground beef
¼ cup Parmesan cheese
5 tablespoons French's® Yellow Mustard
2 tablespoons instant minced onion
2 tablespoons parsley flakes

2 tablespoons capers, drained (optional)
⅓ cup sour cream
4 (6-inch) pita-bread rounds
Sliced tomatoes
Lettuce

Combine beef, cheese, *3 tablespoons* mustard, onion, parsley, and capers; mix well. Firmly shape into 4 burgers. Combine sour cream with remaining *2 tablespoons* mustard; set aside. Grill burgers over high heat or broil 8 minutes or until desired doneness. Top each burger with about *2 tablespoons* of the sour cream sauce. Serve in pita bread with lettuce and tomato.

CHILI MUSHROOM BURGERS

JFC INTERNATIONAL, INC.

Makes 4 servings

1 pound lean, ground beef
¼ pound mushrooms, finely chopped
½ cup Dynasty® Panko
¼ cup minced onion

¼ cup Dynasty® Chinese Stir-Fry Sauce
1 tablespoon Dynasty® Szechwan Chili Sauce

Combine beef, mushrooms, panko, onion, and stir-fry and chili sauces; mix well. Form mixture into 4 equal-size patties. Grill or broil, 4 to 5 inches from heat, 8 to 10 minutes on each side, or until desired degree of doneness is reached. Serve plain or on buns with condiments, as desired.

CORNISH BEEF PASTIES

KELLOGG COMPANY

Makes 6 servings

1 pound beef round steak,
   cut into ¼-inch cubes
½ cup finely cubed, peeled potatoes
½ cup finely cubed, peeled turnips
½ cup finely cubed carrots
½ cup finely chopped onions
¼ teaspoon salt

¼ teaspoon pepper
1 package (11 ounce) pie-crust mix
2 cups KELLOGG'S CORN FLAKES®
   cereal, crushed to ½ cup
7 tablespoons cold water (1 to 2
   teaspoons more if needed)
Gravy (optional)

Preheat oven to 400°F. In large mixing bowl, combine beef, potatoes, turnips, carrots, onions, salt, and pepper. Set aside. Stir together pie-crust mix and crushed cereal. Add water, mixing with fork until dough holds together. Add 1 to 2 teaspoons additional water, if needed. Divide dough into 6 equal portions. On lightly floured surface, roll each portion to a 7-inch circle. Top each with ¾ *cup* meat mixture. Moisten edge with water. Fold in half and press edges to seal, using tines of fork. Cut 2 to 3 slits in pasties for steam to escape. Place on ungreased baking sheet. Bake about 45 minutes or until golden brown. Serve with gravy, if desired.

CALICO MEATBALL STEW

CAMPBELL SOUP COMPANY

Makes 8 servings, 8½ cups total

1 pound ground beef
½ pound bulk pork sausage
1 cup soft breadcrumbs
½ teaspoon dried oregano leaves, crushed
1 egg
¼ cup vegetable oil
2 cans (10¼ ounces each) Franco-
   American® Beef Gravy

1 can (about 14½ ounces) stewed
   tomatoes
3½ cups potatoes, peeled and cut in
   1-inch cubes
1½ cups diagonally sliced carrots
½ cup chopped onion
1 large bay leaf
¼ teaspoon pepper
1 cup frozen peas, thawed

In medium bowl, mix *thoroughly* beef, sausage, breadcrumbs, oregano, and egg.
Shape into 24 meatballs. In 6-quart Dutch oven over medium heat, in hot oil, cook
meatballs until browned on all sides. Spoon off fat. Add gravy, tomatoes, potatoes,
carrots, onion, bay leaf, and pepper. Heat to boiling, stirring occasionally. Reduce
heat to low. Cover; simmer 25 minutes. Stir in peas. Cook uncovered, 5 minutes
more. Discard bay leaf.

STEAK POT PIE

NABISCO FOODS GROUP

Makes 4 servings

1 cup chopped onion
2 tablespoons Blue Bonnet® Margarine
2 tablespoons all-purpose flour
1½ cups College Inn® Beef Broth

½ cup A.1.® Steak Sauce
3 cups (about 1½ pounds) diced cooked
   steak
2 cups frozen peas and carrots, thawed
Prepared pastry for 2-crust pie

Preheat oven to 400°F. In 2-quart saucepan, over medium-high heat, cook onion
in margarine until tender. Blend in flour; cook 1 minute. Add beef broth and steak
sauce; cook and stir until mixture thickens and begins to boil. Stir in steak and
peas and carrots. Spoon mixture evenly into four 16-ounce ovenproof individual
casseroles. Roll out and cut pastry crust to fit over casseroles. Seal crust to edge
of casseroles. Slit tops of crusts to vent. Bake 25 minutes or until golden brown.
Serve warm.

Preparation time: 15 minutes   *Total time:* 50 minutes

THE FIRST PACKAGED BAKING MIX
The Story of Bisquick

The last thing on Carl Smith's mind that cold night in November 1930 was discovering a product concept to alter the way America bakes. Smith had climbed aboard the Southern Pacific car for the late-night run from Portland to San Francisco and just wanted something to eat. He didn't expect much, really. Not at that late hour in a dining car.

What a pleasant surprise to be presented with hot biscuits in no time at all! His naturally curious salesman's mind was intrigued.

"Oh, I always make biscuits right from the oven in the blink of an eye," explained the ingenious chef. "No trouble at all." Before leaving Portland he had blended a mixture of lard, flour, baking powder, and salt that he kept stored in the ice chest.

Smith, a sales executive for General Mills, couldn't wait for morning, when he could take this idea to Charles Kress, head chemist, whose life-long search had been "for the secret hidden in the heart of the wheat kernel."

Before that fateful encounter, homemakers needed time to locate recipes; to scoop flour, shortening, and other ingredients from large bulk containers; and to measure ingredients precisely. The new concept of a baking mixture would streamline the process of making cakes, muffins, and biscuits. Baking became much easier and the results more predictable.

But stumbling blocks had to be overcome before this concept could successfully be brought to market. First, the oil must maintain its sweetness in the package during the many weeks between manufacturer and consumer. Also, the portion of the mixture contacting the wrapping paper must not turn rancid when exposed to the air filtering through the paper. Parchment paper, like the paper used to wrap butter, proved to be the solution to this problem. Finally, the discovery that the ingredients should not be mixed completely in the package foolproofed baking results. Lumps of oil interspersed with layers of flour perfected the product.

General Mills introduced this baking mix in 1931 under the trademark Bisquick. Other manufacturers jumped into the baking market soon after the introduction of Bisquick, but Bisquick grabbed the major share of the business and has remained the leader ever since.

IMPOSSIBLE CHEESEBURGER PIE

GENERAL MILLS, INC.

Makes 6 to 8 servings

1 pound ground beef
1½ cups chopped onion
½ teaspoon salt
¼ teaspoon pepper
1½ cups milk

3 eggs
¾ cup Bisquick® Baking Mix
2 tomatoes, sliced
1 cup shredded Cheddar *or* process
   American cheese

Preheat oven to 400°F. Grease pie plate, 10-by-1½ inches, or square baking dish, 8-by-8-by-2 inches, or six 10-ounce custard cups. Cook and stir ground beef and onion in 10-inch skillet over medium heat until beef is brown; drain. Stir in salt and pepper. Spread in pie plate. Beat milk, eggs, and baking mix 15 seconds in blender on high, or 1 minute with hand beater or wire whisk, until smooth. Pour into pie plate. Bake 25 minutes. Top with tomatoes; sprinkle with cheese. Bake 5 to 8 minutes or until knife inserted in center comes out clean. Cool 5 minutes.

To microwave: Crumble ground beef into ungreased microwave-safe pie plate, 10-by-1½ inches; add onion. Cover with waxed paper and microwave on HIGH 6 to 7 minutes, stirring after 3 minutes, until beef is done; drain. Continue as directed—except place pie plate on inverted microwave-safe dinner plate in microwave oven. Microwave, uncovered, on MEDIUM-HIGH 12 to 18 minutes, rotating pie plate a quarter turn every 6 minutes, until knife inserted in center comes out clean. Top with tomatoes and cheese. Microwave, uncovered, 6 to 8 minutes, rotating pie plate a quarter turn every 3 minutes, until cheese is melted. Let stand on flat, heatproof surface (not on wire rack) 5 minutes.

VARIATIONS

Impossible California Cheeseburger Pie: Just before serving, top with 1½ cups shredded lettuce and 12 to 16 dill-pickle slices.

Impossible Bacon-Cheeeseburger Pie: Arrange 6 slices crisply cooked bacon on pie after baking.

SLOPPY JOES CREOLE

KELLOGG COMPANY

Makes 8 sevings

1 pound ground beef
1 can (1 pound, 2 cups) tomatoes,
  undrained
½ cup chopped green pepper
½ cup chopped onion

2 cups KELLOGG'S CORN FLAKES®
  cereal
1 teaspoon salt
⅛ teaspoon pepper
1 tablespoon Worcestershire sauce
8 hamburger buns, sliced and toasted

In large frying pan, brown ground beef and drain. Stir in tomatoes, cutting into small pieces with spoon. Add green pepper, onion, cereal, salt, pepper, and Worcestershire sauce. Stir to combine. Cover and cook over low heat for 15 minutes, stirring occasionally. Serve on hamburger buns.

VARIATION

Substitute 1 can (15 ounces) tomato sauce with tomato bits for the 1-pound can of tomatoes. Omit salt and pepper.

TURKEY JOES

OSCAR MAYER FOODS CORPORATION

Makes 6 servings

1 package (1 pound) Louis Rich® Ground
  Turkey
1 medium onion, chopped

1 cup barbecue sauce
1 tablespoon sweet pickle relish
6 hamburger buns

Place turkey and onion in skillet. Cook on medium 8 to 10 minutes or until turkey is no longer pink, stirring and separating turkey as it cooks. Stir in barbecue sauce and relish. Cook 2 to 3 minutes more. Serve in buns.

To microwave: Crumble turkey in 2-quart casserole; add onion. Cover with waxed paper. Microwave at HIGH 3 minutes. Stir cooked portions from outside to center. Cover. Microwave 3 minutes more. Add barbecue sauce and relish. Microwave 1 minute more.

PIZZA PROVENÇAL
RAGU FOODS CO.

Makes 6 servings

1 long loaf French bread, split lengthwise
1 jar (14 ounces) Ragú® Pizza Quick Sauce
1 cup thinly sliced yellow pepper
1 cup thinly sliced red pepper
1 cup thinly sliced zucchini
½ cup sliced black olives
1 package (12 ounces) shredded mozzarella cheese
2 tablespoons minced fresh parsley

Preheat oven to 375°F. Place French bread halves on baking sheet. Evenly top each with pizza sauce. Layer yellow and red peppers, zucchini, and black olives. Sprinkle with mozzarella cheese and parsley. Bake 20 to 25 minutes or until cheese is bubbly.

CHICAGO DEEP DISH PIZZA
DURKEE-FRENCH FOODS

Makes 6 servings (1 pizza); 2 cups sauce (enough for 2 pizzas)

1 package (10 ounces) refrigerator pizza crust
1 package (1½ ounces) French's® Spaghetti Sauce Mix
1 can (16 ounces) whole tomatoes, cut up
1 can (6 ounces) tomato paste
2 teaspoons Durkee® RedHot Cayenne Pepper Sauce
1 cup (4 ounces) shredded mozzarella cheese
2 tablespoons grated Parmesan cheese

Preheat oven to 450°F. Press dough into 9-inch greased cake pan; bake, uncovered, 10 minutes. In saucepan combine spaghetti sauce mix, whole tomatoes, tomato paste, and pepper sauce. Simmer 10 minutes. Spoon *1 cup* spaghetti sauce on pizza crust; top with mozzarella and Parmesan cheese. Bake 15 minutes or until crust and cheese are golden.

IMPOSSIBLE PIZZA PIE

GENERAL MILLS, INC.

Makes 6 to 8 servings

⅔ cup chopped onion
⅓ cup grated Parmesan cheese
1½ cups milk
3 eggs
¾ cup Bisquick® Baking Mix
Sauce (see below)

¼ cup grated Parmesan cheese
1 package (3½ ounces) sliced pepperoni
⅓ cup chopped onion
½ cup chopped green bell pepper
1 to 1½ cups shredded mozzarella cheese

Preheat oven to 425°F. Grease pie plate, 10-by-1½ inches. Sprinkle ⅔ *cup* onion and ⅓ *cup* Parmesan cheese in plate. Beat milk, eggs, and baking mix 15 seconds in blender on high, or 1 minute with hand beater, until smooth. Pour into pie plate. Bake 20 minutes. Spread Sauce over top. Layer remaining ingredients on Sauce. Bake 15 to 20 minutes or until cheese is light brown. Cool 5 minutes.

To microware: Sprinkle ⅔ *cup* onion and ⅓ *cup* Parmesan cheese in greased microwave-safe pie plate, 10-by-1½ inches. Continue as directed—except place pie plate on inverted microwave-safe dinner plate in microwave oven. Microwave, uncovered, MEDIUM-HIGH 12 to 16 minutes, rotating pie plate a quarter turn every 6 minutes, until knife inserted in center comes out clean. Spread Sauce over top. Layer remaining ingredients on Sauce. Microwave, uncovered, 5 to 9 minutes, rotating pie plate a quarter turn every 3 minutes, until cheese is melted and bubbly. Let stand on flat, heatproof surface (not on wire rack) 5 minutes.

SAUCE

1 can (6 ounces) tomato paste
¼ cup water
1 teaspoon dried oregano

½ teaspoon garlic salt
½ teaspoon dried basil
¼ teaspoon pepper

Mix together.

VARIATION

Substitute ½ pound ground beef *or* bulk Italian sausage, cooked and drained, for the pepperoni.

ITALIAN-STYLE CHILI
BORDEN, INC.

Makes about 2 quarts

1 pound lean ground beef
¾ cup chopped onion
1 jar (26 ounces) Classico® Di Napoli
   (Tomato & Basil) Pasta Sauce
1½ cups water
1 can (14½ ounces) whole tomatoes,
   undrained and broken up

1 can (4 ounces) sliced mushrooms,
   drained
2 ounces (⅓ cup) sliced pepperoni
1 tablespoon Wyler's® or Steero® Beef-
   Flavor Instant Bouillon or 3 Beef-Flavor
   Bouillon Cubes
1 tablespoon chili powder
2 teaspoons sugar

In large kettle or Dutch oven, brown meat with onion; pour off fat. Add remaining ingredients; bring to a boil. Reduce heat; simmer, uncovered, 30 minutes, stirring occasionally. Garnish as desired. Refrigerate leftovers.

A.I.® TEXAS CHILI
NABISCO FOODS GROUP

Makes 6 servings

2 pounds round or chuck steak, cut into ¼
   inch cubes
1 tablespoon Blue Bonnet® Margarine
1 cup chopped onion

2 cans (16 ounces each) peeled
   tomatoes, coarsely chopped, with
   liquid
½ cup A.I.® Steak Sauce
¼ to ⅓ cup chili powder

In large saucepan, over medium-high heat, brown steak, in batches, in margarine. Add onion; cook until tender. Add tomatoes with liquid, steak sauce, and chili powder. Heat to a boil; reduce heat. Cover and simmer 1¼ to 1½ hours, stirring occasionally.

Preparation time: 15 minutes

Total time: 2 hours

MUSHROOM FRITTATA

LAWRY'S FOODS, INC.

Makes 4 servings

1 teaspoon butter *or* margarine
1 medium zucchini, shredded
1 medium tomato, chopped
1 can (4 ounces) sliced mushrooms,
  drained
6 eggs, beaten

¼ cup milk
2 teaspoons Dijon mustard
½ teaspoon Lawry's® Seasoned Salt
½ teaspoon Lawry's® Seasoned Pepper
2 cups (8 ounces) grated Swiss cheese

In large, ovenproof skillet, melt butter and sauté zucchini, tomato, and mushrooms 1 minute. In large bowl, combine remaining ingredients; blend well. Pour egg mixture into skillet; cook 10 minutes over low heat. To brown top, place skillet under broiler 2 to 3 minutes. Serve directly from skillet or remove frittata to serving dish.

Serve with additional Swiss cheese and fresh fruit.

VARIATION

Try serving frittata with prepared Lawry's® Spaghetti Sauce Seasoning. Blend with Imported Mushrooms.

LAMB CHOPS WITH HORSERADISH-PECAN SAUCE

MCCORMICK & COMPANY, INC.

Makes 6 lamb chops

6 slices bacon
6 boneless lamb loin chops, cut 1½ inches thick
1 tablespoon olive oil
1 tablespoon soy sauce
1 tablespoon lemon juice

⅛ teaspoon McCormick/Schilling® Instant Garlic Powder
⅛ teaspoon McCormick/Schilling Instant Onion Powder
Horseradish-Pecan Sauce (see below)
Fresh mint for garnish (optional)

Cook bacon over low heat until cooked but not crisp. Shape lamb chops into rounds. Wrap each chop with 1 piece bacon. Secure with wooden toothpick. Place lamb chops on broiler pan. Combine next 5 ingredients. Brush chops with mixture. Broil 4 inches from heat 10 minutes or until desired doneness. Turn chops once and brush with marinade occasionally while cooking.

Serve on Horseradish-Pecan Sauce. Garnish with fresh mint, if desired.

HORSERADISH-PECAN SAUCE

Makes 1 cup sauce

1 tablespoon olive oil
1 tablespoon flour
⅛ teaspoon McCormick/Schilling® ground White Pepper
1 teaspoon McCormick/Schilling Bon Appétit®

⅛ teaspoon McCormick/Schilling Instant Minced Garlic
1 cup half-and-half
1 tablespoon horseradish sauce
¼ cup chopped pecans

Combine olive oil and flour in small saucepan. Add white pepper, McCormick/Schilling Bon Appétit®, and minced garlic. Heat until bubbly. Gradually add half-and-half, stirring constantly. Add horseradish sauce and chopped pecans. Cook over medium heat, stirring constantly until mixture thickens.

SPANISH LAMB

LINDSAY INTERNATIONAL, INC.

Makes 4 servings

1 pound boneless lamb, cut into ½-inch
  cubes
1 cup finely chopped onion
2 cloves garlic, minced
2 tablespoons salad oil
1 can (16 ounces) tomatoes, cut up,
  undrained
1 can (8 ounces) tomato sauce

1 can (3 ounces) whole mushrooms,
  undrained
1 bay leaf
1 teaspoon dried basil, crushed
½ cup Lindsay® Salad-Style Green Olives,
  drained
Cooked brown rice
Grated Parmesan cheese

In saucepan, cook the lamb, onion, and garlic in hot oil until meat is brown and onion is tender. Stir in *undrained* tomatoes, tomato sauce, *undrained* mushrooms, bay leaf, and basil. Simmer, uncovered, 20 minutes. Stir in olives; simmer 10 minutes more or until mixture is desired consistency. Discard bay leaf. Serve lamb mixture over rice; sprinkle Parmesan cheese on top.

LAMB KABOBS WITH DUCK SAUCE

JFC INTERNATIONAL, INC.

Makes 4 servings, 2 skewers each

1½ pounds lean, boneless lamb or beef,
  cut into 1-inch chunks
3 tablespoons Dynasty® Oriental
  Marinade

2 medium zucchini, cut crosswise into
  ½-inch widths
1 medium red bell pepper, seeded and
  cut into 1-inch squares
½ cup Dynasty® Duck Sauce

Coat lamb with marinade; cover and refrigerate 2 hours. Thread lamb, zucchini, and pepper alternately onto eight 9-inch bamboo or metal skewers. Arrange threaded skewers, in single layer, on broiler pan or baking rack in baking pan. Brush top sides of skewers with half the Duck Sauce. Broil 3 to 4 inches from heat, 8 to 10 minutes. Turn skewers over; brush with remaining Duck Sauce. Broil 8 to 10 minutes longer, or until desired degree of doneness.

VARIATION

Substitute 2 yellow crookneck squash for zucchini and 1 green bell pepper for red bell pepper.

BEEF AND BACON KABOBS

NABISCO FOODS GROUP

Makes 4 servings

½ cup A.I.® Steak Sauce
¼ cup Regina® Sherry Cooking Wine
2 tablespoons honey
1½ pounds sirloin beef cubes

½ pound bacon slices, halved
Onion wedges
Green *or* red pepper squares
Whole mushroom caps

Blend steak sauce, sherry, and honey. In nonmetal dish, pour marinade over steak cubes. Cover; chill 2 hours, stirring occasionally. Drain beef; reserve marinade. Wrap half bacon slice around each steak cube. On 4 skewers, thread steak, onion wedges, pepper squares, and mushroom caps. Grill or broil 4 inches from heat source for 8 to 10 minutes or until desired doneness, turning occasionally and brushing with reserved marinade. Serve garnished as desired.

Preparation time: 15 minutes   *Total time:* 25 minutes

SKEWERED BEEF WITH HORSERADISH SAUCE

RAGÚ FOODS CO.

Makes 6 servings

6 ounces cream cheese, softened
¼ cup sour cream
1 tablespoon prepared horseradish
2 teaspoons Dijon mustard
1 package Adolph's® Meat Marinade

⅓ cup white vinegar
⅓ cup water
2 teaspoons Worcestershire sauce
1½ pounds beef top round steak, cut into
    cubes for kabobs

Preheat grill or broiler. In small bowl, thoroughly combine cream cheese, sour cream, horseradish, and mustard. Refrigerate until ready to serve.

In medium bowl, thoroughly combine contents of marinade package with vinegar, water, and Worcestershire sauce. Place beef cubes in marinade; pierce deeply with a fork. Marinate 15 minutes, turning occasionally. Thread small skewers with meat. Grill or broil beef 5 to 6 inches from heat, 8 minutes per side for medium. Baste with remaining marinade. Serve beef with horseradish sauce.

PORK AND SHRIMP KABABS

MCCORMICK & COMPANY, INC.

Makes 4 servings, 1 skewer each

¼ cup lime juice
½ cup cream of coconut
1 teaspoon McCormick/Schilling®
Freeze-Dried Shallots
⅛ teaspoon McCormick/Schilling ground
Nutmeg
⅛ teaspoon McCormick/Schilling ground
Cloves

1 McCormick/Schilling Bay Leaf
1 teaspoon McCormick/Schilling Cracked
Black Pepper
1 tablespoon soy sauce
12 (2-inch) cubes lean pork
1 red bell pepper
1 green bell pepper
12 jumbo shrimp, shelled and deveined

Preheat oven to 325°F. Mix first 8 ingredients. Put pork cubes in shallow glass or enamel baking dish. Pour marinade over pork. Bake, covered, 45 minutes. Cool, covered. Remove meat from marinade. Save marinade. Seed bell peppers and cut in bite-size pieces. Thread pork, peppers, and shrimp on 4 skewers. Broil 5 to 6 minutes, brushing frequently with reserved marinade.

OVEN-ROAST PORK HAWAIIAN

DOLE FOOD COMPANY

Makes 12 servings

2 cans (20 ounces each) Dole® Crushed
Pineapple, undrained
2 cups Dole Golden Raisins
1 center-cut pork loin roast (6 pounds)
or 2 pork loin roasts (3 pounds each)
Salt

Pepper
3 large cloves garlic, pressed
½ cup pineapple-apricot jam
¼ cup minced crystalized ginger
¾ cup Dole® Pineapple Juice
1 tablespoon cornstarch

Preheat oven to 350°F. Combine *1 cup* undrained pineapple with *1 cup* raisins. Cover roasting pan with heavy-duty foil. Place pork on foil. Make slit lengthwise through center of roast. Fill with raisin mixture. Sprinkle with salt and pepper; rub with garlic. Tie pork with string. Wrap tightly with foil. Roast 2 hours.

For sauce, combine jam, ginger, and remaining undrained pineapple and raisins. Cook 15 minutes. Uncover roast; baste with drippings. Spoon ¾ *cup* pineapple mixture over roast. Bake, uncovered, 15 to 20 minutes. Mix pineapple juice with cornstarch; add to pineapple mixture. Cook until sauce boils and thickens. Serve sauce with pork roast.

Chicken Paella

COURTESY OF LINDSAY INTERNATIONAL, INC.

Turkey en Croute
COURTESY OF OSCAR MAYER FOODS CORPORATION

PORK CHOPS WITH CREOLE SAUCE

LAWRY'S FOODS, INC.

Makes 4 to 6 servings

1 package (1.5 ounces) Lawry's Extra
 Rich and Thick Spaghetti Sauce
 Seasoning Blend
1 can (6 ounces) tomato paste
1¾ cups water
2 tablespoons butter *or* vegetable oil

1 can (4 ounces) sliced mushrooms,
 finely chopped
1 green bell pepper, finely chopped
½ to 1 teaspoon hot red pepper sauce
¼ teaspoon celery seed
4 to 6 pork chops (about 4 ounces each)

In medium saucepan, prepare spaghetti sauce seasoning blend according to package directions with tomato paste, water, and butter. Add mushrooms, green pepper, pepper sauce, and celery seed. In large, nonstick skillet, pan-fry pork chops 10 to 12 minutes, depending on thickness of chops, until pork is no longer pink. Top with prepared sauce. Serve with oven-browned potatoes and steamed sliced zucchini.

PORK CHOPS IN RAISIN SAUCE

DOLE FOOD COMPANY

Makes 2 servings

2 pork chops, thick cut
Salt (optional)
Pepper (optional)
1 large clove garlic, pressed
1 tablespoon olive oil

½ teaspoon thyme, crumbled
¼ teaspoon sage
1 cup orange juice
2 teaspoons cornstarch
½ cup Dole® Raisins

Sprinkle pork chops with salt and pepper if desired. Rub with garlic. In skillet, brown chops in oil. Cover skillet and shake occasionally during browning. Add thyme and sage; stir into pan juices. Mix 3 tablespoons juice with cornstarch. Set aside. Add remaining juice to skillet. Cover; simmer 10 minutes. Stir in cornstarch mixture until blended. Add raisins. Cook, stirring, until sauce boils and thickens.

Serve with green and yellow vegetables.

ORANGE-HONEY GLAZED PORK CHOPS

RAGÚ FOODS CO.

Makes 6 servings

¾ cup orange juice
3 tablespoons honey
2 tablespoons soy sauce
2 tablespoons apple cider vinegar
4 teaspoons cornstarch
1 tablespoon Dijon mustard

2 teaspoons Worcestershire sauce
1 clove garlic, minced
½ teaspoon dill weed
6 center-cut 1-inch-thick pork chops
(about 3 pounds total)
2 teaspoons Adolph's® 100% Natural
Tenderizer—Unseasoned

Preheat broiler or grill. In medium saucepan, combine first 9 ingredients. Simmer over low heat until thickened; set aside and keep warm.

Moisten meat with water. Evenly sprinkle both sides with tenderizer and pierce deeply with a fork. (*Do Not Add Salt.*) Broil or grill pork chops 4 to 6 inches from heat 12 to 14 minutes per side or until thoroughly cooked. Baste occasionally with sauce. Serve pork chops with remaining heated sauce.

PORK TENDERLOIN WITH PLUM SAUCE

JFC INTERNATIONAL, INC.

Makes about 3 dozen appetizers or 4 to 6 main-dish servings

½ cup Dynasty® Golden Plum Sauce
3 tablespoons Dynasty® Chinese Soy
Sauce

¾ teaspoon Dynasty® Chinese Five Spices
1½ to 2 pounds boneless pork tenderloin

Preheat oven to 375°F. Combine plum and soy sauces and five spices; mix well. Place pork tenderloin on baking rack in baking pan or on broiler pan. Add enough water to cover bottom of pan without touching pork. Generously brush some plum mixture over pork to glaze. Bake, uncovered, 1 hour, 20 minutes or until internal temperature registers 165°F on meat thermometer. Brush with remaining plum mixture every 20 minutes during cooking. Remove from oven; slice crosswise into ¼-inch-thick slices.

PORK STIR-FRY WITH SPICY PLUM SAUCE

JFC INTERNATIONAL, INC.

Makes 2 to 3 servings

1 pound boneless lean pork, cut into thin strips

2 tablespoons Dynasty® Oriental Marinade

2 tablespoons Dynasty® Chinese Stir-Fry Oil, divided

1 small onion, cut into thin wedges

1 green bell pepper, seeded and thinly sliced

2 tablespoons Dynasty® Plum Sauce

1 tablespoon Dynasty® Chinese Soy Sauce

1 teaspoon Dynasty® Hot Chili Oil

Coat pork with marinade; let stand 20 minutes. Heat wok or large frying pan over high heat. Add *1 tablespoon* oil; coat wok. Add half the pork mixture; stir-fry 1 to 2 minutes, or until lightly browned. Remove from wok with slotted spoon. Reheat wok over high heat 1 minute. Add remaining half pork; stir-fry 1 to 2 minutes, or until lightly browned. Remove from wok. Heat remaining *1 tablespoon* oil in same wok. Add onion and green pepper; stir-fry 2 to 3 minutes, or until tender-crisp. Return pork to wok; add plum and soy sauces. Cook and stir 1 minute, or until heated through. Remove from heat; stir in chili oil. Serve while hot.

CHINA SUN PORK

DOLE FOOD COMPANY

Makes 4 servings

1 can (20 ounces) Dole® Pineapple Chunks

½ cup water

3 tablespoons soy sauce

1 tablespoon cornstarch

1 teaspoon white vinegar

¼ teaspoon hot red pepper flakes

1 pound boneless pork loin

1 tablespoon vegetable oil

2 large cloves garlic, pressed

2 tablespoons minced ginger root *or* 1 teaspoon ground ginger

1 onion, cut in wedges

2 medium Dole® Carrots, slivered

1 Dole® Green *or* Red Bell Pepper, slivered

2 cups Dole® Sugar Peas

Drain pineapple and reserve *3 tablespoons* juice. Mix reserved juice with water, soy sauce, cornstarch, vinegar, and pepper flakes; set aside. Cut pork in strips. In skillet, brown pork in hot oil. Add garlic and ginger; cook 1 minute. Add onion and carrots; cook 1 minute. Stir sauce; add to skillet with pineapple, bell pepper, and sugar peas. Cook until sauce boils and thickens.

TROPIC SUN SPARERIBS
DOLE FOOD COMPANY

Makes 4 to 6 servings

3½ to 4 pounds spareribs *or* country-style ribs
3 large cloves garlic, pressed
Salt
Pepper
1 large onion, sliced

1 can (20 ounces) Dole® Crushed Pineapple, undrained
1 bottle (12 ounces) chili sauce
½ cup brown sugar, packed
1 teaspoon ground ginger
½ teaspoon dry mustard

Preheat oven to 350°F.

Rub ribs with garlic. Sprinkle with salt and pepper. Arrange onion in large baking pan. Place ribs on top. Add *¼ cup* water to pan. Cover with foil. Bake 30 minutes. Combine remaining ingredients. Spoon over ribs. Bake, uncovered, 1 hour longer.

ROSEMARY'S FINGER-LICKING RIBS
DURKEE-FRENCH FOODS

Makes about 4 servings

½ cup orange marmalade
1 teaspoon soy sauce
1 teaspoon Durkee® Rosemary, crushed
½ teaspoon Durkee® Garlic Powder

½ teaspoon Durkee® Thyme Leaves or ¼ teaspoon Durkee® Ground Thyme
¾ teaspoon seasoned salt
2 pounds lean pork ribs

In small bowl, combine orange marmalade, soy sauce, rosemary, garlic powder, thyme, and *¼ teaspoon* seasoned salt; mix well. Rub *½ teaspoon* seasoned salt into both sides of ribs. Broil or grill ribs over medium-high heat for 20 minutes, turning frequently. Baste both sides with marmalade sauce. Cook 10 more minutes, or until no longer pink inside.

GLAZED HAM WITH DIJON PINEAPPLE SAUCE
NABISCO FOODS GROUP

Makes 20 servings

1 precooked ham (5 pounds)
Whole cloves
Large maraschino cherries, halved
  (optional)
1 cup firmly packed dark brown sugar

½ cup maple-flavored syrup
¼ cup Grey Poupon® Dijon *or* Country
  Dijon Mustard
1 tablespoon cornstarch
1 can (20 ounces) crushed pineapple in
  its own juice

Preheat oven to 350°F. Score ham; stud with cloves and cherries. Place on rack in shallow baking pan. Bake 2 hours.

Meanwhile, combine brown sugar, syrup, and mustard; use *¾ cup* glaze mixture to baste ham every 10 minutes during last 35 to 40 minutes of baking. In saucepan, blend remaining glaze mixture, cornstarch, and pineapple with juice. Over medium-high heat, cook and stir until sauce thickens and begins to boil. Slice and serve ham with sauce.

JUBILEE HAM WITH RUM TE DUM SAUCE
OSCAR MAYER FOODS CORPORATION

Makes 12 servings

1 can (3 pounds) Oscar Mayer® Ham
1 can (8¼ ounces) crushed pineapple,
  with liquid
½ cup orange juice
½ cup brown sugar
¼ cup raisins

1 tablespoon cornstarch
1 teaspoon dry mustard
¼ teaspoon ground ginger
⅛ teaspoon ground cloves
⅛ teaspoon ground nutmeg
2 tablespoons rum

Heat ham according to label directions. Combine remaining ingredients except rum in saucepan. Bring to a boil. Turn down heat. Simmer 5 minutes until thickened, stirring occasionally. Stir in rum. Brush on ham last 30 minutes of heating. Serve remainder as sauce.

OVEN-BARBECUED BEEF BRISKET

NABISCO FOODS GROUP

Makes 10 to 12 servings

1 beef brisket (5 to 6 pounds)
2 cans (15 ounces each) tomato sauce
½ cup firmly packed light brown sugar
1 bottle (3.5 ounces) Wright's® Natural
  Hickory Seasoning

¼ cup A.1.® Steak Sauce
2 tablespoons lemon juice
½ teaspoon liquid hot pepper seasoning

Preheat oven to 350°F. Place brisket, fat side up, in large roasting pan; set aside.

Blend tomato sauce, brown sugar, hickory seasoning, steak sauce, lemon juice, and hot pepper seasoning; pour over brisket. Bake, covered, 4 to 5 hours or until tender, basting occasionally. If necessary, thicken cooking liquid with flour; serve with sliced meat.

HOT 'N SPICY BROCCOLI BEEF

LAWRY'S FOODS, INC.

Makes 4 servings

3 tablespoons vegetable oil
1 flank *or* round steak (about 1 pound),
  cut into thin strips
3 cups broccoli florets
½ cup water
1 teaspoon crushed red pepper

¼ teaspoon Lawry's® Garlic Powder with
  Parsley
¼ cup ketchup
1 to 2 tablespoons soy sauce
1½ teaspoons cornstarch
½ teaspoon ground ginger
Scallions for garnish

In large skillet, heat oil and stir-fry steak until just browned. Remove steak and set aside. In same skillet, add broccoli, *¼ cup* water, red pepper and garlic powder with parsley. Cover and cook 5 minutes. Meanwhile, in small bowl, combine remaining ingredients except scallions; blend well. Return meat to skillet; blend in ketchup mixture. Bring to a boil. Cook until sauce thickens and glaze develops. Garnish with scallions. Serve over chow mein noodles with sliced cucumbers and carrot sticks on the side.

SIZZLING STEAK FAJITAS
NABISCO FOODS GROUP

Makes 4 servings

½ cup A.I.® Steak Sauce
½ cup Ortega® Mild, Medium, *or* Hot Picante Sauce
1 pound flank *or* bottom round steak, thinly sliced

1 medium onion, thinly sliced
1 medium green pepper, cut into strips
1 tablespoon Blue Bonnet® Margarine
8 flour tortillas, warmed

Blend steak sauce and picante sauce. In nonmetal dish, pour marinade over steak. Cover; chill at least 2 hours, stirring occasionally.

In large skillet, over medium-high heat, cook onion and green pepper in margarine for 3 minutes or until tender. Remove with slotted spoon; reserve. Add steak with marinade to same skillet; cook and stir for 8 minutes or until done. Add onion and pepper; cook until heated through. Serve with tortillas and your favorite fajitas toppings, if desired.

Preparation time: 10 minutes   *Total time:* 25 minutes

FRUITED BEEF WITH RICE
LINDSAY INTERNATIONAL, INC.

Makes 6 servings

1 pound beef stew meat, cut in 1-inch cubes
1 tablespoon cooking oil
1 cup dry red wine
1 can (8 ounces) tomatoes, cut up
1 large onion, sliced ¼-inch thick
1 green pepper, cut in strips
¼ cup raisins
¼ cup dried apricots, halved
1 clove garlic, minced
1 teaspoon dried basil, crushed

1 teaspoon dried thyme, crushed
1 teaspoon dried tarragon, crushed
1 bay leaf
½ teaspoon salt
⅛ teaspoon pepper
½ cup sliced fresh mushrooms
½ cup Lindsay® Medium Pitted Ripe Olives, drained
1 cup cold water
1 tablespoon all-purpose flour
Hot cooked rice

In 10-inch skillet, brown beef in hot oil. Stir in wine, tomatoes, onion, green pepper, raisins, apricots, garlic, basil, thyme, tarragon, bay leaf, salt, and pepper. Simmer, covered, 1 hour. Stir in mushrooms and olives; simmer, covered, 30 minutes more. Discard bay leaf. Stir water into flour; stir into stew. Cook and stir until thickened and bubbly. Cook and stir 1 minute more. Serve over rice.

POPPY BEEF STROGANOFF

DURKEE-FRENCH FOODS

Makes about 6 servings

2 tablespoons vegetable oil
2 pounds sirloin *or* round steak, cut in
  1-inch cubes
1 tablespoon Durkee® Poppy Seed
1 tablespoon Durkee®
  Instant Chopped Onion
1 teaspoon Durkee® Paprika

1 teaspoon Durkee® Garlic Powder
¼ teaspoon Durkee®
  Ground Black Pepper
1 can (10½ ounces) condensed
  beef broth
2 tablespoons all-purpose flour
½ cup sour cream

In large skillet, heat oil on high; add meat and spices. Cook meat about 5 minutes or until browned, stirring frequently. Add broth and flour; stir until flour is blended. Simmer, covered, about 30 to 40 minutes or until meat is tender. Stir in sour cream and heat about 5 minutes.

Serve over noodles or spaghetti squash, if desired.

BOEUF EN DAUBE

LINDSAY INTERNATIONAL, INC.

Makes 8 servings

2 slices bacon, cut up
2 to 2½ pounds beef stew meat, cut into
  1-inch cubes
2 cups dry red wine
1 medium onion, chopped
2 cloves garlic, minced
1 tablespoon vinegar
½ teaspoon instant beef bouillon granules
½ teaspoon dried rosemary, crushed
½ teaspoon dried thyme, crushed

½ teaspoon finely shredded orange peel
½ cup water
¼ teaspoon pepper
6 carrots, bias-sliced into 1-inch pieces
3 medium onions, quartered
1 can 6 ounces; 1½ cups Lindsay® Large
  Pitted Ripe Olives, drained
2 tablespoons cold water
2 tablespoons cornstarch

In Dutch oven, cook bacon until crisp. Add beef; brown. Stir in next 8 ingredients, *½ cup* water, and pepper. Bring to a boil. Reduce heat. Cover; simmer 1 hour. Stir in carrots, onions, and olives. Simmer, covered, about 35 minutes or until tender. Combine cornstarch and *2 tablespoons* cold water; stir into meat mixture. Cook and stir until thickened and bubbly. Cook and stir 2 minutes more.

ITALIAN BRACIOLE
LINDSAY INTERNATIONAL, INC.

Makes 6 servings

2 pounds beef round steak, cut ½-inch
   thick
Salt
Pepper
½ cup chopped onion
¼ cup chili sauce
¼ cup condensed beef broth
1 can 3 ounces sliced mushrooms,
   undrained
2 tablespoons chopped green pepper

½ cup Lindsay® Salad-Style Green Olives,
   drained and sliced
1 teaspoon sugar
1 teaspoon Worcestershire sauce
¼ teaspoon dried oregano, crushed
⅛ teaspoon garlic powder
⅛ teaspoon pepper
Hot cooked spaghetti
½ cup cold water
3 tablespoons all-purpose flour

Preheat oven to 350°F. Cut steak into 6 rectangular pieces; pound each piece to ¼-inch thickness. Season with a little salt and pepper. Spread onion over meat to within ½ inch of edge. Roll up each piece jelly-roll style; secure with wooden toothpicks. Place meat rolls, seam side down, in a 10-by-6-by-2-inch baking dish.

Combine chili sauce, beef broth, undrained mushrooms, green pepper, olives, sugar, Worcestershire sauce, oregano, garlic powder, and *⅛ teaspoon* pepper. Pour over meat rolls. Bake, covered, 1¼ to 1½ hours or until meat is tender.

Arrange meat rolls atop spaghetti on serving platter; keep warm. Pour pan juices into measuring cup; skim off excess fat. Add enough water to juices to make 1½ cups; pour into saucepan. Blend *½ cup* cold water with flour; add to juices. Cook and stir until thickened and bubbly. Spoon some sauce over meat; pass remaining sauce.

FROM HUMBLE BEGINNINGS
The Story of Pepperidge Farm

What good cook hasn't fantasized about introducing a prized recipe to the marketplace and later seeing the product made from it on supermarket shelves nationwide? Margaret Rudkin, a Fairfield, Connecticut, mother of three sons, had this fortune, starting in 1937, when homemakers hardly ventured from their hearths.

Rudkin didn't start out to build a major company. In fact, her success began with dismal news. "We've tried everything known to medical science," the doctors told her, regarding her youngest son, who suffered from severe asthma attacks. "There's nothing more we can do for his allergic condition."

Intuitively, Rudkin knew that there must be something to make her son better. She wondered if a more nutritious diet, starting with better bread, might help her son to breathe more easily. Self-evident as it seems today, few people in 1937 associated good nutrition with good health. The popular, commercially available white bread contained additives and preservatives even then.

Rudkin bought whole-wheat grain from a feed dealer and tracked down an old-time gristmill to stone-grind it. Describing her result years later, she said, "My first loaf of whole wheat tasted like a relic from the Stone Age!" But Rudkin was determined to make the best loaf of bread possible.

After tasting her perfected recipe, her son's doctors insisted on ordering some of the bread to send to other allergic patients. Her Fairfield neighbors started purchasing it at the local grocery. Rudkin could hardly produce enough to meet the ever-increasing local demand.

A natural saleswoman, Rudkin convinced a New York store manager to take on her fledgling product. Already she had enough confidence in her bread to charge twenty-five cents a loaf when the going price was ten cents. But with success came a whole new set of problems. How could she meet deliveries with no real bakery, no distribution network, no bakery trucks?

To the amusement of her stockbroker husband, she set up shop in the garage of their Fairfield home, naming the business after the pepperidge sour gum trees that grew on the property. Praising and criticizing, she taught a few local women to knead and bake bread her way.

With no other means to get the bread into the city, Rudkin prevailed upon her husband, who commuted, to take two "small" twenty-five-pound packages of fresh-baked loaves with him into Grand Central Station each morning. The first official Pepperidge Farm distributor was a railway porter who delivered the packages to a food specialty shop across the street.

By 1938, regular shipments of bread were being distributed to area stores in Dodge panel trucks. Rail express now carried fresh bread to New York specialty food shops. Three short years later, the Pepperidge Farm business outgrew the farm and moved into a rented bakery in Norwalk, Connecticut.

New products were introduced. New bread varieties led to stuffing. Exquisite cookies were modeled after the most delicious varieties the Rudkins had discovered during their trips to Europe.

Ground was broken for plants in Pennsylvania and Illinois, and by 1957, Pepperidge Farm had entered the modern era as a national company. Today, it employs more than five thousand people and makes more than two hundred products in its eight bakeries nationwide—far from its humble beginnings.

BEEF WELLINGTON

PEPPERIDGE FARM, INC.

Makes 6 servings

2½-pound filet of beef
1 sheet Pepperidge Farm® Frozen Puff Pastry, thawed 20 minutes

1½ cups liver pâté
1 egg beaten with 1 tablespoon water
1 cup homemade or canned beef gravy

Preheat oven to 425°F. Roast filet 20 minutes; cool thoroughly. On a lightly floured surface, roll out pastry to a rectangle approximately 4 inches wider and longer than the filet. Spread half the pâté in center of pastry. Place meat on pastry and spread with remaining pâté. Completely enclose the meat in the pastry, sealing the edges. If desired, make decorative designs from pastry scraps and place on top. Brush with egg; place on an ungreased baking sheet seam side down. Bake 25 minutes, or until pastry is browned. Let stand 5 minutes before slicing. Serve with heated gravy.

BURGUNDY BEEF

CAMPBELL SOUP COMPANY

Makes 4 servings, about 3½ cups total

I tablespoon butter *or* margarine
½ cup chopped onion
I large clove garlic, minced
I pound beef for stew, cut into ½-inch pieces

I can (10¼ ounces) Franco-American® Beef Gravy
I cup thinly sliced carrots
¼ cup Burgundy or other dry red wine
¼ cup tomato paste
Hot cooked noodles

In 2-quart microwave-safe casserole, combine butter, onion, and garlic. Cover with lid; microwave on HIGH 3 minutes or until onion is tender, stirring once during cooking. Stir in beef. Cover; microwave on HIGH 5 minutes or until beef is no longer pink, stirring once during cooking. Stir in gravy, carrots, wine, and tomato paste. Cover; microwave on HIGH 5 minutes or until boiling. Stir. Reduce to MEDIUM (50% Power). Cover; microwave 30 minutes or until meat is tender, stirring twice during cooking. Let stand, covered, 5 minutes. Serve over noodles.

SOUTHWEST BARBECUE PEPPER STEAK

NABISCO FOODS GROUP

Makes 6 servings

I cup beer
¾ cup A.I.® Steak Sauce
2 cloves garlic, crushed
2 teaspoons chili powder
I teaspoon ground cumin

1½ pounds round steak, cut into ½-inch strips
3 small red or green peppers, cut into I-inch pieces
I teaspoon cornstarch

Mix first 5 ingredients; add meat. Chill 2 hours. Thread beef and pepper pieces on 6 skewers. Heat marinade and cornstarch to a boil. Grill or broil beef 15 minutes or until done, brushing with marinade often. Heat remaining marinade to serve with steak.

VEAL CUTLET PARMIGIANA

BORDEN, INC.

Makes 4 servings

4 thin veal cutlets, pounded (about 1½ pounds)
Salt
Pepper
3 tablespoons flour
1 egg, beaten with 2 tablespoons water
1½ cups fresh bread crumbs (3 slices bread)

¼ cup olive oil
1 jar (26 ounces) Classico® Di Napoli (Tomato & Basil) *or* Di Sicilia (Ripe Olives & Mushrooms) Pasta Sauce
4 slices (about 6 ounces) mozzarella cheese
½ cup grated fresh Parmesan cheese

Preheat oven to 450°F. Season cutlets with salt and pepper. Coat with flour; dip in egg mixture. Coat with crumbs. In large skillet, over medium heat, brown veal in oil. Arrange veal in 13-by-9-inch baking dish. Top evenly with sauce, then cheeses. Bake 10 minutes or until hot. If desired, broil until lightly browned. Refrigerate leftovers.

FLORENTINE VEAL ROAST

DURKEE-FRENCH FOODS

Makes 8 to 10 servings

4 pounds boneless breast of veal
¼ teaspoon Durkee® Ground Black Pepper
2 teaspoons Durkee® Poultry Seasoning
2 teaspoons Durkee® Basil
1½ teaspoons Durkee® Garlic Powder
2 packages (10 ounces *each*) frozen chopped spinach, thawed and drained

1 teaspoon salt
2 cups (8 ounces) shredded mozzarella cheese
1 red *or* yellow pepper, chopped
2 tablespoons olive oil
1 can (13¾ ounces) chicken broth
¼ cup dry white wine *or* water
3 tablespoons cornstarch

Preheat oven to 350°F. Season outside of meat with black pepper and *½ teaspoon each* poultry seasoning, basil, and garlic powder; turn meat over. Combine spinach, salt, cheese, and red or yellow pepper with remaining *1½ teaspoons each* poultry seasoning and basil and with *1 teaspoon* garlic powder. Spread evenly over meat. Tightly roll up meat; tie with string at 1-inch intervals. Heat oil in Dutch oven or heavy roasting pan; brown roast on all sides. Pour broth on top. Cover tightly; roast for 1½ hours or until 165°F internal temperature. Remove roast to carving board; keep warm. Strain liquid and skim fat. Combine wine and cornstarch; stir into liquid. Bring to a boil; simmer 5 minutes, stirring, until thickened. Serve with roast.

HONEY-MARINATED CHICKEN BREASTS

PET INCORPORATED

Makes 4 servings

1 pound boneless, skinless chicken breast halves

¼ cup Hollywood® Canola *or* Safflower Oil

¼ cup honey

2 tablespoons lemon juice

1 clove garlic, minced

2 teaspoons fresh minced thyme

¼ teaspoon salt

¼ teaspoon ground black pepper

Place chicken in an 8-by-8-inch glass baking dish. In small bowl, whisk together remaining ingredients; pour marinade over chicken. Cover and refrigerate 20 minutes. Grill chicken over hot coals until cooked through, basting occasionally with marinade.

CHICKEN PARMIGIANA

PET INCORPORATED

Makes 4 servings

4 boneless, skinless chicken breast halves

2 eggs, beaten

1 cup Progresso® Italian Style Bread Crumbs

¼ cup Progresso® Olive Oil

1 jar (15 ounces) Progresso® Marinara Sauce

½ cup Progresso® Grated Parmesan Cheese

1 cup (4 ounces) shredded mozzarella cheese

Preheat oven to 400°F. Dip chicken into egg and then into bread crumbs, coating thoroughly. In medium skillet, heat olive oil. Cook chicken in oil until done and well browned on both sides. Pour spaghetti sauce into an 11-by-7-inch baking dish. Place chicken on sauce and top with Parmesan and mozzarella cheeses. Bake for 15 minutes or until cheese is melted and lightly browned.

BRAN PARMESAN CHICKEN

KELLOGG COMPANY

Makes 4 servings

1 ½ cups KELLOGG'S® Bran Flakes cereal
1 egg
¼ cup milk
¼ cup all-purpose flour
⅛ teaspoon salt
Dash pepper

⅛ teaspoon ground sage
3 tablespoons grated Parmesan cheese
4 chicken pieces (1 to 1 ½ pounds),
  washed and patted dry
1 tablespoon margarine *or* butter,
  melted

Preheat oven to 350°F. Crush cereal to measure ¾ *cup*. Set aside. In small mixing bowl, beat egg and milk slightly. Add flour, salt, pepper, sage, and cheese, stirring until smooth. Dip chicken pieces in egg mixture. Coat with cereal. Place in single layer, skin side up, in greased or foil-lined shallow baking pan. Drizzle with margarine. Bake about 45 minutes or until tender. Do not cover pan or turn chicken while baking.

CHICKEN WITH MUSTARD-DILL SAUCE

RAGÚ FOODS CO.

Makes 4 servings

1 package Adolph's® Chicken Marinade
½ cup water
¼ cup lemon juice
1 pound boneless chicken breasts,
  pounded thin

1 tablespoon vegetable oil
1 tablespoon chopped fresh dill
1 teaspoon Dijon mustard
¼ cup light cream
6 slices bacon, cooked and crumbled

In shallow pan, combine marinade mix with water and lemon juice. Place chicken in marinade; pierce deeply with a fork. Marinate 15 minutes, turning chicken occasionally. Remove chicken; reserve ¼ *cup* marinade. In large skillet, thoroughly brown chicken on both sides in hot oil. Cover and cook 15 minutes over low heat. Add reserved marinade, dill, mustard, cream, and bacon. Mix thoroughly; heat through. Serve sauce over chicken.

CHICKEN NOODLE SPINACH BAKE

PET INCORPORATED

Makes 4 servings

4 boneless, skinless chicken breast halves

1 can (19 ounces) Progresso® Chicken Noodle Soup, drained, with broth reserved

½ cup Progresso® Italian Style Bread Crumbs

½ cup sour cream

1 egg

1 clove garlic, minced

1 tablespoon all-purpose flour

⅓ cup chopped onion

1 package (10 ounces) frozen chopped spinach, thawed and well drained

1 cup (4 ounces) Swiss cheese, cut in strips

Preheat oven to 350°F. Dip chicken in reserved soup broth; coat with bread crumbs and set aside. In medium bowl, combine sour cream, egg, garlic, and flour; stir until smooth. Stir in reserved soup pieces, onion, spinach, and half of cheese. Spread mixture evenly in 2-quart rectangular baking dish. Top with chicken and remaining bread crumbs. Bake 35 minutes. Add remaining cheese and bake an additional 10 to 15 minutes or until cheese is melted.

To microwave: Prepare as directed above in a 2-quart rectangular, microwave-safe baking dish. (Do not top chicken with remaining bread crumbs.) Cover and microwave on HIGH (100% Power) 8 to 10 minutes. Combine remaining bread crumbs and cheese and sprinkle on top of casserole. Microwave on MEDIUM (50% Power) 2 to 3 minutes or until cheese is melted. Let stand 5 minutes before serving.

BREADED LEMON CHICKEN

PET INCORPORATED

Makes 4 servings

1 pound boneless, skinless chicken breast halves, pounded to 1/4-inch thick
2 eggs, lightly beaten
1 cup Progresso® Italian Style Bread Crumbs
1/4 cup Progresso® Olive Oil
2 tablespoons butter

1 1/2 tablespoons all-purpose flour
1/4 teaspoon salt
1/4 teaspoon ground black pepper
3/4 cup Progresso® Chicken Broth
2/3 cup white wine
2 teaspoons freshly squeezed lemon juice

Dip chicken in egg, then in bread crumbs, pressing bread crumbs into meat. In large skillet, heat olive oil. Add chicken, cook on medium heat for 3 minutes per side or until done. Remove and keep warm. Remove drippings and any remaining oil from skillet. Melt butter, stir in flour, salt, and pepper. Cook until bubbly. Gradually stir in chicken broth, wine, and lemon juice, stirring constantly until mixture thickens slightly and comes to a boil. Add chicken back to skillet to warm. Serve immediately.

CITRUS GLAZED CHICKEN

RAGÚ FOODS CO.

Makes 4 servings

1 package Adolph's® Marinade in Minutes—Lemon-Pepper Flavor
2/3 cup orange juice
1 tablespoon Dijon mustard

1 teaspoon Worcestershire sauce
1 chicken (about 3 1/2 to 4 pounds), quartered

Preheat over to 350°F. In medium bowl, thoroughly combine contents of marinade package with orange juice, Dijon mustard, and Worcestershire sauce. Place chicken in marinade; pierce deeply with a fork. Marinate 15 minutes, turning chicken occasionally. Remove chicken from marinade. Place on baking sheet. Bake 1 hour and 10 minutes or until thoroughly cooked. Baste occasionally with remaining marinade.

CHICKEN FANFARE

OSCAR MAYER FOODS CORPORATION

Makes 8 servings

8 boneless chicken-breast halves

STUFFING

1 package (6 ounces) chicken-flavored
  stuffing mix
1½ cups water
¼ cup butter, melted
1 cup raisins

TOPPING

1 cup ground pecans
Grated rind from 2 oranges *or*
  2 tablespoons dried orange peel
2 tablespoons sugar
1 package (12 ounces) Oscar Mayer®
  Center-Cut Bacon

Preheat oven to 350°F. Remove skin from chicken; pound between 2 pieces of waxed paper to ¼-inch thick. Remove waxed paper. In large bowl, combine stuffing ingredients; mix thoroughly. Place *⅓ cup* stuffing mixture on each pounded chicken breast. Fold ends of chicken over stuffing. Wrap chicken bundle with 3 slices of bacon. Combine topping ingredients in pie plate. Roll chicken bundle in nut mixture. Place seam side down in shallow baking sheet. Sprinkle with remaining nut mixture. Bake 40 to 45 minutes.

STUFFED CHICKEN BREASTS

LAWRY'S FOODS, INC.

Makes 6 to 8 servings

- 1½ to 2 pounds boneless chicken-breast halves, with skin
- 1 package (10 ounces) frozen chopped spinach, thawed
- 1 cup (4 ounces) grated fontina *or* Monterey Jack cheese
- 1 cup (4 ounces) grated Parmesan cheese
- ½ cup shredded carrot
- ¼ cup sliced green onions
- 2 tablespoons minced fresh basil *or* 2 teaspoons dried basil, crushed
- ½ teaspoons Lawry's® Garlic Powder with Parsley
- ½ teaspoon Lawry's Seasoned Pepper Imperial® Margarine, melted

Preheat oven to 375°F. Rinse chicken thoroughly; pat dry. Place spinach in strainer; press with back of spoon to remove excess liquid. In medium bowl, combine all ingredients except chicken and margarine. Using fingers, carefully stuff thin layer of spinach mixture under skin of chicken. Pat top with paper towel; brush with margarine. Place stuffed chicken pieces in shallow baking dish. Bake 25 to 30 minutes or until chicken is golden brown. Let stand 5 minutes.

Slice chicken crosswise and serve with rice pilaf. Garnish with lemon slices and fresh basil.

VARIATION

To prepare recipe using skinless chicken, slit 1 side of chicken breast to create a "pocket." Place stuffing mixture in "pocket," brush with margarine, and bake as above.

VEGETABLE CONFETTI STUFFED CHICKEN

LAWRY'S FOODS, INC.

Makes 6 servings

1½ pounds boneless chicken breasts, skinned

1 tablespoon vegetable oil

1 carrot, cut into julienne strips

1 zucchini, cut into julienne strips

1 red bell pepper, cut into julienne strips

½ teaspoon Lawry's® Seasoned Salt

¼ teaspoon Lawry's® Garlic Powder with Parsley

4 ounces Cheddar cheese, thinly sliced

½ cup dry white wine *or* chicken broth

Lawry's® Seasoned Salt

Lawry's® Lemon Pepper Seasoning

To microwave: Place chicken breasts between 2 sheets of waxed paper; pound with meat mallet or rolling pin to flatten to ¼-inch thickness. In medium skillet, heat oil and sauté carrot, zucchini, and red pepper with ½ *teaspoon* seasoned salt and with garlic powder with parsley. On each chicken breast, place 1 slice of Cheddar cheese. Divide vegetable mixture evenly among chicken breasts. Roll up each breast and secure with wooden toothpicks. Place chicken rolls in microwave-safe dish; pour wine over rolls. Cover with vented plastic wrap and microwave on HIGH 8 to 12 minutes or until chicken is cooked through. Let stand 5 minutes. Drain off excess liquid. Sprinkle with seasoned salt and lemon pepper seasoning to taste.

Slice chicken rolls into ¼-inch slices. Serve with seasoned rice and garnish with tomato rose.

CARIBBEAN CHICKEN

KELLOGG COMPANY

Makes 4 servings

4 chicken breasts, rinsed and dried
1 egg, slightly beaten
2 cups KELLOGG'S CORN FLAKES®
  cereal, crushed to ½ cup
2 tablespoons margarine *or* butter
¼ cup firmly packed brown sugar

Water *or* rum, light or dark
1 can (10 ounces) mandarin oranges,
  drained, with juice reserved
5 teaspoons concentrated orange juice
1 tablespoon cornstarch
2 tablespoons water

Preheat oven to 350°F. Dip chicken in beaten egg and coat with crushed cereal. Place in a single layer in a greased or foil-lined shallow baking pan. Bake about 1 hour or until chicken is tender.

In medium-size saucepan, melt margarine. Stir in brown sugar. Set aside. Add water or rum to reserved mandarin juice to measure *¾ cup.* Stir into melted margarine and sugar. Stir in orange juice. Dissolve cornstarch in water and add to orange-juice mixture. Bring to a boil and cook until mixture is thickened and clear, stirring constantly. Add mandarin oranges. Heat thoroughly. Pour hot sauce over chicken.

DRUNKEN CHICKEN

MCCORMICK & COMPANY, INC.

Makes 4 servings

4 half chicken breasts, boneless and skinless
¼ cup light rum
¼ teaspoon McCormick/Schilling® ground Nutmeg
1 tablespoon soy sauce
1 tablespoon lime juice
1 tablespoon brown sugar
¾ teaspoon McCormick/Schilling Bon Appétit®

¼ teaspoon McCormick/Schilling Crushed Red Pepper
⅛ teaspoon McCormick/Schilling ground Ginger
2 tablespoons butter
2 cups sliced mushrooms
1 cup dairy sour cream
Additional McCormick/Schilling ground Nutmeg (optional)
Carrot strips for garnish
Celery strips for garnish

Pound chicken breasts to ½-inch thickness. Pierce several times using tines of a fork. Place in single layer in shallow glass dish. Set aside. Combine next 8 ingredients. Mix well. Pour liquid over chicken. Marinate at room temperature 30 minutes, turning once. Melt butter in skillet over medium heat. Reserving marinade, remove chicken and sauté in butter. Remove chicken. Keep warm. Sauté mushrooms. Reduce heat and add marinade. Gradually add sour cream. Stir to blend. Cook, covered, over low heat 5 minutes. Serve sauce over chicken breasts. Sprinkle with additional nutmeg if desired. Garnish with thin strips of carrots and celery.

CHICKEN ITALIENNE
KELLOGG COMPANY

Makes 6 servings

1 can (8 ounces) tomato sauce
¼ teaspoon salt
⅛ teaspoon garlic powder
½ teaspoon ground sweet basil
¼ teaspoon ground oregano
3 pounds frying chicken pieces, rinsed
  and dried

5 cups KELLOGG'S CORN FLAKES®
  cereal, crushed to 2½ cups
3 tablespoons margarine *or* butter,
  melted (optional)

Preheat oven to 350°F. Combine tomato sauce and seasonings. Dip chicken pieces in seasoned tomato sauce; then coat with crushed cereal. Place in single layer, skin side up, in greased or foil-lined shallow baking pan. Drizzle with melted margarine, if desired. Bake about 1 hour or until tender. Do not cover pan or turn chicken while baking.

SOUTH SEAS CHICKEN
DURKEE-FRENCH FOODS

Makes 6 servings

2 tablespoons vegetable oil
1½ pounds boneless, skinless chicken
  breasts, cut into cubes
½ cup chopped onion
3 cups assorted vegetables (red pepper,
  carrots, and snow peas), cut in bite-
  size pieces

1 can (20 ounces) pineapple chuncks,
  drained, with juice reserved
2 tablespoons soy sauce
1 tablespoon cornstarch
1 teaspoon Durkee® Ground Cumin
¼ teaspoon Durkee® Garlic Powder
¼ teaspoon Durkee® Ground Ginger

In large skillet, heat oil. Stir-fry chicken and onion 5 minutes or until chicken is done. Add vegetables and pineapple; stir-fry 2 minutes. In small bowl, combine reserved pineapple juice and remaining ingredients; mix until smooth and stir into chicken mixture. Cook and stir until sauce is thickened and bubbly, about 2 minutes.

Serve over rice.

SUNBURST STIR-FRY

DOLE FOOD COMPANY

Makes 4 servings

I can (20 ounces) Dole® Pineapple Chunks, drained, with ⅓ cup juice reserved

2 chicken breast halves, skinned and boned

2 large cloves garlic, pressed

2 tablespoons minced ginger root *or* I teaspoon ground ginger

2 tablespoons vegetable oil

2 medium Dole® Carrots, sliced

I Dole® Green Bell Pepper, slivered

4 ounces cooked thin spaghetti

⅓ cup soy sauce

I tablespoon cornstarch

I tablespoon sesame oil

3 Dole® Green Onions, chunked

Drain pineapple, reserving ⅓ cup juice for sauce. Chunk chicken. In large skillet, stir-fry chicken with garlic and ginger in oil 2 minutes. Add pineapple, carrots, and bell pepper. Cover; steam 2 to 3 minutes until vegetables are tender-crisp. Stir in spaghetti.

To make sauce; stir together reserved pineapple juice, soy sauce, cornstarch, and sesame oil. Pour into skillet along with green onions. Toss until ingredients are thoroughly mixed and heated through.

CHICKEN CURRY

DOLE FOOD COMPANY

Makes 4 to 6 servings

I can (20 ounces) Dole® Pineapple Chunks, drained, with juice reserved

2 chicken bouillon cubes

4 boneless, skinless chicken breast halves, cubed

I cup chopped onion

2 tablespoons margarine

2 teaspoons curry powder

I cup long-grain rice, uncooked

½ cup Dole® Raisins

2 tablespoons chopped parsley

2 tablespoons Dole® Blanched Slivered Almonds, toasted

Add enough water to reserved pineapple juice to make 2 cups liquid. Heat. Add bouillon to dissolve. Sauté chicken and onion in margarine. Stir in curry powder. Add rice and juice mixture. Bring to a boil. Reduce heat. Simmer, covered, 25 minutes. Stir in pineapple, raisins parsley, and almonds just before serving.

To toast almonds: Preheat oven to 350°F. Place almonds in a shallow pan and bake for 10 minutes. Toasting time will vary depending on the size of the almonds.

TERIYAKI CHICKEN
DOLE FOOD COMPANY

Makes 12 buffet servings

8 chicken breasts halves, boned
2 cups Dole® Pineapple Juice
1 cup soy sauce

3 tablespoons honey
2 pounds quartered mushrooms
¼ cup cornstarch

Preheat oven to 450°F. Place chicken in 3-quart shallow baking dish. Combine juice, soy sauce, and honey. Pour over chicken. Marinate 1 hour or overnight in refrigerator.

Add mushrooms to chicken and coat with marinade. Bake 20 minutes. Spoon *½ cup* pan juices into small bowl. Stir in cornstarch. Pour back into pan, spooning sauce over chicken and mushrooms. Return to oven and bake 20 minutes longer or until chicken is tender. Cut chicken in slices.

GENERAL TSO'S CHICKEN
JFC INTERNATIONAL, INC.

Makes 2 to 3 servings

1½ chicken breasts, skinned, boned, and cut into ¾-inch pieces
1 tablespoon Dynasty® Oriental Marinade
2 tablespoons Dynasty® Hoisin Sauce
2 tablespoons Dynasty® Black Bean Sauce

1 tablespoon dry sherry *or* water
1 tablespoon Dynasty® Chinese Stir-Fry Oil
1 green onion and top, halved lengthwise and cut into ¾-inch lengths
½ cup roasted, salted peanuts
1 teaspoon Dynasty® Hot Chili Oil

Coat chicken with marinade; let stand 20 minutes. Combine hoisin and black bean sauces with sherry; mix well. Heat wok or large frying pan over high heat. Add oil; coat wok. Add chicken; stir-fry 3 to 4 minutes or until lightly browned. Add hoisin sauce mixture and green onion; cook and stir 1 minute or until heated through. Remove from heat; stir in peanuts and chili oil. Serve immediately with hot cooked rice, as desired.

HOT AND SPICY PEANUT CHICKEN

JFC INTERNATIONAL, INC.

Makes 3 to 4 servings

2 whole chicken breasts, skinned, boned, and cut into ¾-inch pieces

2 tablespoons Dynasty® Oriental Marinade

2 tablespoons Dynasty® Chinese Stir-Fry Oil

2 medium zucchini, halved lengthwise and cut crosswise into ½-inch widths

¼ cup Dynasty® Spicy Kung Pao Sauce

1 can (8 ounces) Dynasty® Whole Water Chestnuts, drained and halved vertically

⅓ cup roasted, salted peanuts

Coat chicken with marinade; let stand 20 minutes. Heat wok or large frying pan over high heat. Add oil; coat wok. Add chicken; stir-fry 2 to 3 minutes or until lightly browned. Add zucchini; stir-fry 1 minute. Stir in Kung Pao sauce. Bring to a boil. Cover wok and cook 2 minutes. Add water chestnuts; stir-fry 1 minute, or until sauce is slightly thickened and zucchini is tender-crisp. Remove from heat; stir in peanuts. Serve immediately.

THE PEANUT PRESCRIPTION
The Story of Peanuts and Peanut Butter

Not really a nut at all, the peanut, like a pea, is a seed in a pod, actually a legume, a member of the bean family. The peanut plant is a botanical oddity because it produces its fruit by growing downward instead of upward. After the flower of the plant is fertilized, it withers and drops off. An elongated stalk appears in its place to grow downward and bury itself in the ground. Once covered with soil, the tip of the stalk develops into a peanut pod.

For many years peanuts were thought to have entered the Americas from Africa via slave ships, but actually they are among the many important foods discovered nearly five hundred years ago in the New World. The peanuts found in ancient Peruvian tombs and related legume plants growing wildly in Brazil have confirmed that peanuts are South American natives. Early Portuguese traders exchanged peanuts for ivory and spices on the African coast. From there, the legumes sailed back to the New World with African slaves. At first Southeasterners grew them mainly to feed chickens and pigs; only slaves and poor Southern families ate the "goobers," as they were called.

Seventeenth-century colonists found Indians growing peanuts in Virginia when they arrived there. Virginia landowners began to enjoy eating the seed from shells. Some decided to dedicate fields to raising them. By the middle of the nineteenth century, Georgia was called the Goober State because of its colossal peanut crops. Former President Jimmy Carter is the most famous peanut farmer in the Goober State.

Peanuts were a welcome surprise for hungry Civil War Union soldiers, who developed a taste for the crunchy roasted seed. "Peanut porridge" became a staple of the Union army. The soldiers carried the plants back home to the North, but the seed remained no more than a curiosity there until P. T. Barnum began selling nickel peanut bags at his circuses in the 1880s.

In 1890 a diligent St. Louis physician seeking an easily digestible source of protein for his elderly patients ground peanuts with salt in his kitchen grinder. His peanut-spread prescription became so popular that in 1893 he decided to introduce Chicago World's Fair visitors to the peanutty treat. A decade later, commercially produced peanut butter was on the market, and by 1914 there were several dozen brands.

First sold in 1933, Skippy® Peanut Butter boasted "fuller flavor; smooth as satin" on the package. Skippy® Peanut Butter is now so popular that someone in the United States buys a jar every few seconds. Enough peanut butter is consumed in the United States today to make 10 billion peanut butter and jelly sandwiches annually.

CHICKEN SATÉ WITH PEANUT BUTTER SAUCE

BEST FOODS, A DIVISION OF CPC INTERNATIONAL INC.

Makes 4 servings

3 tablespoons soy sauce
2 tablespoons Mazola® Corn Oil
1 tablespoon lemon juice
½ teaspoon curry powder

1 clove garlic, minced or pressed
1 pound chicken breasts, boned, skinned, and cut into 1-inch cubes
Peanut Butter Sauce (see below)

In small bowl, stir together soy sauce, corn oil, lemon juice, curry powder, and garlic. Add chicken; toss to coat well. Cover; refrigerate at least 2 hours. Drain; reserve marinade. Rinse bamboo skewers in water; thread with chicken cubes. Broil about 6 inches from source of heat, turning and basting frequently with reserved marinade, about 5 minutes or until tender. Serve with Peanut Butter Sauce.

PEANUT BUTTER SAUCE

Makes about 1½ cups

1 teaspoon Mazola® Corn Oil
¼ cup sliced green onions
1 teaspoon minced ginger root
¼ to ½ teaspoon red pepper flakes

½ cup Skippy® Creamy or Super Chunk® Peanut Butter
1 cup water
1 tablespoon soy sauce

In 1-quart saucepan, heat corn oil over medium. Add green onions, ginger root, and red pepper flakes. Stirring frequently, cook 1 minute. Stirring constantly, add peanut butter. Gradually stir in water and soy sauce until well blended. While stirring constantly, bring to a boil until mixture thickens. Serve hot or at room temperature with chicken kabobs.

CHICKEN PAELLA

LINDSAY INTERNATIONAL, INC.

Makes 4 servings

6 ounces chorizo *or* Italian sausage, sliced

1 medium onion, chopped

1 small sweet red *or* green pepper, cut into chunks

1 clove garlic, minced

3 chicken breasts, halved

Salt

Pepper

¾ cup long-grain rice

1½ teaspoons instant chicken bouillon granules

¼ teaspoon ground turmeric

3 cups hot water

4 baby carrots *or* 3-inch carrot chunks

1 package (10 ounces) frozen peas

1 package (9 ounces) frozen artichoke hearts

1 cup Lindsay® Large Pitted Ripe Olives, drained

6 cherry tomatoes, halved

In 12-inch skillet or Dutch oven, cook sausage, onion, pepper, and garlic until sausage is brown and onion and pepper are tender. Drain, reserving drippings in pan; set sausage mixture aside. Season chicken with salt and pepper. Brown in reserved drippings; remove from skillet. Stir in uncooked rice, bouillon granules, turmeric, and water; bring to a boil. Add sausage mixture and carrots. Arrange chicken atop. Reduce heat; cover and simmer 20 minutes.

Meanwhile, rinse peas and artichoke hearts under hot tap water to separate. Arrange atop chicken. Cover and cook 15 to 17 minutes more or until rice and chicken are tender. Add olives and tomatoes; heat through.

CHICKEN AND SPAGHETTI DI NAPOLI

BORDEN, INC.

Makes 6 to 8 servings

6 slices bacon
6 skinned boneless chicken-breast halves
1 cup thinly sliced carrots
1 clove garlic, finely chopped
1 jar (26 ounces) Classico® Di Napoli
  (Tomato & Basil) Pasta Sauce

1 package (1 pound) Creamette®
  Spaghetti
2 tablespoons margarine *or* butter,
  softened

In large skillet, cook bacon until crisp; removed and crumble. In same skillet, brown chicken in *2 tablespoons* drippings; remove. Cook and stir carrots and garlic until tender-crisp. Add pasta sauce and chicken. Simmer, uncovered, 10 to 15 minutes or until chicken is tender. Meanwhile, cook spaghetti according to package directions; drain. Toss with margarine. Slice chicken; serve on hot cooked spaghetti with sauce. Garnish with crumbled bacon. Refrigerate leftovers.

CHICKEN CORDON BLEU

SARGENTO CHEESE COMPANY, INC.

Makes 4 servings

4 large chicken breast halves, boned and
  skinned
1 tablespoon Dijon mustard
½ teaspoon dried thyme
4 slices (4 ounces) lean cooked ham
2 slices (1½ ounces) Sargento® Preferred
  Light® Sliced Swiss Cheese

¼ cup seasoned bread crumbs
1 tablespoon Sargento® Grated
  Parmesan
4 teaspoons melted light margarine

Preheat oven to 400°F. Place chicken breast between 2 pieces of waxed paper. Pound to ¼-inch thickness. Divide mustard and spread down center of chicken. Sprinkle with thyme. Top each chicken breast with a slice of ham and half a slice of Swiss cheese. Roll up jelly-roll style, tucking in sides of ham and chicken to seal. Secure with skewers or large sandwich picks. Combine breadcrumbs and Parmesan cheese. Brush chicken with melted margarine and roll in crumb mixture. Place on a 9-by-9-inch baking pan. Bake 10 minutes. Reduce heat to 350°F and continue baking 20 to 25 minutes or until chicken is done. Remove picks. Serve immediately.

CHICKEN TAQUITOS

LAWRY'S FOODS, INC.

Makes 6 servings

12 corn tortillas
1 pound chicken breasts, boneless and skinless, cooked and shredded
1 package (1.25 ounces) Lawry's® Taco Spices and Seasonings
½ cup hot water
½ cup minced green onions

¼ teaspoon Lawry's® Garlic Powder with Parsley
1 cup finely chopped tomatoes
Vegetable oil for frying
Lettuce, shredded
Guacamole for garnish
Red onion, sliced, for garnish

Preheat oven to 200°F. Sprinkle tortillas lightly with water; wrap in aluminum foil and place in oven 10 minutes to soften. Leave in foil until ready to use. In skillet, combine chicken, spices and seasonings, water, onions, and garlic powder with parsley; blend well. Bring to a boil, reduce heat, and simmer 10 minutes. Stir in tomatoes. Place *2 tablespoons* chicken mixture down center of each warmed tortilla. Roll up tortillas tightly; secure with toothpicks. In deep, large saucepan, heat oil to 375°F. Fry rolled tortillas in oil until golden brown and crisp. Drain well on paper towels. Keep warm in oven; remove toothpicks before serving. Serve on shredded lettuce. Garnish with guacamole and sliced red onion.

To microwave: Sprinkle tortillas lightly with water; wrap in plastic wrap and microwave on HIGH 30 seconds to soften. Leave in plastic until ready to use. In large microwave-safe dish, combine chicken, spices and seasonings, water, onions, and garlic powder with parsley; blend well. Cover and microwave on HIGH 5 to 6 minutes, stirring after 4 minutes. Stir in tomatoes. Fill and roll tortillas and fry as above.

Fish Rolls Primavera
COURTESY OF BORDEN, INC.

Chicken Saté with Peanut Butter Sauce
COURTESY OF SKIPPY PEANUT BUTTER / CPC INTERNATIONAL, INC.

Salmon Curry with Melon

COURTESY OF McCORMICK / SCHILLING SPICES

Garlic Shrimp with Noodles

COURTESY OF THOMAS J. LIPTON CO.

CHICKEN RISOTTO

SARGENTO CHEESE COMPANY, INC.

Makes 6 servings

6 tablespoons butter *or* margarine, divided
1 pound chicken breasts, boned, skinned, and cut into thin strips
1½ cups rice
1 clove garlic, minced

¼ pound mushrooms, sliced
3 green onions, thinly sliced
3 cups chicken broth
1 teaspoon basil
1 cup (4 ounces) Sargento® Fancy Shredded Cheddar Cheese

In large skillet, melt 2 tablespoons butter. Add chicken and cook over medium heat, stirring constantly, until browned, about 5 minutes. Remove chicken from skillet. Add remaining butter, rice, and garlic to skillet and cook, stirring constantly, until rice is lightly browned, about 5 minutes. Add mushrooms and green onions. Continue cooking, stirring occasionally, until mushrooms are tender, about 2 minutes. Stir in chicken broth and basil. Bring to a boil; cover and simmer 15 minutes. Gently stir in chicken. Continue simmering until chicken is heated through and rice is tender, about 5 minutes. Top with cheese and serve immediately.

VERSATILE CHICKEN
BORDEN, INC.

Makes 4 to 6 servings

¾ cup Borden® or Meadow Gold®
  Buttermilk
1 tablespoon Wyler's® or Steero®
  Chicken-Flavor Instant Bouillon
½ teaspoon oregano leaves (optional)

3 pounds chicken pieces
1 cup unsifted flour
1 teaspoon paprika
¼ cup margarine or butter, melted

Preheat oven to 350°F. In 1-cup measure, combine buttermilk, bouillon, and oregano; let stand 10 minutes. Stir. Place chicken in large bowl. Pour bouillon mixture over chicken; toss to coat. Let stand 30 minutes to blend flavors. In plastic bag, combine flour and paprika. Add chicken, a few pieces at a time; shake to coat. Place in 13-by-9-inch baking dish. Drizzle with margarine. Bake 1 hour or until golden. Refrigerate leftovers.

To fry: Omit melted margarine; fry in vegetable oil.

SWEET 'N SPICY BAKED CHICKEN
DURKEE-FRENCH FOODS

Makes 4 servings

2½ to 3 pounds cut-up chicken, skinned if
  desired
1 tablespoon dehydrated minced onion
1 cup Ketchup
⅓ cup packed brown sugar

¼ cup red wine vinegar or white distilled
  vinegar
¼ teaspoon Durkee® Ground Cloves
¼ teaspoon Durkee® Ground Black
  Pepper

Preheat oven to 350°F. Arrange chicken pieces meaty side up, in single layer, in shallow 9-by-13-inch baking dish. Combine remaining ingredients and pour over chicken. Bake, uncovered, 45 to 50 minutes, basting halfway through.

BROCCOLI-OLIVE STUFFED CORNISH HENS

LINDSAY INTERNATIONAL, INC.

Make 4 servings

1 package (10 ounces) frozen chopped
  broccoli
¼ cup chopped onion
1 cup cooked long-grain rice
½ cup (2 ounces) shredded process Swiss
  cheese
½ cup Lindsay® Medium Pitted Ripe
  Olives, drained and sliced

2 tablespoons butter *or* margarine,
  melted
¼ teaspoon salt
Dash pepper
4 Cornish game hens 1 to 1½ pounds
  each
Melted butter *or* margarine
⅓ cup orange marmalade

Preheat oven to 375°F. For stuffing, cook chopped broccoli according to package directions except omit salt and add chopped onion; drain well. Combine with cooked rice, cheese, olives, *2 tablespoons* butter, salt, and pepper.

Rinse Cornish hens; pat dry with paper towels. Lightly salt cavities. Stuff cavities with stuffing mixture. (Reserve some stuffing mixture to serve separately.) Secure neck skin to back with small skewers. Tie legs to tail. Twist wing tips under back.

Place stuffed hens on a rack in a large roasting pan. Brush with a little melted butter. Cover loosely with foil and roast 30 minutes. Uncover; roast about 1 hour more or until done, brushing with additional melted butter every ½ hour. In saucepan, melt marmalade. Brush hens with marmalade during last 5 minutes of roasting. Just before serving, cook and stir reserved stuffing mixture in a saucepan until heated through.

DUCK WITH
CRANBERRY–WILD RICE STUFFING
CAMPBELL SOUP COMPANY

Makes 4 servings

1 can (14 ounces) chicken broth
½ cup regular rice, uncooked
¼ cup regular wild rice, uncooked
2 tablespoons butter *or* margarine
1 package (12 ounces) Campbell's® Fresh Mushrooms, coarsely chopped (about 2½ cups)
¼ cup finely chopped green onions
1 cup whole cranberry sauce
¼ teaspoon salt
⅛ teaspoon pepper
1 duckling (4 to 5 pounds)
¼ cup orange marmalade
1 tablespoon lemon juice
Lemon leaves for garnish
Campbell's® Fresh Mushrooms, fluted, for garnish
Lemon peel twist for garnish

To make stuffing: In 1½-quart saucepan, combine broth, regular rice, and wild rice. Over high heat bring to a boil. Reduce heat to low; simmer, covered, 30 minutes or until rice is tender and all liquid is absorbed, stirring occasionally. In 10-inch skillet over medium heat, in hot butter, cook chopped mushrooms and onions until tender and liquid has evaporated, stirring occasionally. Remove from heat. Stir in cooked rice, cranberry sauce, salt, and pepper.

Remove neck and giblets from inside bird. Remove excess fat. Cut off and discard neck skin. Rinse duck with cold running water; drain well. Spoon stuffing loosely into body cavity. Fold skin over stuffing; secure with skewer. With breast side up, lift wings toward neck, then fold tips under back of bird to balance. Tie legs. With fork, prick skin in several places.

To make glaze: In small saucepan, combine marmalade and lemon juice. Over low, heat until marmalade is melted, stirring constantly.

To grill: Arrange preheated coals around drip pan; test for medium heat above pan. Insert a meat thermometer into thickest part of meat between breast and thigh, without touching fat or bone. On grill rack, place duck, breast side up, over pan but not over coals. Grill, covered, 1¼ to 1½ hours or until well done, or 180°F. Adjust vents and add more charcoal as necessary. Brush often with glaze during the last 30 minutes. Garnish with lemon leaves, mushrooms, and lemon peel twist.

To roast: Preheat oven to 350°F. Place stuffed bird, breast side up, on rack in roasting pan. Roast, uncovered, 2 hours or until well done, or 180°F. Brush often with glaze during the last 30 minutes.

TURKEY WITH FRUIT STUFFING

MCCORMICK & COMPANY, INC.

Makes 12 generous servings

2 turkey-breast halves, boneless
1 package (10 ounces) pitted dates
1 package (6 ounces) dried apricot halves
1 cup walnut pieces
2 cups water
¼ teaspoon McCormick/Schilling® Ginger

½ teaspoon McCormick/Schilling ground Cinnamon
¼ teaspoon McCormick/Schilling ground Black Pepper
¼ teaspoon McCormick/Schilling Nutmeg
¼ teaspoon McCormick/Schilling ground Cloves

Preheat oven to 325°F. Cut 3 parallel, lengthwise, 1-inch-deep slits in each turkey-breast half. Place turkey-breast halves flat in a buttered roasting pan. Cut dates in thirds. Cut apricot halves in fourths. Combine dates, apricots, and remaining ingredients in saucepan. Heat, stirring constantly. Simmer 2 minutes, stirring. Cool slightly. Fill slits in turkey with fruit mixture. Cook 2 hours. Cut each half breast in 6 slices.

TURKEY OSCAR

OSCAR MAYER FOODS CORPORATION

Makes 4 servings

2 tablespoons margarine
1 package (about 1 pound) Louis Rich® Fresh Turkey Breast Slices
1 can (8½ ounces) asparagus tips, drained

1 can (6½ ounces) crabmeat, drained
1 package (⅞ ounces) hollandaise sauce mix, prepared according to package directions.

Melt *1 tablespoon* margarine in skillet on medium. When margarine begins to brown, add half the turkey: Cook 3 minutes, turn. Top with half the asparagus and crabmeat. Cover. Cook 2 minutes more. Place on platter; cover to keep warm. Repeat with remaining margarine, turkey, asparagus, and crabmeat. Top with warm hollandaise sauce.

TURKEY EN CROÛTE

OSCAR MAYER FOODS CORPORATION

Makes 2 to 4 servings

1 package (about 1 pound) Louis Rich® Fresh Turkey Breast Tenderloins
1 tablespoon margarine

1 package (17½ ounces) frozen puff pastry, thawed

SAUCE

1¼ cups half-and-half
1 tablespoon cornstarch
½ teaspoon dill weed

⅛ teaspoon dried basil leaves
⅛ teaspoon pepper
⅛ teaspoon onion powder

Preheat oven to 375°F. Cook turkey in margarine in skillet on medium-high 5 minutes, turning to brown. Remove turkey and allow to cool slightly. Cut pastry in half; wrap each half around a tenderloin, gently stretching pastry to cover turkey. Pinch edges of pastry together to seal. Decorate with additional pastry. Place seam side down on ungreased baking sheet. Bake 25 to 30 minutes until golden brown.

Meanwhile, combine sauce ingredients in skillet used to brown turkey. Cook on medium, stirring constantly until thickened. Serve with turkey.

TURKEY SLICES PROVENÇAL

LAWRY'S FOODS, INC.

Makes 4 servings

1 tablespoon olive *or* vegetable oil
1¼ pounds turkey-breast slices
1 cup sliced onions
¾ cup sliced fresh mushrooms
1 cup water
½ cup chicken broth
¼ cup dry red wine

1 package (1.5 ounces) Lawry's® Extra Rich and Thick Spaghetti Sauce Spices and Seasonings
1 can (6 ounces) tomato paste
1 can (3¼ ounces) ripe olives, drained and sliced
Parsley for garnish

In large skillet, heat oil and sauté turkey 2 minutes on each side. Remove and keep warm. To skillet, add onions and mushrooms; sauté 3 minutes or until tender. Stir in water, broth, wine, spaghetti sauce spices and seasonings, and tomato paste. Bring to a boil; reduce heat and simmer, uncovered, 10 minutes, stirring occasionally. Add turkey slices and olives. Heat through.

Serve over cooked egg noodles. Garnish with parsley.

TURKEY AND CRAN-ORANGE SAUCE
DURKEE-FRENCH FOODS

Makes 4 servings

1 pound fresh turkey breast slices
1 teaspoon paprika
¾ teaspoon Italian seasoning
1 tablespoon olive oil

½ cup orange juice
2 tablespoons honey
2 tablespoons French's® Yellow Mustard
1 cup fresh or frozen cranberries

Season both sides of turkey slices with paprika and Italian seasoning. In medium skillet, sauté turkey in hot oil about 5 minutes or until cooked. Remove from pan and keep warm. Combine orange juice, honey, and mustard. Stir into pan and bring to a boil. Reduce heat; simmer about 2 minutes until slightly thickened. Add cranberries, stirring until heated. Serve sauce over turkey.

HUMANITY'S OLDEST CONDIMENT
The Story of Mustard

Used for flavoring in prebiblical times, mustard is the oldest condiment known. Prehistoric people chewed the tiny seed of the mustard plant with meat. Romans took a giant culinary step toward modern mustard preparation by learning to ferment the ground seed with verjuice, the unripe juices of grapes and other fruits, which produced a zesty paste they called *mustum ardens,* burning must. Ardently devoted to the eating of mustard with sausages, stuffed cow's udders, and boiled ostriches, Roman legions planted mustard seed throughout the empire.

Eventually monasteries husbanded knowledge of mustard making, with some royal households and monasteries becoming so particular that a "mustardarius" was employed to ensure proper selection of seed and grinding of paste. The 1336 festival of the Duke of Burgundy and his cousin Philip the Fair, King of France, demonstrated the popularity of mustard eating in the medieval period when seventy gallons of the relished paste were consumed for one feast. At that time, the poor as well as the rich could enjoy mustard as their favorite spice because it was cheaply grown on their native soil, unlike pepper and other spices that were imported at great expense from exotic lands.

In 1634 a law was passed in Dijon, France, to promote high standards in mustard making. The privileged shop proprietors granted the exclusive right to make mustard had to guarantee that they would wear clean clothes and keep only one shop each so that any suspect jar could be traced to its origins.

Until the clever Mrs. Clements of Durham, England, experimented in her kitchen in the eighteenth century, preparing mustard meant mixing little clumps of coarsely ground seed with honey or vinegar. More vinegar mixed in at the time of use made a grainy, paste condiment. Clements developed the modern method of milling mustard seed to the consistency of fine flour. Adding only water or vinegar to make a smooth texture greatly simplified the process. In addition, Clements added secret ingredients to her mustard flour.

In 1729, Clements galloped on horseback from town to town to promote her product. King George I became her loyal patron and issued a royal warrant declaring her dry Durham mustard to be of high quality. Throughout England, her mustard became famous. Then she died without sharing the secrets of her ingredients and the acclaimed Durham mustard became only a mouth-watering memory.

Seventy years later, Jeremiah Colman hulled, milled, and blended the yellow-and-black mustard seed of the English growing fields, then considered the finest in the world. He exported his hot, smooth mustard worldwide, and his name became the most acclaimed in mustard making in England.

Early in the twentieth century, French brothers George and Francis took the helm of their father's thriving spice business in New York City. Francis French had observed that people in the United States didn't really care for the taste of mustard and used it very cautiously. He wondered how to awaken them to this savory delight. His understanding of U.S. preference for mild tastes led to a yellow, smooth recipe made from white mustard seed, salt, vinegar, and turmeric, which gives mustard its bright yellow color.

Visitors at the 1904 St. Louis World's Fair, produced to celebrate the one hundredth anniversary of the Louisiana Purchase, saw such wonders as the John Philip Sousa Marching Band, electricity, the world's first ice cream cones, the world's first hot dogs served on warm hot dog–shaped buns, and bright yellow French's® Cream Salad Mustard debuting atop the hot dogs. All were stunning successes.

CLAM FRITTERS

MCCORMICK & COMPANY, INC.

Makes 40 fritters

2 cups sifted flour
1 tablespoon baking powder
1 teaspoon McCormick/Schilling® Bon
   Appétit®
½ teaspoon McCormick/Schilling ground
   Black Pepper
1 teaspoon McCormick/Schilling Instant
   Onion Powder
1½ teaspoons McCormick/Schilling
   Chesapeake Bay Style Seafood
   Seasoning

1 tablespoon sugar
4 egg yolks, beaten
⅔ cup milk
2 tablespoons melted butter
4 egg whites, beaten
2 cups drained, coarsely chopped clams
   (or 4 cans, 6½ ounces each, minced
   clams, drained)
Vegetable oil for deep-fat frying
Orange-Dijon Dipping Sauce (see below)

Sift together flour and baking powder. Mix with next 5 ingredients. Mix beaten egg yolks with milk and butter. Stir into flour mixture. Fold in beaten egg whites, lightly but thoroughly. Stir in clams. Drop by spoonfuls into deep, hot vegetable oil, 350°F. Fry until brown on 1 side. Turn and brown other side. Drain on paper towels. Keep hot. Serve with Orange-Dijon Dipping Sauce.

ORANGE-DIJON DIPPING SAUCE

Makes ¾ cup

¾ cup orange marmalade
2 teaspoons Dijon mustard

1 tablespoon orange juice
Dash ground McCormick/Schilling® Mace

Combine all ingredients. Mix well. Serve at room temperature.

SALMON CURRY WITH MELON

MCCORMICK & COMPANY, INC.

Makes 6 servings, ½ cup each

1 can (1 pound) red salmon (or 1 pound
    fresh salmon, poached and separated
    into bite-size pieces)
1⅔ cups water
1 teaspoon McCormick/Schilling®
    Chicken Flavor Base
1 tablespoon butter
1 teaspoon McCormick/Schilling
    Seasoning Salt
¼ teaspoon McCormick/Schilling
    Dill Weed

1 tablespoon McCormick/Schilling
    Madras Curry Powder, *or* to taste
1 teaspoon McCormick/Schilling Instant
    Minced Onion
1 tablespoon cornstarch
1 tablespoon cold water
1 cup sliced water chestnuts
Cooked rice
Melon Garnish (see below)

Drain salmon, saving ⅓ *cup* of the liquid. Break salmon in bite-size pieces, removing skin and bones. Combine liquid from salmon with next 7 ingredients. Heat to a boil. Mix cornstarch with water. Stir into curry sauce. Stir until slightly thickened. Add salmon and water chestnuts. Heat 2 to 3 minutes over low heat without stirring. Serve over rice with Melon Garnish.

MELON GARNISH

Cantaloupe
Honeydew
1 tablespoon honey
2 tablespoons gin

¼ teaspoon McCormick/Schilling®
    Orange Extract
1 sprig fresh mint

Cut melon balls from cantaloupe and honeydew. Mix honey with gin and orange extract. Toss with melon balls; cover and chill. Arrange several melon balls at one side of plate. Add a sprig of fresh mint.

SALMON ORIENTAL

LAWRY'S FOODS, INC.

Makes 4 servings

½ cup soy sauce

¼ cup rice vinegar

3 tablespoons sesame *or* vegetable oil

2 tablespoons chopped green onion

1½ tablespoons minced fresh ginger

1 tablespoon brown sugar

½ teaspoon Lawry's® Garlic Powder with Parsley

¾ teaspoon Lawry's® Lemon Pepper Seasoning

1½ pounds salmon fillets

In medium bowl, combine all ingredients except fish; blend well. Place fish in marinade. Marinate in refrigerator 30 minutes. Grill or broil 5 to 7 minutes on each side or until fish flakes easily.

Serve with grilled or steamed vegetables and a rice side dish.

VARIATION

Substitute chicken breasts for salmon fillets.

SPICY SCALLOPS WITH PEA PODS

JFC INTERNATIONAL, INC.

Makes 2 to 3 servings

1 pound scallops

1 tablespoon Dynasty® Oriental Marinade

2 tablespoons Dynasty® Chinese Stir-Fry Oil, divided

1 small onion, cut into thin wedges

½ pound Chinese pea pods

2 tablespoons Dynasty® Black Bean Sauce

1 teaspoon Dynasty® Hot Chili Oil

Coat scallops with marinade; let stand 20 minutes. Heat wok or large frying pan over high heat. Add *1 tablespoon* oil; coat wok. Add scallops; stir-fry 1 to 2 minutes or until cooked through. Remove from wok. Heat remaining *1 tablespoon* oil in same wok. Add onion and pea pods; stir-fry 2 to 3 minutes, or until tender-crisp. Return scallops to wok along with black bean sauce; cook and stir 1 minute, or until heated through. Remove from heat; stir in chili oil. Serve immediately with hot, cooked rice, as desired.

VARIATION

If pea pods are unavailable, substitute 1 package (6 ounces) frozen Chinese pea pods, thawed and drained. Stir-fry onion only and add pea pods with black bean sauce. Continue as directed.

FISH STEAKS VERONIQUE

LAWRY'S FOODS, INC.

Makes 2 servings

12 ounces orange roughy *or* halibut
    steaks
2 tablespoons Imperial® Margarine
2 tablespoons dry white wine
½ teaspoon Lawry's® Seasoned Salt

¼ teaspoon dried rosemary, crushed
⅛ teaspoon dried thyme, crushed
¼ cup milk
1 teaspoon all-purpose flour
½ cup seedless green grapes, halved

In medium skillet, sauté fish in margine 8 to 10 minutes or until almost done. Add wine, seasoned salt, rosemary, and thyme. Simmer, covered, about 5 minutes or until fish flakes easily. Remove fish from skillet; keep warm. Bring pan juices to a boil; boil 1 minute. In *1-cup* measure, combine milk and flour; blend well. Add to skillet; bring just to a boil. Reduce heat and cook, stirring, until thickened. Stir grapes into cream mixture; heat through. Spoon sauce over fish steaks.

    Serve with wild rice pilaf.

VARIATION

Substitute 2 tablespoons water for white wine.

MEDITERRANEAN BROILED FISH

SARGENTO CHEESE COMPANY, INC.

Makes 4 servings

¼ cup light mayonnaise
¼ cup (1 ounce) Sargento® Preferred
    Light Fancy Shredded Cheddar Cheese
1 tablespoon Sargento® Grated
    Parmesan Cheese
1 small clove garlic, minced

5 pitted ripe olives, sliced
2 tablespoons minced green onion
4 Orange Roughy *or* Sole fillets (about 5
    ounces each)
Paprika

Combine all ingredients except fish and paprika. Set aside. Place fish fillets on a broiler pan that has been coated with a nonstick vegetable spray. Sprinkle fish with paprika. Broil 4 to 5 inches from heat until fish begins to flake with a fork, 5 to 7 minutes. Divide cheese mixture and spread evenly over each fillet. Broil until topping puffs and cheese melts, 2 to 3 minutes. Serve immediately.

GARLIC SHRIMP WITH NOODLES

THOMAS J. LIPTON CO.

Makes about 4 servings

4 tablespoons butter
¼ cup finely chopped onion
2 cups water
1 package Lipton® Noodles & Sauce—
  Butter & Herb
2 tablespoons olive oil
1 tablespoon finely chopped garlic

1 pound uncooked medium shrimp,
  cleaned
1 can (14 ounces) artichoke hearts,
  drained and halved
¼ cup finely chopped parsley
Pepper to taste
Watercress for garnish (optional)

In medium saucepan, melt *2 tablespoons* butter and cook onion until tender. Add water and bring to a boil. Stir in Noodles & Butter & Herb Sauce and continue boiling over medium heat, stirring occasionally, 8 minutes or until noodles are tender.

Meanwhile, in large skillet, heat remaining *2 tablespoons* butter with olive oil and cook garlic over medium-high heat 30 seconds. Add shrimp and artichokes and cook, stirring occasionally, 3 minutes or until shrimp turn pink. Stir in parsley and pepper. To serve, combine shrimp mixture with hot noodles. Garnish, if desired, with watercress.

To microwave: In 2-quart microwave-safe casserole, microwave *2 tablespoons* butter with onions, uncovered, at HIGH (100% Power) 2 minutes or until tender. Stir in water and noodles and butter and herb sauce and microwave 11 minutes or until noodles are tender. Stir; then cover and set aside.

In 1-quart microwave-safe casserole or 9-inch glass pie plate, microwave remaining *2 tablespoons* butter, olive oil, and garlic at HIGH (100% Power) 2 minutes. Stir in shrimp and artichokes and microwave 3 minutes or until shrimp are almost pink, stirring once; stir in parsley and pepper. Combine shrimp mixture with noodles and microwave, covered, 1 minute or until heated through. Let stand, covered, 2 minutes.

SHRIMP CREOLE

THOMAS J. LIPTON CO.

Makes about 4 servings

½ cup Wish-Bone® Italian Dressing
1 medium green pepper, cut into chunks
1 medium onion, sliced
1 can (14½ ounces) whole peeled
  tomatoes, undrained and chopped

1 pound uncooked medium shrimp,
  cleaned
⅛ teaspoon crushed red pepper
2 cups hot cooked rice

In medium skillet, heat Italian dressing and cook green pepper and onion over medium heat, stirring occasionally, 5 minutes or until tender. Stir in tomatoes and simmer, covered, 15 minutes. Add shrimp and red pepper and simmer, covered, an additional 5 minutes or until shrimp turn pink. To serve, arrange shrimp mixture over hot rice.

VARIATIONS

Also terific with Wish-Bone® Robusto Italian *or* Lite Italian Dressing.

CAJUN SPICY SHRIMP

LAWRY'S FOODS, INC.

Makes 4 to 6 servings

¼ cup butter *or* margarine
¼ cup dry white wine
1 teaspoon Lawry's® Garlic Salt
½ teaspoon rosemary, crushed
½ teaspoon paprika
¼ teaspoon basil

¼ to ½ teaspoon cayenne pepper
⅛ teaspoon oregano, crushed
1 pound fresh large shrimp, peeled,
  deveined, and butterflied, with tails
  left on

In large skillet, melt butter and add white wine and spices. Bring to a boil; reduce heat, and simmer, uncovered, 5 minutes. Wash shrimp and pat dry. Add to skillet and sauté until shrimp is pink and edges curl.

Serve on a bed of rice.

ORANGE ROUGHY AU GRATIN

LAWRY'S FOODS, INC.

Makes 4 servings

4 orange roughy fillets (about 1 pound)
1 tablespoon butter *or* margarine
2 tablespoons diced celery
4 green onions, cut into ½-inch pieces
2 teaspoons all-purpose flour

½ teaspoon Lawry's® Seasoned Salt
½ teaspoon Lawry's® Seasoned Pepper
⅓ cup milk
½ cup (2 ounces) grated Swiss cheese
Parsley, chopped, for garnish

Preheat oven to 350°F. Wash fillets; pat dry with paper towels. Place fillets in 10-by-6-by-2-inch greased baking dish. In small skillet, melt butter and sauté celery and onions 5 minutes. Stir in flour, seasoned salt, and seasoned pepper; cook 1 minute. Gradually blend in milk and cheese. Cook until cheese is melted. Pour mixture over fillets. Cover and bake 25 minutes or until fish begins to flake when tested with a fork. Carefully drain off excess liquid.

Garnish with chopped parsley. Serve with boiled potatoes.

To microwave: Place fillets in microwave-safe 10-by-6-by-2-inch baking dish. Microwave on HIGH 4 minutes; drain. Prepare sauce as directed; pour over fillets. Cover with vented plastic wrap and microwave on HIGH 3 to 5 minutes longer or until fish begins to flake when tested with a fork. Carefully drain off excess liquid.

CRAB-STUFFED TROUT

CAMPBELL SOUP COMPANY

Makes 6 servings

⅓ cup butter *or* margarine, divided
2 cups chopped Campbell's® Fresh
   Mushrooms
½ cup finely chopped onion
½ cup shredded carrot
1 cup crabmeat, flaked
¼ cup fine dry breadcrumbs
3 tablespoons chopped fresh parsley,
   divided

1 tablespoon white wine Worcestershire
   sauce
6 brook trout *or* salmon (8 ounces each),
   pan-dressed
2 teaspoons lemon juice
Arugula for garnish
Cherry tomatoes for garnish

To make filling: In 10-inch skillet over medium heat, in *3 tablespoons* hot butter, cook mushrooms, onion, and carrot until tender and liquid has evaporated, stirring occasionally. In medium bowl, combine onion mixture, crabmeat, breadcrumbs, *2 tablespoons* parsley, and Worcestershire sauce; toss gently to coat. Spoon ½ cup filling loosely into each fish cavity; secure with toothpicks.

Arrange fish in oiled grill basket. In covered grill, arrange preheated coals around drip pan; test for hot coals above pan. On grill rack, place grill basket over pan but not over coals. Cover, grill 16 to 20 minutes or until fish begins to flake when tested with fork, turning once.

To make sauce: In 1-quart saucepan, combine remaining butter, remaining parsley, and lemon juice. Over medium heat, melt butter, stirring occasionally.

To serve, garnish with arugula and tomatoes. Serve with sauce.

To broil: Arrange fish on rack in broiler pan. Broil 6 inches from heat 16 to 20 minutes or until fish begins to flake when tested with fork, turning once.

BRAISED SNAPPER WITH SPICY SAUCE

JFC INTERNATIONAL, INC.

Makes 4 servings

1½ pounds red snapper *or* sea bass fillets
1 tablespoon Dynasty® Chinese Stir-Fry Oil
2 tablespoons Dynasty® Chinese Barbecue
 Sauce

1 tablespoon Dynasty® Chinese Soy
 Sauce
½ teaspoon Dynasty® Hot Chili Oil
½ green onion and top, slivered

Cut fillets into serving pieces. Heat large frying pan over high heat. Add oil; coat pan. Add fillets in single layer. Cook, uncovered, 1 to 2 minutes on each side. Meanwhile, combine barbecue and soy sauces. Spoon over fillets. Reduce heat; cover and simmer 3 to 5 minutes, or until fish flakes easily with fork. Lift fillets from pan to serving platter; keep warm. Remove frying pan from heat. Stir chili oil into sauce in pan. Spoon over fillets and sprinkle with green onion to serve.

To microwave: Omit stir-fry oil. Cut fillets into serving pieces. Place in single layer in microwave-safe 9-inch pie plate or shallow baking dish. Cover with waxed paper. Microwave on HIGH 5 to 8 minutes, or until fish flakes easily with fork. Drain well. Combine barbecue sauce, soy sauce, and chili oil; mix well. Spoon over fillets; sprinkle with green onion. Cover and microwave on HIGH 1 minute, or until heated through. Remove from microwave and serve immediately.

SOLE WITH VEGETABLES

SARGENTO CHEESE COMPANY, INC.

Makes 4 servings

4 Sole fillets, about 4 ounces each
½ teaspoon salt
¼ teaspoon pepper
1 cup sliced mushrooms
1 medium tomato, seeded and chopped

1 cup (4 ounces) Sargento® Shredded *or*
 Fancy Shredded Mozzarella Cheese
½ cup (2 ounces) Sargento® Grated
 Parmesan Cheese

Preheat oven to 325°F. Place fish fillets in lightly greased 13-by-9-inch baking dish. Sprinkle with salt and pepper. Sprinkle mushrooms and tomatoes equally over fillets. Bake, covered, 20 to 25 minutes or until fish is cooked through. Uncover; sprinkle with cheeses. Broil 4 inches from heat source until cheese is melted and top is lightly browned, about 3 minutes.

CRISPY OVEN FISH

BORDEN, INC.

Makes 4 servings

1⅔ cups finely crushed Kruncher's!® Potato Chips

⅓ cup grated Parmesan cheese

1 tablespoon chopped parsley

½ cup Bennett's® Tartar Sauce

1 tablespoon ReaLemon® Lemon Juice from Concentrate

1 pound fish fillets

Flour

Preheat oven to 400°F. Combine potato chips, cheese, and parsley. In medium bowl, combine tartar sauce and ReaLemon® brand. Coat fish with flour; dip in tartar-sauce mixture, then chip mixture. Arrange on baking sheet. Bake 5 to 10 minutes or until fish flakes with fork. Refrigerate leftovers.

FISH ROLLS PRIMAVERA

BORDEN, INC.

Makes 4 servings

1 cup shredded carrots

1 cup shredded zucchini

2 tablespoons finely chopped onion

½ cup fresh bread crumbs (1 slice bread)

⅛ teaspoon thyme leaves

¼ cup margarine *or* butter, melted

¼ cup ReaLemon® Lemon Juice from Concentrate

4 sole, orange roughy, or other fish fillets (about 1 pound), fresh or frozen, thawed

Preheat oven to 375°F. In medium bowl, combine carrots, zucchini, onion, breadcrumbs, and thyme. Combine margarine and ReaLemon® brand; add *¼ cup* to vegetable mixture. Place equal amounts of mixture on fillets; roll up. Arrange in shallow baking dish; pour remaining margarine mixture over fillets. Bake 15 minutes or until fish flakes with fork. Refrigerate leftovers.

CONDIMENTS
& SAUCES

SOY MARINADE
BORDEN, INC.

Makes about 1½ cups

½ cup ReaLemon® Lemon Juice from
   Concentrate
½ cup soy sauce
½ cup vegetable oil

3 tablespoons ketchup
3 to 4 cloves garlic, finely chopped
¼ teaspoon pepper
Beef, pork, or poultry

In small bowl, combine first 6 ingredients. Pour over beef, pork, or poultry. Cover; refrigerate 6 hours or overnight, turning occasionally. Remove meat from marinade; grill or broil as desired.

SWEET 'N SPICY ONION GLAZE
THOMAS J. LIPTON CO.

Makes about 2½ cups

1 envelope Lipton® Onion Recipe Soup
   Mix
1 jar (20 ounces) apricot preserves

1 cup (8 ounces) Wish-Bone® Sweet 'n
   Spicy French Dressing
Chicken, spareribs, kabobs, hamburgers,
   or frankfurters

In small bowl, blend soup mix, preserves, and dressing. Use as a glaze for chicken, spareribs, kabobs, hamburgers, or frankfurters. Brush on during the last half of cooking. Can be stored covered in refrigerator up to 2 weeks.

VARIATIONS

Also terrific with Wish-Bone® Lite Sweet 'n Spicy French, Russian, *or* Lite Russian Dressing.

GARLIC MAYONNAISE SAUCE
LAWRY'S FOODS, INC.

Makes 1½ cups

1 cup mayonnaise
¼ cup milk
1 teaspoon Lawry's® Garlic Powder with
  Parsley

1 teaspoon lemon juice
½ teaspoon Lawry's® Seasoned Pepper

In blender or food processor, combine all ingredients; process until well blended. Cover and refrigerate. Use as a sandwich spread or as a sauce for vegetables or grilled steak.

VARIATION

For a low-cal version, use reduced-calorie mayonnaise and skim milk *or* plain non-fat yogurt; omit lemon juice if using yogurt.

WRIGHT'S® TANGY BARBECUE SAUCE
NABISCO FOODS GROUP

Makes 4½ cups

3 medium onions, finely chopped
3 cloves garlic, minced
3 tablespoons vegetable oil
3 cups ketchup
½ cup firmly packed light brown sugar
⅓ cup Regina® White Wine Vinegar

3 tablespoons Wright's® Natural Hickory
  Seasoning
2 tablespoons Grey Poupon® Dijon
  Mustard
1 teaspoon liquid hot pepper seasoning
Poultry, beef, or pork

In large saucepan, over medium-high heat, cook onions and garlic in oil until tender. Stir in ketchup, brown sugar, vinegar, hickory seasoning, mustard, and hot pepper seasoning. Heat to a boil; reduce heat. Simmer 10 minutes. Use as a barbecue sauce when cooking poultry, beef, or pork. Cover and store in refrigerator for up to 2 weeks.

AN A.1. SAUCE, FIT FOR A KING
The Story of A.1. Steak Sauce

An extravagant and self-indulgent epicure, King George IV of England, circa 1820, was a ceaseless challenge to his royal chef, Brand, who was expected to produce a continual stream of culinary delights. One of Brand's original recipes, a blend of soy, vinegar, shallots, and anchovies, particularly titillated his majesty's finely tuned palate. "This is an A-one sauce!" he is reported to have raved.

The expression, A-one, was commonly used as a slang term during George IV's reign to denote first class or top of the line, as in an A-one theater production. The saying originated with businessmen familiar with Lloyd's of London's terms for rating ships for insurance purposes, capital letter A, number 1 being the top rating.

After the king's death, Brand resigned from his royal kitchen duties to commercially produce his masterpiece blend. For many years the Brand Company marketed A.1. exclusively in Great Britain. The condiment was introduced in the United States in 1906 when the Heublein Company, a spirits-making concern, became an agent for distribution.

When World War I interrupted the flow of supplies from England, Heublein acquired all U.S. rights to the recipe. Manufacturing began at the Heublein plant in Hartford, Connecticut, with slight alteration of ingredients to suit U.S. tastes. A.1. Steak Sauce has since become one of the fine Nabisco Foods Group products.

QUICK BARBECUE SAUCE
NABISCO FOODS GROUP

Makes 1 cup

½ cup A.1.® Steak Sauce
½ cup tomato ketchup

½ teaspoon liquid hot pepper seasoning
Steak

In small bowl, combine steak sauce, ketchup, and liquid hot pepper seasoning. Use as a basting sauce on steak. Serve steak with remaining sauce.

STIR-FRY SAUCE MIX

BEST FOODS, A DIVISION OF CPC INTERNATIONAL INC.

Makes 4 cups

½ cup Argo® or Kingsford's® Corn Starch
¼ cup firmly packed brown sugar
1½ tablespoons minced fresh ginger
4 large cloves garlic, minced
¼ teaspoon ground red pepper

⅔ cup soy sauce
⅓ cup cider vinegar
1 can (13¾ or 14½ ounces) chicken *or* beef broth
⅔ cup dry sherry

In 1-quart jar, combine corn starch, brown sugar, ginger, garlic, and red pepper. Add soy sauce and vinegar; shake until blended. Add broth and sherry; shake well. Store covered in refrigerator up to 2 weeks; shake before using. Mix may be frozen in tightly covered containers in 1-cup portions; thaw and shake before using.

CRUNCHY CORN RELISH

DURKEE-FRENCH FOODS

Makes about 4 to 6 servings

¼ cup red wine vinegar
2 tablespoons French's® Yellow Mustard
1 teaspoon sugar
¼ teaspoon seasoned salt

1 package (16 ounces) frozen whole-kernel corn, thawed and drained
½ cup chopped celery
¼ cup chopped red pepper
¼ cup chopped green onions

In large bowl, combine vinegar, mustard, sugar, and seasoned salt; stir well. Add remaining ingredients; toss. Cover and chill several hours. Toss before serving.

MEXICAN SALSA

DURKEE-FRENCH FOODS

Makes about 5 cups

1 cup ripe olives
2 cans (4 ounces *each*) chopped green
   chilies
2 tomatoes, chopped
2 green onions, chopped
1½ tablespoons red wine vinegar

1 tablespoon French's® Worcestershire
   Sauce
1 tablespoon olive oil
1 teaspoon chili powder
1 teaspoon oregano

Combine in a large bowl all ingredients; stir until well mixed. Chill 1 hour or overnight.

Serve with tortilla chips.

PINEAPPLE SALSA

DOLE FOOD COMPANY

Makes 8 servings

1 can (20 ounces) Dole® Crushed
   Pineapple in Juice
½ cup minced Dole® Red Bell Pepper
¼ cup minced Dole® Green Bell Pepper

1 tablespoon minced Dole® Green onion
2 teaspoons minced cilantro
2 teaspoons minced jalapeño peppers
1 teaspoon lime zest

Drain ½ cup juice from pineapple. Use drained juice for a beverage. Combine remaining undrained pineapple with all other ingredients. Serve salsa at room temperature or slightly chilled. Salsa is also tasty heated slightly.

Serve over chicken or fish, as a dip with tortilla chips, or spooned over quesadillas or tacos.

AMERICA'S FAVORITE DESSERTS

REALEMON® MERINGUE PIE
Borden, Inc.
273

CHOCOLATE CHEESECAKE PIE
Pet Incorporated
273

HERSHEY'S® BAVARIAN
CHOCOLATE MINT PIE
Hershey Foods Corporation
274

CHERRY CHEESE PIE
Borden, Inc.
274

BANANA CREAM CHEESE PIE
Kellogg Company
275

CREAMY YOGURT PIE
Kellogg Company
275

CHOCOLATE-PECAN
AND CARAMEL PIE
Thomas J. Lipton Co.
276

NO-BAKE OLD-FASHIONED
COCONUT CREAM PIE
Thomas J. Lipton Co.
277

DREAM PIE
Kraft General Foods, Inc.
277

PINEAPPLE PISTACHIO ICE CREAM PIE
Dole Food Company
278

FAMOUS PUMPKIN PIE
Libby's, Nestlé Food Company
278

THY OWN PUMPKIN PIE
The Story of Libby's Pumpkin
279

HARVEST CHERRY PIE
Borden, Inc.
280

OLD-FASHIONED APPLE CRUMB PIE
Pet Incorporated
280

PEACHY MINCE PIE
WITH CHEDDAR CRUST
Borden, Inc.
281

MAPLE PECAN PIE
Borden, Inc.
281

SOUTHERN CHOCOLATE
PRALINE CREME SWIRL PIE
Pet Incorporated
282

CINNAMON FRUIT TART
WITH SOUR CREAM FILLING
Thomas J. Lipton Co.
283

HERSHEY'S® PREMIUM
DOUBLE CHOCOLATE DROP COOKIES
Hershey Foods Corporation
298

HERSHEY'S® DOUBLE CHOCOLATE
MINT COOKIES
Hershey Foods Corporation
298

HERSHEY'S® VANILLA CHIP
CHOCOLATE COOKIES
Hershey Foods Corporation
299

HERSHEY'S® VANILLA
MILK CHIP COOKIES
Hershey Foods Corporation
299

MAGIC COOKIE BARS
Borden, Inc.
300

CHOCOLATE SPICE COOKIES
Borden, Inc.
301

PECAN PIE BARS
Best Foods, a division of
CPC International Inc.
302

CAKE MIX COOKIES
General Mills, Inc.
303

GIANT SKIPPY® OAT COOKIES
Best Foods, a division of
CPC International Inc.
304

BEST EVER PEANUT BUTTER COOKIES
Best Foods, a division of
CPC International Inc.
304

WHOLE-WHEAT ORANGE
PEANUT BUTTER COOKIES
Best Foods, a division of
CPC International Inc.
305

HONEY NUT PEANUT BUTTER
OAT BARS
Best Foods, a division of
CPC International Inc.
306

PEANUT BUTTER RAISIN BARS
Nabisco Foods Group
307

PEANUT BUTTER CHIPS
AND JELLY BARS
Hershey Foods Corporation
307

DATE ALMOND FINGERS
Dole Food Company
308

FRUIT AND NUT COOKIES
Dole Food Company
308

Easy, Yet Impressive

EASY CHERRIES JUBILEE
Pepperidge Farm, Inc.
323

NAPOLEONS
Pepperidge Farm, Inc.
323

ELEPHANT EARS
Pepperidge Farm, Inc.
324

FRUIT 'N CHEESE DESSERT SALAD
Sargento Cheese Company, Inc.
324

Toppings

WHIPPED TOPPING
Nestlé Food Company
325

NUTMEG BRANDY SAUCE
Nestlé Food Company
325

DEEP DARK CHOCOLATE CAKE

HERSHEY FOODS CORPORATION

Makes 8 to 10 servings

2 cups sugar
1¾ cups all-purpose flour
¾ cup Hershey's® Cocoa *or* Hershey's®
   Premium European-Style Cocoa
1½ teaspoons baking powder
1½ teaspoons baking soda
1 teaspoon salt

2 eggs
1 cup milk
½ cup vegetable oil
2 teaspoons vanilla extract
1 cup boiling water
One-Bowl Buttercream Frosting
   (see below)

Heat oven to 350°F. Grease and flour two 9-inch round baking pans or one 13-by-9-by-2-inch baking pan. In large mixer bowl, stir together sugar, flour, cocoa, baking powder, baking soda, and salt. Add eggs, milk, oil, and vanilla; beat on medium speed 2 minutes. Remove from mixer; stir in boiling water (batter will be thin). Pour batter into prepared pans. Bake 30 to 35 minutes for round pans, 35 to 40 minutes for rectangular pan, or until toothpick inserted in center comes out clean. Cool 10 minutes; remove from pans to wire racks. Cool completely. (Cake may be left in rectangular pan, if desired.) Frost with One-Bowl Buttercream Frosting.

ONE-BOWL BUTTERCREAM FROSTING

Makes about 2 cups

6 tablespoons butter *or*
   margarine, softened
2⅔ cups confectioners' sugar
½ cup Hershey's Cocoa *or* Hershey's®
   Premium European-Style Cocoa

⅓ cup milk
1 teaspoon vanilla extract

In small mixer bowl, beat butter. Add confectioners' sugar and cocoa alternately with milk; beat to spreading consistency. (Additional milk may be needed.) Blend in vanilla.

Cinnamon Fruit Tart with Sour Cream Filling
COURTESY OF THOMAS J. LIPTON CO.

Cookies and Cream Cheesecake
COURTESY OF KRAFT GENERAL FOODS, INC.

Easy-As-Pie Crust

COURTESY OF MAZOLA CORN OIL/CPC INTERNATIONAL, INC.

THE SAUCE OF MAHON
The Story of Mayonnaise

The origin of mayonnaise is mysterious. One story claims that the sauce was first created in the French town of Bayonne and was called Bayonnaise sauce. A more plausible story is that the chef of the French Duke Richelieu couldn't locate the eggs and cream he needed to prepare a sauce for the victory feast to celebrate the capture of Port Mahon on the island of Minorca in 1756. Undaunted, the chef blended what was available: raw egg yolks and Spanish olive oil. Duke Richelieu, thrilled with the new taste, called the exotic condiment "The Sauce of Mahon" and brought the recipe back to France. The great French chefs decided the difficult-to-prepare "mahonnaise" sauce, with its exquisite taste, was haute cuisine. They reserved it for the finest meals.

Mayonnaise first crossed the Atlantic Ocean as a silken French sauce, far too sophisticated for standard American fare. "Mayo" wasn't popularized until the turn of the twentieth century, when it debuted in a small Manhattan delicatessen. Richard Hellmann, an ambitious German immigrant, was besieged with compliments from customers on his prepared salads. Deciding the mayonnaise mixed by his wife was the key, the deli operator began to envision the commercial possibilities of producing quality, premixed mayonnaise on a larger scale. He placed two large jars filled with the sauce on his countertop and watched with satisfaction as customers eagerly bought his wife's creation for ten cents per "wooden boat" (a one-pound container he used for weighing butter).

The demand for the mayonnaise was so great that Hellmann started a small production facility in back of the deli and sold what he called his Blue Ribbon formula in large glass jars. He soon bought a truck for deliveries, and before long the truck was part of a fleet. By 1915 he had built his first manufacturing plant in Queens, New York, a facility large enough to satisfy production for an ever-growing list of consumers and retail stores.

Twenty-five years later the now-famous chocolate mayonnaise cake was born. In 1937 the Hellmann's Company managers learned that Mrs. Paul Price, wife of a sales distributor, had created an astonishingly rich cake. The deep, dark chocolate flavor and moist texture were attributed to the addition of an unconventional ingredient: mayonnaise. Today, real, light, and cholesterol free mayonnaise make three versions of the famous cake possible.

Hellmann's® Real Mayonnaise is still based on the original Blue Ribbon formula. Thanks to Richard Hellmann, the exotic and difficult-to-prepare sauce of the great French chefs is now a common condiment for U.S. tuna salads, potato salads, burgers, and much more.

CHOCOLATE MAYONNAISE CAKE

BEST FOODS, A DIVISION OF CPC INTERNATIONAL INC.

Makes one 9-inch layer cake

2 cups unsifted flour *or* 2¼ cups unsifted
   cake flour
⅔ cup unsweetened cocoa
1¼ teaspoons baking soda
¼ teaspoon baking powder

3 eggs
1⅔ cups sugar
1 teaspoon vanilla
1 cup Hellmann's® Best Foods®
   Mayonnaise
1⅓ cups water

Preheat oven to 350°F. Grease and flour bottoms of two 9-by-1½-inch round cake pans. In medium bowl, stir flour, cocoa, baking soda, and baking powder; set aside. In large bowl with mixer at high speed, beat eggs, sugar, and vanilla, scraping bowl occasionally, 3 minutes or until light and fluffy. Reduce speed to low; beat in real mayonnaise until blended. Add flour mixture in 4 additions alternately with water, beginning and ending with flour. Pour into prepared pans. Bake 30 to 35 minutes or until cake tester inserted in center comes out clean. Cool in pans on wire racks 10 minutes. Remove; cool completely on racks. Frost as desired.

To microwave: Prepare Chocolate Mayonnaise Cake. Line bottoms of two 8-by-2½-inch round glass cake dishes with circles of waxed paper or microwave paper towels. Pour batter into prepared cake dishes. Microwave 1 layer at a time. Place 1 cake dish on inverted pie plate in microwave oven. Microwave on MEDIUM (50% Power) 5 minutes. If cake appears to be rising unevenly, rotate dish. Microwave on HIGH (100% Power) 3 to 5 minutes longer or just until cake begins to set up on the outer edge. Although center may appear to be slightly soft, it will firm up as it cools. Let stand in dish 10 minutes. Remove; let cool completely on rack. Repeat with remaining layer. Frost as desired. Makes one 8-inch layer cake.

GERMAN SWEET CHOCOLATE CAKE

KRAFT GENERAL FOODS, INC.

Makes 1 cake

1 package (4 ounces) Baker's®
  German's® Brand Sweet Chocolate
⅓ cup boiling water
2 cups sifted cake flour *or* 1¾ cups
  unsifted all-purpose flour
¾ teaspoon baking soda
¼ teaspoon salt

¾ cup Parkay® Margarine
1⅓ cups sugar
3 egg yolks
¾ teaspoon vanilla
¾ cup buttermilk
3 egg whites, stiffly beaten
Coconut-pecan filling and frosting (see
  page 326)

Preheat oven to 350°F. Melt chocolate in boiling water. Cool. Sift flour with soda and salt (or mix together, if using all-purpose flour). Cream butter. Gradually beat in sugar and continue beating until light and fluffy. Add egg yolks, 1 at a time, beating after each. Blend in vanilla and chocolate; mix until blended. Add flour mixture alternately with buttermilk, beating after each addition until smooth. Fold in egg whites.

Pour into pans lined on the bottom with waxed paper. Bake until cake springs back when lightly pressed in center: about 35 minutes for two 9-inch layer pans, 45 to 50 minutes for one 13-by-9-inch pan, or 30 to 35 minutes for two 8½-inch heart-shaped pans. Immediately run spatula around sides between cake and pans. Cool in pans 15 minutes. Then remove from pans and finish cooling on racks. Spread coconut-pecan filling and frosting between layers and over top of cake.

SUPREME CHOCOLATE ALMOND TORTE

HERSHEY FOODS CORPORATION

Makes 10 to 12 servings

3 eggs
1¼ cups sugar
1 cup (2 sticks) butter *or* margarine,
    melted
1 teaspoon vanilla exract
Dash salt
½ cup Hershey's® Premium European-
    Style Cocoa

⅓ cup all-purpose flour
¾ cup toasted almonds, very finely
    chopped
Supreme Cocoa Glaze (see below)
Sliced almonds (optional)

Heat oven to 350°F. Line 9-by-1½-inch round baking pan with aluminum foil; butter bottom only. In large mixer bowl, beat eggs, sugar, butter, vanilla, and salt; beat on high speed 3 minutes until smooth and thick, scraping bowl often. Add cocoa and flour; blend well. Stir in almonds. Spread into prepared pan. Bake 35 to 40 minutes or until wooden toothpick inserted in center comes out clean. Cool on wire rack 15 minutes; remove from pan. Carefully peel off foil; cool thoroughly. Place on serving plate. Spread Supreme Cocoa Glaze over top and sides; garnish with sliced almonds, if desired.

SUPREME COCOA GLAZE

Makes about ¾ cup

2 tablespoons butter *or* margarine
2 tablespoons Hershey's® Premium
    European-Style Cocoa
2 tablespoons water

1 cup confectioners' sugar
½ teaspoon vanilla extract

In small saucepan, over low heat, melt butter; add cocoa and water, stirring constantly until mixture thickens. Do not boil. Remove from heat; gradually add confectionary sugar and vanilla, beating with spoon until smooth. Add additional water, ½ teaspoon at a time, until desired consistency.

SOUR CREAM BROWNIE CAKE

BORDEN, INC.

Makes one 15-by-10-inch sheet cake

1 cup Borden® Country Store® *or* Meadow Gold® Butter

2 squares (1 ounce each) unsweetened chocolate

1 cup water

2 cups firmly packed brown sugar

2 cups unsifted flour

1 teaspoon baking soda

½ teaspoon salt

1 container (8 ounces) Borden® *or* Meadow Gold® Sour Cream

2 eggs

1 tablespoon vanilla extract

1 cup chopped nuts, optional

Preheat oven to 350°F. In saucepan, melt butter and chocolate with water. Combine dry ingredients. In mixer bowl, beat sour cream, eggs, vanilla, and chocolate mixture, then flour mixture, until smooth. Add nuts. Pour into greased and floured 15-by-10-inch baking pan. Bake 25 minutes or until wooden toothpick comes out clean. Cool. Frost. Refrigerate.

FUDGY FROSTING

2 cups confectioners' sugar

½ cup Borden® *or* Meadow Gold® Sour Cream

1 tablespoon butter

2 squares (1 ounce each) unsweetened chocolate, melted

1 teaspoon vanilla

In mixer bowl, beat all ingredients until smooth.

MICROWAVE ROCKY ROAD BROWNIES

KRAFT GENERAL FOODS, INC.

Makes 8 brownies

1 cup sugar
4 squares (1 ounce each) Baker's® Semi-
    Sweet Chocolate
⅓ cup Miracle Whip® Salad Dressing
2 eggs
½ teaspoon vanilla

1 cup flour
¾ teaspoon Calumet® Baking Powder
½ teaspoon salt
2 cups Kraft® Miniature Marshmallows
½ cup peanuts

Microwave sugar and 3 ounces chocolate on HIGH 3 minutes. Stir until blended. Beat in salad dressing, eggs, and vanilla. Blend in combined dry ingredients. Pour into 8-inch square baking dish. Cover corners of dish with foil; do not overlap foil. Microwave on HIGH 7 to 8 minutes, turning dish halfway after 4 minutes. Top with marshmallows and peanuts. Microwave on HIGH 30 seconds. Microwave remaining 1 ounce of chocolate on High 1 to 2 minutes, stirring after 1 minute. Stir until smooth. Drizzle over brownies.

Preparation time: 10 minutes   *Microwave time:* 13 minutes

Note: Since 1976 it has been considered safe to use aluminum foil in the microwave oven. The general guidelines are that the foil should not touch the side of the oven and the proper ratio is ¼ foil to ¾ food. The foil is used as a shielding technique for baking, a method of achieving even cooking. Without foil, the corners of the brownies get too brown.

CHEWY DOUBLE CHOCOLATE BROWNIES

KRAFT GENERAL FOODS, INC.

Makes 24 brownies

2 eggs, beaten
½ cup Miracle Whip® Salad Dressing
¼ cup cold water
1 package (21.5 ounces) fudge brownie
  mix

1 cup Baker's® Real Semi-Sweet
  Chocolate Chips
Confectioners' sugar (optional)

Preheat oven to 350°F. Mix eggs, salad dressing, and water until well blended. Stir in brownie mix, mixing just until moistened. Add chocolate chips; mix lightly. Pour into greased 13-by-9-inch pan. Bake 25 minutes or until edges begin to pull away from sides of pan. Cool; sprinkle with sifted confectioners' sugar, if desired. Cut into squares.

VARIATION

Substitute Miracle Whip® Light Reduced Calorie Salad Dressing for regular Salad Dressing.

Preparation time: 5 minutes   *Cooking time:* 30 minutes, plus cooling

DOUBLE FUDGE SAUCEPAN BROWNIES

HERSHEY FOODS CORPORATION

Makes about 18 brownies

½ cup sugar
2 tablespoons butter *or* margarine
2 tablespoons water
2 cups (12-oz. pkg.) Hershey's Semi-
  Sweet Chocolate Chips, divided

2 eggs, slightly beaten
1 teaspoon vanilla extract
⅔ cup all-purpose flour
¼ teaspoon baking soda
¼ teaspoon salt
½ cup chopped nuts (optional)

Heat oven to 325°F. Grease 9-inch square baking pan. In medium saucepan over low heat, cook sugar, butter, and water, stirring constantly, until mixture comes to a boil. Remove from heat; immediately add *1 cup* chocolate chips, stirring until melted. Stir in eggs and vanilla until blended. Stir together flour, baking soda, and salt; stir into chocolate mixture. Stir in remaining 1 cup chips and nuts, if desired. Pour batter into prepared pan. Bake 25 to 30 minutes or until brownies begin to pull away from sides of pan. Cool completely in pan on wire rack; cut into squares.

CHOCOLATE CARAMEL BROWNIES

NESTLÉ FOOD COMPANY

Makes 48 brownies

1 package (18.25 to 18.5 ounces) devil's food *or* chocolate cake mix
1 cup finely chopped nuts
½ cup butter
½ cup *undiluted* Carnation® Evaporated Milk

35 light caramels (10 ounces)
⅓ cup *undiluted* Carnation® Evaporated Milk
1 cup Nestlé® Toll House® Semi-Sweet Chocolate Morsels (6 ounces)

Preheat oven to 350°F. In large bowl, combine cake mix and nuts; cut in butter. Stir in ½ *cup* evaporated milk. Batter will be thick. Spread half of batter in greased 13-by-9-by-2-inch baking pan. Bake 15 minutes. In small saucepan, combine caramels and ⅓ *cup* evaporated milk. Cook over low heat, stirring occasionally, until caramels are melted. Sprinkle chocolate pieces over baked layer. Drizzle caramel syrup over chocolate pieces, carefully spreading to cover chocolate layer. Drop remaining half of batter in heaping teaspoons over caramel mixture. Return to oven and bake 20 to 25 minutes longer (top layer will be soft). Cool completely before cutting.

ORANGE DREAM CAKE

KRAFT GENERAL FOODS, INC.

Makes 12 servings

¾ cup Miracle Whip® Salad Dressing
1 (2-layer) yellow cake mix
1 envelope Dream Whip® Whipped
  Topping Mix
¾ cup orange juice

3 eggs
2 teaspoons grated orange peel
1½ cups confectioners' sugar
2 tablespoons milk
1 tablespoon red and green sprinkles

Preheat oven to 350°F. Mix together first 6 ingredients at medium speed of electric mixer for 2 minutes. Pour into greased and floured 10-inch fluted tube pan. Bake 35 to 40 minutes or until wooden toothpick inserted near center comes out clean. Let stand 10 minutes; remove from pan. Cool.

Combine confectioners' sugar and milk. Drizzle over cake. Decorate with sprinkles.

Preparation time: 10 minutes   *Cooking time:* 40 minutes

ORANGE ZUCCHINI CAKE

KELLOGG COMPANY

Makes 12 servings

1 cup all-purpose flour
1 teaspoon baking powder
½ teaspoon baking soda
¼ teaspoon salt
1 teaspoon ground cinnamon
½ teaspoon ground nutmeg
¾ cup sugar
½ cup vegetable oil

2 eggs
½ cup KELLOGG'S® ALL-BRAN® cereal
1½ teaspoons grated orange peel
1 teaspoon vanilla flavoring
1 cup grated zucchini
½ cup chopped nuts
Orange Cream Cheese Frosting (see
   below)

Preheat oven to 325°F. Combine flour, baking powder, soda, salt, cinnamon, and nutmeg. Set aside. In large mixing bowl, beat sugar, oil, and eggs until well combined. Stir in cereal, peel, and vanilla. Add flour mixture, zucchini, and nuts. Mix well. Spread evenly in greased 10-by-6-by-2-inch (1½-quart) glass baking dish. Bake 35 minutes or until toothpick inserted near center comes out clean. Cool completely. Spread with Orange Cream Cheese Frosting.

ORANGE CREAM CHEESE FROSTING

1 package (3 ounces) cream cheese,
   softened
1 tablespoon margarine *or* butter,
   softened

½ teaspoon grated orange peel
1½ cups sifted confectioners' sugar
Milk, if needed

In small mixing bowl, beat cream cheese, margarine, and peel until light and fluffy. Gradually add sugar, beating until fluffy and of spreading consistency. If mixture is too thick, add 1 to 2 teaspoons of milk.

THE MYSTERY CAKE
The Story of Chiffon Cake

In 1948, after nearly a year of hushed, behind-closed-doors experimentation and intrigue, Betty Crocker of General Mills finally announced to the country that a totally new cake, the *chiffon* cake, had been created. This was the first important contribution to cake baking since the introduction of baking powder one hundred years earlier and was expected to cause the revision of textbooks on the subject.

Made with a "mystery ingredient," this unique cake had an airiness, moistness, and velvetiness that surpassed the qualities of the two basic cake types then recognized, the butter cake and the angel food (or sponge) cake. It had the melt-in-your-mouth feel of the butter cake, but was higher in volume, richer, and more delicate. It was made with only seven eggs rather than the thirteen required for an angel food cake, yet was more tender. And the easy-to-make chiffon cake required only ten minutes of beating time rather than the twenty-five minutes necessary for angel food perfection—no small matter when you realize that electric beaters were not a standard household appliance of the time.

A Los Angeles insurance salesman, Harry Baker, had originated the cake twenty years earlier and spent the intervening two decades preparing his custom masterpieces for famous Hollywood restaurants like The Brown Derby and for posh parties given by luminary hostesses of the period like Eleanor Roosevelt, Lily Pons, and Barbara Stanwyck. Although he received countless requests for the recipe, Harry Baker had always kept it a closely guarded secret.

Nearing retirement, he decided to give his creation to the homemakers of America. He had listened to the Betty Crocker radio program and helpful cooking hints for years and decided to present his great secret to Betty Crocker.

After purchasing the idea from Baker, Betty Crocker tested the baking techniques for a year to best adapt them for a typical household. The Mazola® and Wesson® oil salespeople were delighted when General Mills announced the "first really new cake in one hundred years." The mysterious ingredient? Familiar salad or cooking oil.

ORANGE CHIFFON CAKE

GENERAL MILLS, INC.

Makes 1 cake

2¼ cups Softasilk® Cake Flour *or* 2 cups Gold Medal® All-Purpose Flour

1½ cups sugar

3 teaspoons baking powder

1 teaspoon salt

½ cup vegetable oil

5 egg yolks (with Softasilk®) *or* 7 egg yolks (with Gold Medal® Flour)

¾ cup cold water

2 tablespoons grated orange peel

1 cup egg whites (7 or 8)

½ teaspoon cream of tartar

Orange Butter Frosting (see below)

Preheat oven to 325°F. Mix flour, sugar, baking powder, and salt in bowl. Make a well and add in order: oil, egg yolks, water, and orange peel. Beat with spoon until smooth. Beat egg whites and cream of tartar in large bowl until very stiff peaks form. Gradually pour egg yolk mixture over beaten whites, gently folding with rubber spatula just until blended. Pour into ungreased tube pan, 10-by-4 inches. Bake about 1 hour 15 minutes or until top springs back when touched lightly. Hang upside down on heatproof funnel until cake is completely cold. Frost with Orange Butter Frosting.

ORANGE BUTTER FROSTING

⅓ cup margarine *or* butter, softened

3 cups confectioners' sugar

1½ tablespoons grated orange *or* lemon peel

About 3 tablespoons orange *or* lemon juice

Mix all ingredients until smooth.

VARIATIONS

Lemon Chiffon Cake: Omit orange peel; add 2 teaspoons grated lemon peel and 2 teaspoons vanilla.

Spice Chiffon Cake: Omit orange peel; add with the flour 1 teaspoon ground cinnamon and ½ teaspoon each ground nutmeg, allspice, and cloves.

Chocolate Chip Chiffon Cake: Increase sugar to 1¾ cups. Omit orange peel; add 2 teaspoons vanilla. Gently fold 3 squares (1 ounce each) shaved sweet, semisweet, or unsweetened chocolate into batter.

Maple-Pecan Chiffon Cake: Substitute ¾ cup granulated sugar and ¾ cup packed brown sugar for the 1½ cups sugar. Omit orange peel; add 2 teaspoons maple flavoring. Gently fold 1 cup very finely chopped pecans into batter.

EASY CARROT CAKE

KRAFT GENERAL FOODS, INC.

Makes 10 to 12 servings

1 (2-layer) yellow cake mix
1¼ cups Miracle Whip® Salad Dressing
4 eggs
¼ cup cold water

2 teaspoons ground cinnamon
2 cups finely shredded carrots
½ cup chopped walnuts
Vanilla "Philly" Frosting (see below)

Preheat oven to 350°F. Beat cake mix, salad dressing, eggs, water, and cinnamon at medium speed with electric mixer until well blended. Stir in carrots and walnuts. Pour into greased 13-by-9-inch baking pan. Bake 30 to 35 minutes or until wooden toothpick inserted in center comes out clean. Cool. Frost.

VANILLA "PHILLY" FROSTING

1 package (8 ounces) Philadelphia® Brand
  Cream Cheese, softened

1 tablespoon vanilla
3 to 3½ cups sifted confectioners' sugar

Beat cream cheese and vanilla at medium speed with electric mixer until well blended. Gradually add sugar, beating well after each addition.

Preparation time: 25 minutes   *Cooking time:* 35 minutes

AMAZIN' RAISIN CAKE

BEST FOODS, A DIVISION OF CPC INTERNATIONAL INC.

Makes 12 servings

3 cups unsifted flour
2 cups sugar
2 teaspoons baking soda
1½ teaspoons cinnamon
½ teaspoon nutmeg
½ teaspoon salt
¼ teaspoon cloves

1 cup Hellmann's® *or* Best Foods®
   Mayonnaise
⅓ cup milk
2 eggs
3 cups coarsely chopped apples
1 cup raisins
1 cup coarsely chopped walnuts
1 cup heavy *or* whipping cream, whipped

Preheat oven to 350°F. Grease and flour two 9-inch layer cake pans. In large bowl, combine flour, sugar, baking soda, cinnamon, nutmeg, salt, and cloves. Add mayonnaise, milk, and eggs. Beat at low speed 2 minutes, scraping bowl frequently. (Batter will be thick.) With spoon, stir in apples, raisins, and nuts. Spoon into pans. Bake 40 to 45 minutes or until cake tester inserted in center comes out clean. Cool in pans 10 minutes. Remove; cool on racks. Fill and frost with whipped cream.

GELATIN POKE CAKE

KRAFT GENERAL FOODS, INC.

Makes 1 cake

1 package (2-layer size) white cake mix
   or pudding-included cake mix
1 package (4-serving size) Jell-O® Brand
   Gelatin, any flavor
1 cup boiling water
½ cup cold water

3½ cups (8 ounces) Cool Whip®
   Nondairy Whipped Topping, thawed,
   for garnish
Fruit for garnish (optional)
Marzipan for garnish (optional)

Preheat oven to 350°F. Prepare cake batter as directed on package and pour into well-greased and floured 13-by-9-inch pan. Bake 30 to 35 minutes, or until cake tester inserted in center comes out clean. Cool cake in pan 15 minutes; then pierce with utility fork at ½-inch intervals.

Meanwhile, dissolve gelatin in boiling water. Add cold water and carefully pour over cake. Chill 3 to 4 hours. Garnish with whipped topping and fruit or marzipan, if desired.

Alternate baking pans: Bake in one 10-inch tube pan for 45 to 50 minutes; remove from pan and place on waxed paper before adding gelatin. *Or* bake in two 8-inch or 9-inch layer pans for 30 to 35 minutes; remove from pans and place in clean pans or on waxed paper before adding gelatin. Fill and frost with 3½ cups (8 ounces) Cool Whip® Nondairy Whipped Topping, thawed.

PINEAPPLE UPSIDE DOWN CAKE

DOLE FOOD COMPANY

Makes 8 servings

⅔ cup margarine
⅔ cup brown sugar, packed
1 can (20 ounces) Dole® Pineapple Slices
10 maraschino cherries
¾ cup granulated sugar
2 eggs, separated

Zest and juice from 1 Dole® Lemon
1 teaspoon vanilla extract
1½ cups all-purpose flour
1¾ teaspoons baking powder
¼ teaspoon salt
½ cup dairy sour cream

Preheat oven to 350°F. Melt ⅓ *cup* margarine in 9- or 10-inch cast iron skillet. Remove from heat. Add brown sugar and stir until blended. Drain pineapple well, reserving *2 tablespoons* syrup. Arrange pineapple slices in brown sugar mixture. Place a cherry in the center of each pineapple slice. In large bowl, beat remaining ⅓ *cup* margarine with ½ *cup* granulated sugar until fluffy. Beat in egg yolks, *1 teaspoon* lemon zest, *1 tablespoon* lemon juice, and vanilla. Combine flour, baking powder, and salt. Blend into creamed mixture alternately with sour cream and reserved *2 tablespoons* pineapple syrup. Beat egg whites to soft peaks. Gradually beat in remaining ¼ *cup* granulated sugar to make stiff meringue. Fold into batter. Pour over pineapple in skillet. Bake 35 minutes or until cake springs back when touched. Let stand in pan on rack for 10 minutes, then invert onto serving plate.

PIÑA COLADA CAKE

BORDEN, INC.

Makes one 10-inch cake

1 package (18¼ to 18½ ounces) yellow cake mix

1 package (4-serving size) *instant* vanilla-flavored pudding mix

1 can (15 ounces) Coco Lopez® Cream of Coconut

½ cup plus 2 tablespoons rum

⅓ cup vegetable oil

4 eggs

1 can (8 ounces) crushed pineapple, well drained

Pineapple chunks for garnish (optional)

Maraschino cherries for garnish (optional)

Toasted coconut for garnish (optional)

Coconut Cream Sauce (see below)

Preheat oven to 350°F. In large mixer bowl, combine cake mix, pudding mix, ½ *cup* cream of coconut, ½ *cup* rum, oil, and eggs. (Note: If using cake mix "with pudding in", omit pudding mix.) Beat on medium speed 2 minutes. Stir in crushed pineapple. Pour into well-greased and floured 10-inch fluted or tube pan. Bake 50 to 55 minutes. Cool 10 minutes. Remove from pan. With a table knife or skewer, poke holes about 1 inch apart in cake almost to bottom. Combine remaining cream of coconut and remaining *2 tablespoons* rum; slowly spoon over cake. Chill thoroughly. Garnish. Serve with Coconut Cream Sauce. Store in refrigerator.

COCONUT CREAM SAUCE

Makes about 2 cups

1 cup (½ pint) Borden® *or* Meadow Gold® Whipping Cream

½ cup Coco Lopez® cream of coconut

In small mixer bowl, combine ingredients; beat *only* until stiff. Sauce can be held in refrigerator 2 to 3 hours.

SKIPPY'S HONEY NUT
PEANUT BUTTER CUPCAKES

BEST FOODS, A DIVISION OF CPC INTERNATIONAL INC.

Makes 24 cupcakes

1 package (18¼ or 18½ ounces) yellow cake mix (non-pudding type)

1 cup Roasted Honey Nut™ Skippy® Creamy Peanut Butter

½ cup grape jelly

Chocolate Peanut Butter Frosting (see below)

Preheat oven to 350°F. Line twenty-four 2½-inch muffin cups with paper liners. In large bowl with mixer at medium speed, beat cake mix and peanut butter until coarse crumbs form. Continue, following package directions for yellow cake, omitting oil. Spoon some of the batter into cups, filling each about half full. Top each with *1 teaspoon* jelly. Carefully add enough batter to cover jelly and fill each cup three-fourths full. Bake 22 to 25 minutes or until toothpick inserted in center of 1 cupcake comes out clean. Cool in pan on wire rack 10 minutes; remove from pan and cool completely. Frost with Chocolate Peanut Butter Frosting.

CHOCOLATE HONEY NUT FROSTING

⅓ cup unsweetened cocoa

¼ cup Mazola® Corn Oil Margarine

2 cups confectioners' sugar

3 to 4 tablespoons milk

½ teaspoon vanilla

⅓ cup Roasted Honey Nut™ Skippy® Creamy Peanut Butter

In large bowl, with mixer at medium speed, beat cocoa and margarine until smooth. Gradually beat in confectioners' sugar alternately with milk and vanilla. Beat in peanut butter until frosting is fluffy. Spread on cupcakes.

MAHOGANY POUND CAKE

BORDEN, INC.

Makes one 10-inch cake

2½ cups unsifted flour
½ cup unsweetened cocoa
¼ teaspoon baking soda
2 cups granulated sugar
1 cup firmly packed light brown sugar
1½ cups Borden® Country Store® or
  Meadow Gold® Butter, softened

6 eggs, separated
1 teaspoon vanilla extract
1 container (8 ounces) Borden® or
  Meadow Gold® Sour Cream
Confectioners' sugar (optional)

Preheat oven to 325°F. Combine flour, cocoa, and baking soda; set aside. In large mixer bowl, beat sugars and butter until light and fluffy. Add egg yolks, 1 at a time, beating well after each addition; add vanilla. Beat in sour cream alternately with dry ingredients. (Batter is very thick.) In medium bowl, beat egg whites until stiff but not dry; fold half into batter. Fold in remaining egg whites. Pour into well-greased and floured 10-inch tube pan. Bake 1½ hours or until wooden toothpick inserted in center comes out clean. Cool 10 minutes; remove from pan. Sprinkle with confectioners' sugar, if desired.

COCONUT-PECAN FILLING AND FROSTING

KRAFT GENERAL FOODS, INC.

Makes about 2 cups, enough to cover tops of two 9-inch layers

⅔ cup (one 5.33 fluid-ounces can)
  evaporated milk
⅔ cup sugar
2 egg yolks, slightly beaten
⅓ cup butter *or* margarine

¾ teaspoon vanilla
1 cup Baker's® Angel Flake® Brand
  Coconut
⅔ cup chopped pecans

Combine milk, sugar, egg yolks, butter, and vanilla in saucepan. Cook and stir over medium heat until mixture thickens, about 10 minutes. Remove from heat; add coconut and pecans. Beat until cool and of spreading consistency.

VELVETY CHEESECAKE

PET INCORPORATED

Makes 9 servings

1 cup graham-cracker crumbs
¼ cup butter *or* margarine, melted
2 packages (8 ounces each) cream
   cheese, softened
2 eggs
1 cup Pet® Evaporated Milk

1 cup sugar
1 teaspoon vanilla
½ teaspoon lemon peel
1 can (21 ounces) cherry *or* peach pie
   filling

Preheat oven to 350°F. In 8-inch square baking pan, combine graham-cracker crumbs and butter. Press mixture into bottom of pan and set aside. In medium mixing bowl, beat cream cheese until fluffy. Add eggs and continue beating until smooth. Gradually add evaporated milk, beating until smooth. Stir in sugar, vanilla, and lemon peel. Pour blended mixture over graham-cracker crust and bake 45 to 50 minutes until slightly puffed and firm to the touch. Allow cake to cool and then top with pie filling. Chill thoroughly before serving.

NORTHWEST CHEESECAKE SUPREME

KRAFT GENERAL FOODS, INC.

Makes 10 to 12 servings

CRUST

1 cup graham cracker crumbs

3 tablespoons sugar

3 tablespoons Parkay® Margarine, melted

FILLING

4 packages (8 ounces each) Philadelphia®
  Brand Cream Cheese, softened

1 cup sugar

3 tablespoons flour

4 eggs

1 cup Breakstone's® Sour Cream

1 tablespoon vanilla

Sweet Cherry Sauce (see below)

Preheat oven to 350°F. Mix together crumbs, sugar, and margarine; press onto bottom of 9-inch springform pan. Bake 10 minutes.

In large mixing bowl, beat cream cheese, sugar, and flour, mixing at medium speed with electric mixer, until well blended. Add eggs; mix well. Blend in sour cream and vanilla; pour over crust. Bake 1 hour, 10 minutes. Loosen cake from rim of pan; cool before removing rim of pan. Chill. Top with sweet cherry sauce just before serving.

SWEET CHERRY SAUCE

Makes 2 cups

1 can (17 ounces) pitted dark sweet
  cherries

1 tablespoon sugar

1 tablespoon cornstarch

1 teaspoon lemon juice

2 tablespoons kirsch

Drain cherries, reserving liquid. Add enough water to reserved liquid to measure *1¼ cups.* Combine sugar and cornstarch in saucepan; gradually add liquid and lemon juice. Cook, stirring constantly, until mixture is clear and thickened. Remove from heat; stir in cherries and kirsch. Cool.

Preparation time: 20 minutes

Cooking time: 1 hour, 20 minutes

COOKIES AND CREAM CHEESECAKE

KRAFT GENERAL FOODS, INC.

Makes 8 servings

2 cups (24) crushed creme-filled chocolate cookies

6 tablespoons Parkay® Margarine, softened

1 envelope unflavored gelatin

¼ cup cold water

1 package (8 ounces) Philadelphia® Brand Cream Cheese, softened

½ cup sugar

¾ cup milk

1 cup whipping cream, whipped

1¼ cups (10) chopped creme-filled chocolate cookies

Combine cookie crumbs and margarine; press onto bottom and sides of 9-inch springform pan. (Use a food processor to crush the creme-filled chocolate cookies in an instant.)

Soften gelatin in water; stir over low heat until dissolved. Combine cream cheese and sugar, mixing at medium speed on electric mixer until well blended. Gradually add gelatin and milk, mixing until blended. Chill until mixture is thickened but not set. Fold in whipped cream. Reserve *1½ cups* cream-cheese mixture; pour remaining cream-cheese mixture over crust. Top with chopped cookies and reserved cream-cheese mixture. Chill until firm.

Preparation time: 25 minutes, plus chilling

MARBLE CHEESECAKE

KRAFT GENERAL FOODS, INC.

Makes 10 to 12 servings

1 cup graham cracker crumbs
3 tablespoons sugar
3 tablespoons Parkay® Margarine, melted
3 packages (8 ounces each) Philadelphia®
  Brand Cream Cheese, softened

¾ cup sugar
1 teaspoon vanilla
3 eggs
1 square (1 ounce) Bakers®
  Unsweetened Chocolate, melted

Preheat oven to 350°F. Combine crumbs, sugar, and margarine; press onto bottom of 9-inch springform pan. Bake 10 minutes.

Turn oven up to 450°F. Combine cream cheese, sugar, and vanilla, mixing at medium speed on electric mixer until well blended. Add eggs, 1 at a time, mixing well after each addition. Blend chocolate into 1 cup batter. Spoon plain and chocolate batters alternately over crust; cut through batters with knife several times for marble effect. Bake 10 minutes. Reduce oven temperature to 250°F; continue baking 30 minutes. Loosen cake from rim of pan; cool before removing rim of pan. Chill.

Preparation time: 20 minutes, plus chilling

Cooking time: 40 minutes

BEAT-THE-HEAT CHEESECAKE

THOMAS J. LIPTON CO.

Makes about 12 servings

2 envelopes Knox® Unflavored Gelatine
¾ cup sugar
1 cup boiling water
2 packages (8 ounces each) cream
  cheese, softened
1 cup (8 ounces) creamed cottage
  cheese

1 cup (½ pint) whipping *or* heavy cream
1 tablespoon vanilla extract
1 tablespoon fresh grated lemon peel
  (optional)
Graham-Craker Almond Crust (see
  below)
Fruit for garnish (optional)

In large bowl, mix gelatine with *¼ cup* sugar; add boiling water and stir until gelatine is completely dissolved, about 5 minutes. With electric mixer, add remaining *½ cup* sugar, cream cheese, cottage cheese, cream, vanilla, and lemon peel, 1 at a time, beating well after each addition. Continue beating an additional 5 minutes or until mixture is smooth. Turn into Graham-Cracker Almond Crust; chill until firm, about 5 hours. Garnish, if desired, with fruit.

GRAHAM-CRACKER ALMOND CRUST

1 cup grahm-cracker crumbs
½ cup ground almonds
2 tablespoons sugar

¼ cup melted butter *or* margarine
½ teaspoon almond extract

In small bowl, combine all ingredients. Press onto bottom and sides of 9-inch springform pan; chill.

PINEAPPLE CHEESECAKE SQUARES

DOLE FOOD COMPANY

Makes 12 servings

2¼ cups all-purpose flour, divided
½ cup Dole® Chopped Almonds
½ cup confectioners' sugar
⅔ cup margarine, softened
2 packages (8 ounces each) cream
   cheese, softened

¾ cup sugar, divided
2 eggs
⅔ cup Dole® Pineapple Juice
I can (20 ounces) Dole® Crushed
   Pineapple, drained, with juice reserved
½ cup whipping cream, whipped

Preheat oven to 350°F. To make crust, combine *2 cups* flour, almonds, and confectioners' sugar in medium bowl. Cut in margarine until crumbly. Press firmly and evenly in bottom of ungreased 13-by-9-by-2-inch pan. Bake until very light golden brown, 15 to 20 minutes.

To make filling, beat cream cheese in medium bowl until smooth and fluffy. Beat in *½ cup sugar* and the eggs. Stir in *⅔ cup* pineapple juice. Pour over hot crust. Bake just until center is set, about 20 minutes. Cool completely.

To make topping, mix *¼ cup* flour and remaining *¼ cup* sugar in 2-quart saucepan. Stir in juice from drained pineapple. Heat to boiling over medium, stirring constantly. Boil and stir 1 minute. Remove from heat; fold in pineapple. Cool. Fold in whipped cream. Spread carefully over dessert. Cover loosely and refrigerate until firm, about 4 hours.

EASY-AS-PIE CRUST

BEST FOODS, A DIVISION OF CPC INTERNATIONAL INC.

Makes 1 (9-inch) pie crust

1 1/4 cups flour	1/2 cup Mazola® margarine
1/8 teaspoon salt	2 tablespoons cold water

In medium bowl mix flour and salt. With pastry blender or 2 knives, cut in margarine until mixture resembles fine crumbs. Sprinkle water over flour mixture while tossing with fork to blend well. Press dough firmly into ball. On lightly floured surface roll out to 12-inch circle. Fit loosely into 9-inch pie plate. Trim and flute edge. Fill and bake according to recipe.

LIGHT 'N LUSCIOUS LEMON PIE

NESTLÉ FOOD COMPANY

Makes one 8-inch pie

2 cups water	1 envelope unflavored gelatin
1 1/3 cups Carnation® Nonfat Dry Milk, divided	1/4 cup lemon juice
	1/2 teaspoon grated lemon zest
1 package (3 1/8 ounces) vanilla cook and serve pudding and pie filling mix	1/3 cup ice water
	1 tablespoon lemon juice
1/4 cup granulated sugar	8-inch graham cracker crust

In large saucepan, combine water, *1 cup* nonfat dry milk, pudding and pie filling mix, sugar, and gelatin. Bring to a boil over medium heat, stirring constantly. Chill until mixture mounds from spoon. Beat in *1/4 cup* lemon juice and zest until smooth. In small mixer bowl, combine remaining nonfat dry milk and ice water. Beat at high speed about 3 to 4 minutes, until soft peaks form. Add *1 tablespoon* lemon juice; continue beating 1 to 2 minutes until stiff peaks form. Fold into pudding mixture. Spoon into crust; chill for 2 hours.

REALEMON® MERINGUE PIE

BORDEN, INC.

Makes one 9-inch pie

1⅔ cups sugar
6 tablespoons cornstarch
½ cup ReaLemon® Lemon Juice from
    Concentrate
4 eggs, separated

1½ cups boiling water
2 tablespoons margarine *or* butter
1 (9-inch) baked pastry shell
¼ teaspoon cream of tartar

Preheat oven to 300°F. In heavy saucepan, combine *1⅓ cups* sugar and cornstarch; add ReaLemon® brand. In small bowl, beat egg *yolks;* add to lemon mixture. Gradually add water, stirring constantly. Over medium heat, cook and stir until mixture boils and thickens, about 8 to 10 minutes. Remove from heat. Add margarine; stir until melted. Pour into prepared pastry shell. In small mixer bowl, beat egg whites with cream of tartar until soft peaks form; gradually add remaining *⅓ cup* sugar, beating until stiff but not dry. Spread on top of pie, sealing carefully to edge of shell. Bake 20 to 30 minutes or until golden. Cool. Chill before serving. Refrigerate leftovers.

CHOCOLATE CHEESECAKE PIE

PET INCORPORATED

Makes 8 servings

1 package (8 ounces) cream cheese,
    softened
1 cup powdered sugar
1 teaspoon vanilla extract
1 cup semi-sweet chocolate chips,
    melted

2 cups La Creme® Whipped Topping,
    thawed
1 Pet•Ritz® Deep Dish Pie Crust Shell,
    baked
½ cup caramel dessert topping
¾ cup pecan halves

In medium bowl, combine cream cheese, powdered sugar, and vanilla. Stir in melted chocolate chips, mixing well. Fold in whipped topping. Spoon cream cheese mixture into pie crust. Spread caramel topping evenly over top of pie. Arrange pecan halves on top. Chill 1 to 2 hours.

HERSHEY'S® BAVARIAN CHOCOLATE MINT PIE

HERSHEY FOODS CORPORATION

Makes 8 servings

1 envelope unflavored gelatin
1½ cups milk
1⅔ cups (10-oz. pkg.) Hershey's® Mint
    Chocolate Chips
1 teaspoon vanilla extract

½ cup chilled whipping cream
8-inch packaged chocolate-flavored
    crumb crust (6 ounces)
Sweetened Whipped Cream (see below)

In medium saucepan, sprinkle gelatin over milk; let stand at least 5 minutes to soften. Stir in mint chocolate chips. Cook over low heat, stirring constantly with wire whisk, until chips are melted, chocolate flecks disappear, and mixture is smooth; do not boil. Remove from heat; add vanilla. Chill, stirring occasionally, until mixture begins to set. Beat ½ *cup* whipping cream until stiff; carefully fold into chocolate mixture. Pour into crust; cover and chill until set. Garnish with Sweetened Whipped Cream.

SWEETENED WHIPPED CREAM

Makes about 1 cup

½ cup chilled whipping cream
1 tablespoon confectioners' sugar

¼ teaspoon vanilla extract

In small mixer bowl, beat ingredients until stiff.

CHERRY CHEESE PIE

BORDEN, INC.

Makes one 9-inch pie

1 package (8 ounces) cream cheese,
    softened
1 can (14 ounces) Eagle® Brand
    Sweetened Condensed Milk (*not*
    evaporated milk)

⅓ cup ReaLemon® Lemon Juice from
    Concentrate
1 teaspoon vanilla extract
1 graham cracker crumb crust (9 inch) *or*
    baked pastry shell
1 can (21 ounces) cherry pie filling,
    chilled

In large mixer bowl, beat cheese until fluffy. Gradually beat in sweetened condensed milk until smooth. Stir in ReaLemon® brand and vanilla. Pour into prepared crust. Chill 3 hours or until set. Top with desired amount of pie filling before serving. Refrigerate leftovers.

BANANA CREAM CHEESE PIE

KELLOGG COMPANY

Makes one 9-inch pie

4 cups KELLOGG'S CORN FLAKES®
  cereal, crushed to 1 cup
2 tablespoons sugar
¼ cup margarine *or* butter, melted
3 medium-size bananas

1 package (8 ounces) cream cheese,
  softened
1 can (14 ounces, 1⅓ cups) sweetened
  condensed milk
⅓ cup lemon juice
1 teaspoon vanilla flavoring

In medium-size mixing bowl, combine crushed cereal, sugar, and margarine. Press evenly and firmly in bottom and around sides of buttered 9-inch pie pan. Chill. Slice *2 bananas* over bottom of pie shell. Beat softened cream cheese until light and fluffy. Gradually beat in condensed milk. When mixture is smooth, stir in lemon juice and vanilla. Pour over sliced bananas and chill until firm, about 6 hours or overnight. Just before serving, slice remaining banana and use to garnish pie.

CREAMY YOGURT PIE

KELLOGG COMPANY

Makes 8 servings

2 cups Kellogg's® RICE KRISPIES®
  cereal, crushed to 1 cup
½ cup chopped nuts
⅓ cup margarine, melted
¼ cup firmly packed brown sugar
1 envelope (1 tablespoon) unflavored
  gelatin

⅓ cup granulated sugar
2 containers (8 ounces each) low-fat
  yogurt, any flavor
½ pint (1 cup) nondairy whipped topping,
  thawed Fruit for garnish (optional)

Preheat oven to 350°F. Combine crushed cereal, nuts, margarine, and brown sugar. Mix well. Press evenly in 9-inch pie pan to form crust. Bake 8 minutes or until lightly browned. Cool completely. In saucepan, combine gelatin and granulated sugar. Stir in *1 container* of yogurt. Cook over low heat, stirring constantly 4 to 5 minutes or until gelatin dissolves. Stir in remaining yogurt. Chill, stirring occasionally, until mixture mounds slightly when dropped from a spoon. Stir whipped topping into thickened yogurt mixture. Spoon into pie crust. Chill until set, about 1 hour. Garnish with fruit, if desired.

CHOCOLATE-PECAN AND CARAMEL PIE

THOMAS J. LIPTON CO.

Makes about 8 servings

1 envelope Knox® Unflavored Gelatine
¼ cup cold water
2 cups (1 pint) whipping *or* heavy cream
1 package (6 ounces) semi-sweet
   chocolate chips
2 eggs

1 teaspoon vanilla extract
1 cup (about 22) caramels
2 tablespoons butter
Chocolate-Pecan Crust (see below)
Pecans for garnish (optional)

In small saucepan, sprinkle unflavored gelatine over cold water; let stand 1 minute. Stir over low heat until gelatine is completely dissolved, about 3 minutes. Stir in *1 cup* cream. Bring just to the boiling point; then immediately add to blender with chocolate. Process until chocolate is completely melted, about 1 minute. While processing, through feed cap, add *½ cup* cream, eggs, and vanilla; process until blended. Pour into large bowl and chill until thickened, about 15 minutes.

Meanwhile, in small saucepan, combine caramels, *¼ cup* cream, and butter. Simmer over low heat, stirring occasionally, until caramels are completely melted and mixture is smooth. Pour onto Chocolate-Pecan Crust to cover bottom; let stand at room temperature to cool, about 10 minutes.

With wire whisk or spoon, beat gelatin mixture until smooth. Pour into prepared crust; chill until firm, about 3 hours. Garnish with remaining *¼ cup* cream, whipped, and, if desired, pecans.

CHOCOLATE-PECAN CRUST

1 box (8½ ounces) chocolate wafer
   cookies

¾ cup finely chopped pecans
½ cup melted butter *or* margarine

Preheat oven to 350°F. Crumble cookies to make about 2 cups crumbs. Combine with pecans and butter. Press into 9-inch pie pan and press up sides to form high rim. Bake 10 minutes. Cool.

NO-BAKE OLD-FASHIONED
COCONUT CREAM PIE

THOMAS J. LIPTON CO.

Makes about 12 servings

2 envelopes Knox® Unflavored Gelatine
¼ cup cold water
1 can (15 ounces) cream of coconut
1 cup (½ pint) light cream *or* half-and-half
3 eggs

1 (9-inch) baked pastry shell *or* graham
   cracker crust
4 cups whipped cream or whipped
   topping
2 tablespoons coconut, toasted

In small saucepan, sprinkle unflavored gelatine over cold water; let stand 1 minute. Stir over low heat until gelatine is completely dissolved, about 3 minutes.

In blender or food processor, process cream of coconut, light cream, and eggs until blended. While processing, through feed cap, gradually add gelatine mixture and process until blended. Chill blender container until mixture is slightly thickened, about 15 minutes. Turn into pastry shell; chill until firm, about 3 hours. Top with whipped cream and coconut.

VARIATION

Instead of 3 eggs, use ¾ cup frozen cholesterol-free egg product, 1½ tablespoons butter or margarine, and ⅛ teaspoon salt.

DREAM PIE

KRAFT GENERAL FOODS, INC.

Makes one 8-inch pie

1 envelope, Dream Whip® Whipped
   Topping Mix *or* 1¾ cups (4 ounces)
   Birds Eye® Cool Whip® Non-Dairy
   Whipped Topping, thawed
1 package (4-serving size) Jell-O® Instant
   Pudding and Pie Filling, any flavor

1⅓ cups cold milk
1 baked 8-inch pie shell *or* graham
   cracker crumb crust, cooled
   Sweetened sliced strawberries
   (optional)

Prepare whipped topping mix (if using Dream Whip®) as directed on package. Prepare pie filling mix with the milk as directed on package for pie. Blend in *1 cup* of whipped topping. Pour into pie shell. Chill at least 2 hours. Top each serving with strawberries and garnish with remaining whipped topping.

PINEAPPLE PISTACHIO ICE CREAM PIE

DOLE FOOD COMPANY

Makes 8 servings

⅓ cup shelled Dole® Natural Pistachios

1 can (8 ounces) Dole® Crushed
   Pineapple, drained

2 tablespoons orange-flavored liqueur

Grated peel from 1 orange

1 quart vanilla ice cream, softened

1 (9-inch) prepared graham cracker crust

Toast pistachios. Fold pistachios, pineapple, liqueur, and orange peel into ice cream. Turn filling into graham cracker crust. Freeze 4 hours or until firm. Garnish with additional pistachios before serving.

To toast pistachio nutmeats (shelled pistachios): Preheat oven to 200°F. Toast nutmeats 10 to 15 minutes.

FAMOUS PUMPKIN PIE

LIBBY'S, NESTLÉ FOOD COMPANY

Makes one 9-inch pie

1 9-inch (4-cup volume) unbaked pie
   crust

2 eggs, lightly beaten

1¾ cups (16-ounce can) Libby's® Solid
   Pack Pumpkin

¾ cup granulated sugar

½ teaspoon salt

1 teaspoon ground cinnamon

½ teaspoon ground ginger

¼ teaspoon ground cloves

1½ cups (12-ounce can) *undiluted*
   Carnation® Evaporated Milk

Preheat oven to 425°F. In large mixing bowl, combine eggs, pumpkin, sugar, salt, cinnamon, ginger, cloves, and evaporated milk. Pour into unbaked pie crust. (Note: When using metal or foil pie pan, bake on preheated cookie sheet. When using glass or ceramic pie plate, *do not* use cookie sheet.) Bake 15 minutes. Reduce temperature to 350°F. Bake an additional 40 to 50 minutes, or until knife inserted near center comes out clean. Top cooled pie as desired.

Chocolate-Pecan and Caramel Pie

COURTESY OF THOMAS J. LIPTON CO.

*Peanut Butter
Cereal Muffins,
Best Ever
Peanut Butter Cookies,
Peanut Butter
Oat Bars*

COURTESY OF SKIPPY PEANUT BUTTER /
CPC INTERNATIONAL, INC.

St. Tropez Holiday Cranberry Mousse

COURTESY OF DOLE FOOD COMPANY

THY OWN PUMPKIN PIE
The Story of Libby's Pumpkin

The versatile pumpkin became a highly regarded vegetable in America after some generous Indians introduced starving colonists to the large golden orb. For food in bitter winters, pumpkins could be stored in dugout root cellars along with winter squash, apples, and potatoes. In times of barley- and hop-crop failure, innovative colonists discovered that fermented pumpkins and persimmons, flavored with maple sugar, made an appealing-tasting substitiute for beer. More importantly, the effect of the two drinks was the same.

Early pumpkin pies were simple dishes made by slicing off the tops of the fruit, scooping out the seed, adding milk, spices, and a sweetener like molasses, honey, or maple sugar, replacing the lid, and baking the whole pumpkin.

The familiar Halloween icon, the jack-o'-lantern, was introduced to America by Irish settlers. The Druid priests of their Celtic ancestors had believed the unearthly light emanating from carved faces warded off evil.

The type of pumpkin sold in markets for jack-o'-lanterns at Halloween is watery and not very sweet. The Dickinson variety, a meatier and sweeter version, is known as the eating pumpkin. By selectively breeding the sweet and rich Dickinson, Libby's was able to hybridize a variety, called the Libby's® Select, that has a richer, more golden color; a creamier texture; and a fresher flavor. Libby's introduction of solid-packed canned pumpkin in 1929 dramatically transformed America's humble pumpkin-pie-making efforts.

Besides being scrumptious, pumpkin is a rich, natural source of many important nutrients: vitamin A in the beta carotene form, vitamin C, potassium, iron, riboflavin, calcium, and protein. The calorie count, at 80 calories per cup, is low. One-third of the solids in a can of Libby's® pumpkin is natural dietary fiber.

Poet John Greenleaf Whittier has given us this beautiful thought for pumpkin pie makers: "And thy life be as sweet and its last sunset sky, golden-tinted and fair as thy own pumpkin pie!"

HARVEST CHERRY PIE

BORDEN, INC.

Makes one 9-inch pie

½ jar (1⅓ cups) None-Such® Ready-to-Use
   Mincemeat (Regular *or* Brandy & Rum)
¾ cup chopped nuts

Pastry for 2-crust pie
1 can (21 ounces) cherry pie filling
1 egg yolk *plus* 2 tablespoons water
   (optional)

Place rack in lower half of oven; preheat oven to 425°F. Combine mincemeat and nuts; turn into pastry-lined 9-inch pie plate. Spoon cherry pie filling over mincemeat. Cover with top crust; cut slits near center. Seal and flute. For a more golden crust, mix egg yolk and water; brush over entire surface of pie. Bake 25 to 30 minutes or until golden brown. Serve warm or cool. Garnish as desired.

OLD-FASHIONED APPLE CRUMB PIE

PET INCORPORATED

Makes 8 servings

⅔ cup granulated sugar
2 tablespoons all-purpose flour
¼ teaspoon cinnamon
¼ teaspoon nutmeg
5 cups cored and sliced apples

1 Pet•Ritz® Deep Dish Pie Crust Shell
¾ cup flour
¼ cup butter *or* margarine
¼ cup firmly packed brown sugar
La Creme® Whipped Topping, thawed

Preheat oven and baking sheet to 400°F. In large bowl, combine granulated sugar, 2 tablespoons flour, cinnamon, and nutmeg; mix well. Add apple slices and mix until apples are evenly coated; spoon into pie crust. For crumb topping, in a small bowl, combine ¾ *cup* flour, butter, and brown sugar until crumbly. Sprinkle topping over apples. Place pie on baking sheet and bake for 30 to 40 minutes. Allow to cool 1 hour before serving. Top with whipped topping.

PEACHY MINCE PIE WITH CHEDDAR CRUST

BORDEN, INC.

Makes one 9-inch pie

1 package (9 ounces) pie crust mix
1 cup (4 ounces) shredded sharp
   Cheddar cheese
1 jar (27 ounces) None Such® Ready-to-
   Use Mincemeat (Regular *or* Brandy &
   Rum)

1 can (16 ounces) sliced peaches, drained
1 egg yolk *plus* 2 tablespoons water
   (optional)

Place rack in lower half of oven; preheat oven to 425°F. Prepare pie-crust mix as package directs for 2-crust pie, adding cheese. Turn mincemeat into pastry-lined 9-inch pie plate. Top with peach slices. Cover with top crust; cut slits near center. Seal and flute. For a more golden crust, mix egg yolk and water; brush over entire surface of pie. Bake 20 minutes or until golden. Serve warm or cool. Garnish as desired.

MAPLE PECAN PIE

BORDEN, INC.

Makes one 9-inch pie

3 eggs, beaten
1 cup Cary's®, Maple Orchards®, *or*
   MacDonald's™ Pure Maple Syrup
½ cup firmly packed light brown sugar

2 tablespoons butter *or* margarine,
   melted
1 teaspoon vanilla extract
1¼ cups pecan halves *or* pieces
1 (9-inch) unbaked pastry shell

Place rack in lowest position in oven; preheat oven to 350°F. In bowl, combine all ingredients except pastry shell. Pour into pastry shell. Bake 35 to 40 minutes or until golden. Cool. Chill if desired. Refrigerate leftovers.

SOUTHERN CHOCOLATE
PRALINE CREME SWIRL PIE
PET INCORPORATED

Makes 8 servings

½ cup granulated sugar
¼ cup brown sugar
3 tablespoons cornstarch
½ teaspoon salt
1 can (12 fluid ounces) Pet® Evaporated
  Milk
3 egg yolks, beaten
1 cup sour cream
1 tablespoon butter

3 tablespoons praline liqueur
1 teaspoon vanilla extract
½ cup semisweet chocolate chips
1 Pet•Ritz® Deep Dish Pie Crust Shell,
  baked
1 container (8 ounces) La Creme®
  Whipped Topping, thawed
2 tablespoons semisweet chocolate chips
  for garnish

In medium bowl, combine granulated sugar, brown sugar, cornstarch, and salt; mix well. In heavy saucepan on medium heat, cook and stir sugar mixture and evaporated milk until mixture thickens and begins to boil. Gradually stir one-fourth of hot mixture into beaten egg yolks; add back to remaining hot mixture, stirring constantly. Stir in sour cream and butter and continue to cook until mixture thickens. Remove from heat and stir in praline liqueur and vanilla, mixing well. Stir in chocolate chips until distributed but *not* melted. Pour mixture into pie crust. Let stand 2 minutes; gently swirl mixture with knife blade, creating a marbled effect. Refrigerate 30 minutes. Spoon dollops of whipped topping around edge of pie, leaving center open with marbling showing. Sprinkle chocolate chips over topping. Refrigerate several hours before serving.

CINNAMON FRUIT TART
WITH SOUR CREAM FILLING

THOMAS J. LIPTON CO.

Makes 1 tart, 12 servings

1 envelope Knox® Unflavored Gelatine
¼ cup cold water
1 cup (8 ounces) creamed cottage cheese
¾ cup pineapple juice
½ cup sour cream
½ cup milk
¼ cup sugar

1 teaspoon lemon juice
Cinnamon Graham-Cracker Crust (see below)
2 cups any combination of fresh sliced strawberries, kiwi, or oranges; blueberries; and raspberries
2 tablespoons orange or apricot marmalade, melted

In small saucepan, sprinkle unflavored gelatine over cold water; let stand 1 minute. Stir over low heat until gelatine is completely dissolved, about 3 minutes.

In blender or food processor, process cottage cheese, pineapple juice, sour cream, milk, sugar, and lemon juice until blended. While processing, through feed cap, gradually add gelatine mixture and process until blended. Pour into Cinnamon Graham-Cracker Crust; chill until firm, about 3 hours. To serve, top with fresh fruit; then brush with marmalade.

CINNAMON GRAHAM-CRACKER CRUST

¼ cup melted butter
1 tablespoon water
2 cups graham-cracker crumbs

1 tablespoon sugar
½ teaspoon ground cinnamon

Blend butter and water. In small bowl, combine all ingredients. Press into 10-inch tart pan. Refrigerate about 30 minutes before filling.

MAPLE BREAD PUDDING

BORDEN, INC.

Makes 6 to 8 servings

12 slices 1-inch-thick French bread
  or 5 cups (about 6 ounces) French
  bread cubes
3 eggs
2½ cups Borden® *or* Meadow Gold® milk
⅓ cup Cary's®, Maple Orchards®, *or*
  MacDonald's™ Pure Maple Syrup

¼ cup firmly packed light brown sugar
3 tablespoons margarine *or* butter,
  melted
½ teaspoon ground cinnamon
⅛ teaspoon ground nutmeg
Maple Almond Sauce (see below)

Preheat oven to 325°F. Arrange bread in 8-inch square baking dish or pan. In medium bowl, beat eggs. Add remaining ingredients except Maple Almond Sauce; mix well. Pour over bread, moistening completely. Bake 50 minutes or until knife inserted near center comes out clean. Serve warm or cold with warm Maple Almond Sauce. Refrigerate leftovers.

MAPLE ALMOND SAUCE

Makes about ¾ cup

¼ cup water
2 teaspoons cornstarch
2 tablespoons margarine *or* butter

½ cup Cary's®, Maple Orchards®, *or*
  MacDonald's™ Pure Maple Syrup
2 tablespoons toasted sliced almonds

Combine water and cornstarch. In small saucepan, melt margarine. Add pure maple syrup and cornstarch mixture; cook and stir until slightly thickened. Remove from heat. Stir in almonds.

THE GAIL BORDEN STORY
The Story of Sweetened Condensed Milk

The name Borden has blazed brightly in American food-product history. The son of a frontiersman, Gail Borden was born in New York in 1801 and started his career as a schoolteacher in Mississippi. He worked his way further across the country, landing in Texas in time to work in politics and help write that state's first constitution. Borden is credited with originating the battle cry "Remember the Alamo!" as a headline while writing newspaper reports of the heroic Texan struggle for independence from Mexico.

Borden became interested in scientific food preservation and developed his first product, a dehydrated meat biscuit, in Galveston, Texas. This nutritious hardtack sustained California gold seekers and the U.S. Army in 1849. For this invention, Borden was awarded a Gold Medal from Queen Victoria at the International Exposition in London in 1851. The meat biscuit wasn't a commercial success, however, because it didn't taste good.

His funds depleted, Borden was forced to return to America in steerage class with poor southern and eastern European immigrants. The cows that had been brought on board to provide milk were diseased. Borden witnessed many sick infants dying in their mothers' arms from the infected raw milk. Haunted by the sadness of those scenes, he vowed to do something about it.

In Lebanon, New York, he watched the Shakers, a religious sect, to learn their method of vacuum cooking to preserve fruit. Borden spent many months with the religious community developing and refining a similar procedure for removing water from milk to condense it.

In France at the time, Louis Pasteur was experimenting with ways to preserve milk, but he didn't yet understand the complete process of sterilization. Gail Borden learned that enough sugar in a product could retard bacterial growth. His genius was to add sugar to his condensed milk to prevent spoilage. In 1856, at age fifty-five, he received the first patent for the sweetened condensed milk that would be the beginning of one of America's greatest food corporations.

The Union Army ordered such large quantities of Borden's condensed milk to feed the troops during the Civil War that Borden was forced to license other manufacturers to help fill the quotas. He was incensed when he discovered that many licensees were selling an inferior product and chose the American Bald Eagle to represent the safe and wholesome qualities of his milk. Eagle Brand remains the name of his product today.

The Civil War propelled the Borden canned milk product into national consciousness. Returning to the North when the fighting had ended, Union soldiers remembered the sweet taste of the convenient food, and the ravaged South relied heavily on canned foods like Borden's milk to stave off starvation during the Reconstruction period.

Borden's milk also saved the lives of many infants in North America. Mothers followed feeding instructions on every Eagle Brand label until 1938, when doctors took over the business of prescribing infant formulas.

Refrigerators as standard household appliances capable of storing fresh whole milk changed the role of canned milk after World War I. But during the forties, sugar became scarce, and Eagle Brand found a second role as a popular and convenient ingredient for homemade desserts.

Through the years, the Borden Company has been a milk-industry leader with a flow of innovations. Borden was the first company to sell fresh milk in bottles in 1885, the first to homogenize milk in 1927, and the first to fortify milk with vitamin D. Research at the company's Endicott, New York, plant led to the first federal pasteurization standards. And Borden continues to satisfy the needs of today's consumers with high-quality and wholesome product innovations in the Gail Borden tradition.

CREAMY BANANA PUDDING
BORDEN, INC.

Makes 8 to 10 servings

1 can (14 ounces) Eagle® Brand Sweetened Condensed Milk (*not* evaporated milk)

1½ cups cold water

1 package (4-serving size) *instant* vanilla-flavor pudding mix

2 cups (1 pint) Borden® *or* Meadow Gold® Whipping Cream, whipped

36 vanilla wafers

3 medium bananas, sliced and dipped in ReaLemon® Lemon Juice from Concentrate

In large bowl, combine sweetened condensed milk and water. Add pudding mix; beat well. Chill 5 minutes. Fold in whipped cream. Spoon *1 cup* pudding mixture into 2½-quart glass serving bowl. Top with one-third *each* of the wafers, bananas, and pudding. Repeat layering twice, ending with pudding. Cover; chill. Garnish as desired. Refrigerate leftovers.

(Tip: Mixture can be layered in individual serving dishes.)

ALL-TIME FAVORITE PUFF PUDDING

KRAFT GENERAL FOODS, INC.

Makes 8 servings

¼ cup (½ stick) Parkay Margarine
½ cup sugar *or* honey
1 teaspoon grated lemon rind
2 egg yolks
3 tablespoons lemon juice
2 Tablespoons all-purpose flour

¼ cup Post® Grape-Nuts® *or* Raisin Grape-Nuts® Cereal *or* ½ C. W. Post® Hearty Granola Cereal
1 cup milk
2 egg whites, stiffly beaten
Cream *or* prepared whipped topping (optional)

Preheat oven to 325°F. Beat butter with sugar and lemon rind until light and fluffy. Beat in egg yolks. Stir in lemon juice, flour, cereal, and milk. (Mixture will look curdled, but this will not affect finished product.) Fold in beaten egg whites. Pour into greased 1-quart baking dish; place dish in pan of hot water. Bake 1 hour and 15 minutes or until top springs back when lightly touched. When done, pudding has a cakelike layer on top with custard below. Serve warm or cold with cream or prepared whipped topping, if desired.

For individual puddings, pour mixture into five 5-ounce or four 6-ounce custard cups or soufflé cups. Bake about 40 minutes.

INDIAN PUDDING
NABISCO FOODS GROUP

Makes 8 servings

4 cups skim milk
¾ cup uncooked Regular, Quick, or Instant
   Cream Of Wheat® Cereal
2 tablespoons Blue Bonnet® Margarine
½ cup Brer Rabbit® Light Molasses

I egg, slightly beaten, *or* ¼ cup Egg
   Beaters® 99% Real Egg Product
¼ cup firmly packed light brown sugar
¾ teaspoon ground cinnamon
½ teaspoon ground ginger
Ice milk, (optional)

Preheat oven to 350°F. In large saucepan, over medium heat, bring milk to a boil; gradually sprinkle in cereal, stirring constantly. Heat to a boil, stirring constantly; reduce heat. Cook 5 minutes for regular, 3 to 4 minutes for quick, and 2 to 3 minutes for instant, stirring occasionally until thickened. Remove from heat; stir in margarine, molasses, egg, brown sugar, cinnamon, and ginger.

   Spoon mixture into 8 greased custard cups (6-ounce size) or 1½-quart greased casserole. Bake 20 minutes for custard cups or 35 minutes for casserole. Serve warm with ice milk, if desired.

CHEESY APPLE YORKSHIRE PUDDING
BEATRICE CHEESE, INC.

Makes 4 to 5 servings

2 eggs
½ cup all-purpose flour, sifted
¼ teaspoon salt
½ cup milk

2 medium apples, thinly sliced
⅓ cup County Line® Medium Sharp
   Cheddar Cheese, grated
¼ cup melted butter

Preheat oven to 425°F. In mixer bowl, beat eggs until light and fluffy. Sift together flour and salt; mix with *¼ cup* milk. Add to eggs along with remaining milk; beat until smooth. Fold in apples, cheese, and melted butter; pour into a greased 8-inch baking pan. Bake 30 minutes.

   Serve hot with butter and powdered sugar.

ORIGINAL BANANA PUDDING

NABISCO FOODS GROUP

Makes 8 servings

½ cup sugar
3 tablespoons all-purpose flour
Dash salt
4 eggs
2 cups milk

½ teaspoon vanilla extract
43 Nilla® Wafers
5 to 6 medium-ripe bananas, sliced
(about 4 cups)

Preheat oven to 425°F. Reserve 2 tablespoons sugar. In top of double boiler, combine remaining sugar, flour, and salt. Beat in 1 whole egg and 3 egg yolks; reserve 3 egg whites. Stir in milk. Cook, uncovered, over boiling water, stirring constantly 10 minutes or until thickened. Remove from heat; stir in vanilla.

In bottom of 1½-quart round casserole, spoon ½ *cup* custard; cover with 8 wafers. Top with generous layer of sliced bananas; pour ⅔ *cup* custard over bananas. Arrange 10 wafers around outside edge of dish; cover custard with 11 wafers. Top with sliced bananas and ⅔ *cup* custard. Cover custard with 14 wafers; top with sliced bananas and remaining custard.

In small bowl, with electric mixer at high speed, beat reserved egg whites until soft peaks form. Gradually add reserved *2 tablespoons* sugar, beating until mixture forms stiff peaks. Spoon on top of custard, spreading to cover entire surface.

Bake 5 minutes, or until surface is lightly browned. Garnish with additional banana slices if desired. Serve warm or cold.

VARIATION

Quick Banana Pudding: Prepare 1 package (6-serving size) Royal® Instant Vanilla Pudding and Pie Filling according to package directions. Layer prepared pudding with wafers and bananas as above. Cover; chill at least 3 hours. Garnish with 2 cups prepared whipped topping and additional banana slices.

MEXICAN CUSTARD
DURKEE-FRENCH FOODS

Makes 10 to 12 servings

1 cup sugar
1/4 cup water
6 large eggs
2 cups milk

1 teaspoon Durkee® Vanilla
1/2 teaspoon Durkee® Ground Cinnamon
1/4 teaspoon Durkee® Ground Ginger
Assorted fruit (optional)

Preheat oven to 350°F. In heavy saucepan, combine 1/2 *cup* sugar and water. Bring to a boil, stirring until sugar dissolves. Continue boiling 6 minutes or until mixture becomes a light caramel color, stirring occasionally. Pour sugar syrup into greased 6-cup ring mold. Holding mold with pot holders, quickly rotate mold so syrup coats the bottom evenly. In a medium bowl, combine 1/2 *cup* sugar, eggs, milk, vanilla, and spices; mix well. Pour egg mixture into mold. Place mold in roasting pan filled with water 1 inch deep. Bake, uncovered, 55 minutes or until knife inserted in center comes out clean. Cool to room temperature. Loosen edge of custard with spatula and invert onto serving dish. Spoon any remaining caramel on top of custard; garnish with fruit, if desired.

ST. TROPEZ HOLIDAY CRANBERRY MOUSSE
DOLE FOOD COMPANY

Makes 8 to 10 servings

1 can (20 ounces) Dole® Crushed
   Pineapple
1 cup water
2 packages (3 ounces each) strawberry
   gelatin

1 can (16 ounces) whole-berry
   cranberry sauce
Zest and juice from 1 Dole® Lemon
1/4 teaspoon ground nutmeg
2 cups dairy sour cream
1/2 cup Dole® Chopped Almonds, toasted

Drain pineapple well; reserve all juice. Heat juice and water to boiling. Stir into gelatin to dissolve. Blend in cranberry sauce. Add 1 teaspoon lemon zest, 3 table-spoons lemon juice, and nutmeg. Chill until mixture thickens slightly. Blend in sour cream. Fold in pineapple and almonds. Pour into 2-quart mold. Chill until firm. Unmold onto serving plate.

WHITE CHOCOLATE MOUSSE

MCCORMICK & COMPANY, INC.

Makes 3 cups

16 ounces white chocolate
2 egg whites
¼ cup sugar
1 cup whipping cream
¼ cup confectioners' sugar

1 teaspoon pure McCormick/Schilling®
Vanilla Extract
½ teaspoon McCormick/Schilling imitation
Rum Extract
Cherry Sauce (optional; see below)

Melt white chocolate in stainless steel bowl over hot water. Beat egg whites until foamy. Gradually add sugar, beating until stiff peaks form when beaters are lifted. Whip cream with confectioners' sugar and extracts. Fold together chocolate, egg whites, and cream. Spoon into dessert glasses. Chill. If desired, layer with Cherry Sauce or serve sauce separately.

CHERRY SAUCE

Makes 1 cup

1 cup cherry pie filling
¼ teaspoon McCormick/Schilling®
Cinnamon

⅛ teaspoon McCormick/Schilling Almond
Extract

In food processor, mix ingredients. Run food processor 3 seconds. Scrape down sides of bowl and run 2 more seconds.

PIÑA COLADA SOUFFLÉ

MCCORMICK & COMPANY, INC.

Makes 16 servings, ½ cup each

2 envelopes unflavored gelatin
1½ cups canned pineapple juice, chilled
8 eggs, separated
½ teaspoon salt
1 cup sugar
⅛ teaspoon ground McCormick/Schilling® Mace
⅛ teaspoon ground McCormick/Schilling Cardamom

½ teaspoon McCormick/Schilling imitation Rum Extract
1 cup whipping cream
2 tablespoons confectioners' sugar
¼ cup dark rum
1 cup cream of coconut
Sweetened whipped cream

Soften gelatin in *½ cup* cold pineapple juice. In top of double boiler, combine egg yolks, salt, *¼ cup* sugar, mace, cardamom, and remaining *1 cup* pineapple juice. Cook over boiling water, stirring constantly, until slightly thickened. Add gelatin mixture and rum extract. Stir until gelatin is dissolved. Pour into large bowl. Cool. To prepare 6-cup soufflé dish, fold a 30-inch strip of foil in half lengthwise. Tie foil with string around outside of dish to make a collar standing about 5 inches above rim. Beat egg whites until foamy. Gradually add remaining *¾ cup* sugar. Beat until stiff peaks form when beaters are lifted. Whip cream with confectioners' sugar. Add rum and cream of coconut to gelatin mixture. Stir well. Gently fold in egg whites and whipped cream. Pour into prepared soufflé dish. Refrigerate at least 3 hours. Cut string and carefully remove foil collar. Garnish soufflé with sweetened whipped cream.

FOOD OF THE GODS
The Story of Chocolate and Milton S. Hershey

More than two thousand years ago, the ancient Mayans worshiped the cacao bean as an idol. In fact, the scientific name for the cacao bean, *Theobraom cacao*, means "food of the gods."

The Spanish adventurers in Hernando Cortés' 1518 Mexican expedition watched with fascination as the last Aztec emperor, Montezuma II, drank from golden goblets filled with a bitter, spicy liquid prepared from roasted and ground cacao beans and chilled with snow carried down from the high sierra slopes. The drink was considered so prestigious that the golden goblets in which it was served were discarded after one use.

Cortés brought cacao beans back to Spain, where the nobility reserved for themselves exclusive rights to enjoy a heated chocolate drink prepared with cane sugar, another New World food discovery. The formula was too delicious to keep secret for long, however, and by the mid-1600s the chocolate drink was widely appreciated throughout France. The first chocolate shop was opened in England, and by the 1700s chocolate houses flourished and competed with coffeehouses throughout the country.

The New World's first chocolate-manufacturing facility was opened near Dorchester, Massachussetts, in 1765. Sixty years later a Dutch chemist, Conrad Van Houten, devised a chocolate press to mold cocoa butter and finely ground sugar into bar shapes.

Two Swiss contributions greatly enhanced the pleasures to be derived from the cacao bean. The Swiss learned to make smoother chocolate using a process called *conching*. The word *conch* comes from a Greek word meaning seashell and refers to the shape of the vat used to grind chocolate particles into a satiny texture. To cocoa liquor, a nonalcoholic end product of the bean, the Swiss added condensed milk to make the world's first milk chocolate. The later addition of fresh milk to produce superior candy would establish one of the United States' great fortunes.

Milton S. Hershey started life on a central Pennsylvania farm as a poor boy who dropped out of school before he was fourteen years old to apprentice with a printer. Soon he was fired after he dropped his straw hat into the printing press. His mother found him work as a candy maker's apprentice. Hershey spent his younger years learning to make good candy. He failed in several candy-making ventures before he began work with a Denver candy manufacturer who taught him to make incomparable caramels by adding milk to them.

Hershey raised capital to start the Lancaster Caramel Company in Lancaster, Pennsylvania. The German chocolate-manufacturing equipment displayed at the Chicago International Exposition in 1893 captured his interest. He purchased the equipment and was soon producing chocolate-covered caramels. Other chocolate experiments during this period led to some of today's major chocolate products: HERSHEY'S milk chocolate bar, HERSHEY'S milk chocolate bar with almonds, HERSHEY'S cocoa, and HERSHEY'S baking chocolate.

Hershey sold the Lancaster Caramel Company for $1 million in 1900 but retained the chocolate-manufacturing equipment and the rights to produce chocolate. His concept of a quality and affordable chocolate bar for the masses would make him the Henry Ford of the chocolate business.

In 1903 Hershey began building the world's largest chocolate-manufacturing facility to mass-produce milk chocolate. The chocolate business flourished. Hershey built a community for the workers, including churches, a school, a bank, a department store, golf courses, a zoo, and a trolley system to bring employees from nearby towns. The company is still headquartered in Hershey, Pennsylvania, where the aroma of chocolate wafts over the town.

Milton S. Hershey died at age eighty-eight, leaving the legacy that makes the company the leading chocolate and confectionery manufacturer in North America. He is remembered as the rarest of men, a dreamer as well as a builder, a philanthropic man who was acutely aware of the moral need to share the fruits of his success. The Milton Hershey School for orphaned boys, founded by Milton Hershey and his wife in 1909, became and continues to be the principal recipient of the Hershey fortune.

REESE'S® CHEWY CHOCOLATE COOKIES

HERSHEY FOODS CORPORATION

Makes about 4½ dozen cookies

1¼ cups (2½ sticks) butter *or* margarine, softened

2 cups sugar

2 eggs

2 teaspoons vanilla extract

2 cups all-purpose flour

¾ cup Hershey's® Cocoa

1 teaspoon baking soda

½ teaspoon salt

1⅔ cups (10-oz. pkg.) Reese's® Peanut Butter Chips

Heat oven to 350°F. In large mixer bowl, beat butter and sugar until light and fluffy. Add eggs and vanilla; beat well. Stir together flour, cocoa, baking soda, and salt; gradually blend into butter mixture. Stir in chips. Drop by rounded teaspoonfuls onto ungreased cookie sheet. Bake 8 to 9 minutes. (Do not overbake; cookies will be soft. They will puff while baking and flatten while cooling.) Cool slightly; remove from cookie sheet to wire rack. Cool completely.

VARIATIONS

Pan Recipe: Spread batter in greased 15½-by-10½-by-1-inch jelly-roll pan. Bake at 350°F for 20 minutes or until set. Cool completely in pan on wire rack; cut into bars. Makes about 4 dozen bars.

Ice Cream Sandwiches: Prepare cookies as directed; cool. Press small scoop of vanilla ice cream between flat sides of cookies. Wrap and freeze.

REESE'S® COOKIES

HERSHEY FOODS CORPORATION

Makes about 5 dozen cookies

1 cup shortening *or* ¾ cup (1½ sticks) butter *or* margarine, softened

1 cup granulated sugar

½ cup packed light brown sugar

1 teaspoon vanilla extract

2 eggs

2 cups all-purpose flour

1 teaspoon baking soda

1⅔ cups (10-oz. pkg.) Reese's® Peanut Butter Chips

⅔ cup Hershey's® Semi-sweet *or* Milk Chocolate Chips

Heat oven to 350°F. In large mixer bowl beat shortening, granulated sugar, brown sugar, and vanilla. Add eggs; beat well. Stir together flour and baking soda; blend into sugar mixture. Stir in chips. Drop by rounded teaspoonfuls onto ungreased cookie sheet. Bake 8 to 10 minutes or until lightly browned. Cool slightly; remove from cookie sheet onto wire rack. Cool completely.

MINI CHIPS BLONDIES

HERSHEY FOODS CORPORATION

Makes about 3 dozen bars

¾ cup (1½ sticks) butter *or* margarine, softened

1½ cups packed light brown sugar

2 eggs

2 tablespoons milk

1 teaspoon vanilla extract

2 cups all-purpose flour

1 teaspoon baking powder

¼ teaspoon baking soda

¼ teaspoon salt

2 cups (12-oz. pkg.) Hershey's® Mini Chips® Semi-sweet chocolate

Heat oven to 350°F. Grease 13-by-9-by-2-inch pan, set aside. In large mixer bowl, cream butter and brown sugar until light and fluffy. Add eggs, milk, and vanilla; beat well. Combine flour, baking powder, baking soda, and salt; add to creamed mixture. Stir in chocolate. Spread into prepared pan. Bake 30 to 35 minutes or until lightly browned. Cool completely; cut into bars.

CHOCOLATE-CARAMEL BARS

GENERAL MILLS, INC.

Makes 32 bars

1 package (14 ounces) vanilla caramels
⅔ cup evaporated milk
1 package Betty Crocker® SuperMoist®
  German Chocolate Cake Mix
½ cup margarine *or* butter, melted

¼ teaspoon vanilla
1 package (6 ounces) semi-sweet
  chocolate chips
¼ cup chopped nuts
¼ cup flaked coconut

Preheat oven to 350°F. Heat caramels and ⅓ *cup* evaporated milk in 2-quart sauce-pan over low heat, stirring occasionally, until caramels are melted and mixture is smooth. Mix cake mix (dry), margarine, remaining ⅓ *cup* evaporated milk, and vanilla in large bowl (mixture will be thick). With rubber spatula, pat half of mixture in bottom of ungreased 13-by-9-by-2-inch pan. Bake 6 minutes. Sprinkle with chocolate chips; pour caramel mixture over chocolate chips. Break remaining cake mixture into small pieces evenly over caramel mixture; sprinkle with nuts and coconut. Bake about 16 minutes or until coconut is light golden brown; cool. Cut into 2-by-½-inch bars.

THE ULTIMATE CHOCOLATE CHIP COOKIE

GENERAL MILLS, INC.

Makes 18 cookies

1 cup packed brown sugar
¾ cup granulated sugar
1 cup margarine *or* butter, softened
1 teaspoon vanilla
2 eggs
2½ cups Gold Medal® All-Purpose Flour
  (*not* self-rising flour)

¾ teaspoon baking soda
¾ teaspoon salt
12 ounces semi-sweet chocolate *or* milk
  chocolate, coarsely chopped, *or* semi-
  sweet chocolate chips (2 cups)
1 cup chopped walnuts

Preheat oven to 375°F. Beat sugars and margarine in large bowl on medium speed about 5 minutes or until fluffy. Beat in vanilla and eggs. Beat in flour, baking soda, and salt on low speed. Stir in chocolate and walnuts. Drop dough by ¼ cupfuls about 2 inches apart onto ungreased cookie sheet; flatten slightly with fork. Bake 11 to 14 minutes or until edges are light brown. Let stand 3 to 4 minutes before removing from cookie sheet. Cool on wire rack.

HERSHEY'S® PREMIUM
DOUBLE CHOCOLATE DROP COOKIES

HERSHEY FOODS CORPORATION

Makes about 3½ dozen cookies

1 cup (2 sticks) butter, softened
1½ cups sugar
2 eggs
2 teaspoons vanilla extract
2 cups all-purpose flour

⅔ cup Hershey's® Cocoa
¾ teaspoon baking soda
¼ teaspoon salt
½ cup toasted, slivered almonds
1¾ cups (10-oz. pkg.) Hershey's®
  Premium Milk Chocolate Chunks

Heat oven to 350°F. In large mixer bowl, beat butter, sugar, eggs, and vanilla until light and fluffy. Stir together flour, cocoa, baking soda, and salt; add to creamed mixture. Stir in almonds and milk chocolate chunks. Drop by tablespoonfuls onto ungreased cookie sheets. Bake 8 to 10 minutes or just until set. Cool slightly; remove from cookie sheet onto wire rack. Cool completely.

To toast almonds: Preheat oven to 350°F. On shallow baking pan, place slivered almonds; toast until lightly browned, about 8 to 10 minutes.

HERSHEY'S® DOUBLE CHOCOLATE
MINT COOKIES

HERSHEY FOODS CORPORATION

Makes about 2½ dozen cookies

⅔ cup butter or margarine, softened
1 cup sugar
1 egg
1 teaspoon vanilla extract
1 cup all-purpose flour

½ cup Hershey's Cocoa
½ teaspoon baking soda
¼ teaspoon salt
1⅔ cups (10-oz. pkg.) Hershey's® Mint
  Chocolate Chips

Heat oven to 350°F. In large mixer bowl, beat butter and sugar until light and fluffy. Add egg and vanilla; beat well. Combine flour, cocoa, baking soda, and salt; gradually blend into butter mixture. Stir in mint chocolate chips. Drop by rounded teaspoonfuls onto ungreased cookie sheet. Bake 8 to 9 minutes, or just until set; do not overbake. Cool slightly; remove from cookie sheet onto wire rack. Cool completely.

HERSHEY'S® VANILLA CHIP CHOCOLATE COOKIES

HERSHEY FOODS CORPORATION

Makes about 4½ dozen cookies

1¼ cups (2½ sticks) butter *or* margarine, softened

2 cups sugar

2 eggs

2 teaspoons vanilla extract

2 cups all-purpose flour

¾ cup Hershey's® Cocoa

1 teaspoon baking soda

½ teaspoon salt

1⅔ cups (10-oz. pkg.) Hershey's® vanilla milk chips

Heat oven to 350°F. In large mixer bowl, beat butter and sugar until creamy. Add eggs and vanilla extract; beat until light and fluffy. Stir together flour, cocoa, baking soda, and salt; gradually blend into butter mixture. Stir in vanilla milk chips. Drop by rounded teaspoonfuls onto ungreased cookie sheet. Bake 8 to 9 minutes. (Do not overbake; cookies will be soft. They will puff while baking; flatten upon cooling.) Cool slightly; remove from cookie sheet to wire rack. Cool completely.

HERSHEY'S® VANILLA MILK CHIP COOKIES

HERSHEY FOODS CORPORATION

Makes about 5 dozen cookies

1 cup (2 sticks) butter, softened

¾ cup granulated sugar

¾ cup packed light brown sugar

1 teaspoon vanilla extract

2 eggs

2¼ cups all-purpose flour

1 teaspoon baking soda

½ teaspoon salt

1⅔ cups (10-oz. pkg.) Hershey's® Vanilla Milk Chips

1 cup chopped nuts (optional)

Heat oven to 375°F. In large mixer bowl, beat butter, granulated sugar, brown sugar, and vanilla until light and fluffy. Add eggs; beat well. Stir together flour, baking soda, and salt; gradually add to butter mixture. Beat well. Stir in vanilla milk chips and nuts, if desired. Drop by rounded teaspoonfuls onto ungreased cookie sheet. Bake 8 to 10 minutes or until very lightly browned. Cool slightly; remove from cookie sheet to wire rack. Cool completely.

MAGIC COOKIE BARS

BORDEN, INC.

Makes 24 to 36 bars

½ cup margarine *or* butter

1½ cups graham cracker crumbs

1 can (14 ounces) Eagle® Brand Sweetened Condensed Milk (*not evaporated milk*)

1 cup (6 ounces) semi-sweet chocolate chips

1 can (3½ ounces; 1⅓ cups) flaked coconut

1 cup chopped nuts

Preheat oven to 350°F. (325°F. for glass dish). In 13-by-9-inch baking pan, melt margarine in oven. Sprinkle crumbs over margarine; pour sweetened condensed milk evenly over crumbs. Top with remaining ingredients; press down firmly. Bake 25 to 30 minutes or until lightly browned. Cool. Chill, if desired. Cut into bars. Store, loosely covered, at room temperature.

VARIATION

Seven-Layer Magic Cookie Bars: Add 1 package (6 ounces) butterscotch-flavored chips after chocolate chips.

CHOCOLATE SPICE COOKIES

BORDEN, INC.

Makes about 6 dozen cookies

2 cups unsifted flour
½ cup unsweetened cocoa
I teaspoon baking soda
½ teaspoon salt
I¼ cups sugar
¾ cup shortening
¼ cup margarine *or* butter, softened

2 eggs
2 teaspoons vanilla extract
I package (9 ounces) None Such®
  Condensed Mincemeat, crumbled
I cup chopped nuts (optional)
Chocolate Glaze (see below)
Candied cherry halves (optional)

Preheat oven to 350°F. Stir together flour, cocoa, baking soda, and salt; set aside. In large mixer bowl, beat sugar, shortening, and margarine until fluffy. Beat in eggs and vanilla. Add flour mixture; mix well. Stir in mincemeat and, if desired, nuts. Roll into 1-inch balls; place 2 inches apart on ungreased baking sheets. Flatten slightly. Bake 8 to 10 minutes or until almost no imprint remains when lightly touched (*do not overbake*). Cool. Spread with Chocolate Glaze. Garnish with candied cherries, if desired.

CHOCOLATE GLAZE

Makes about ¾ cup

3 squares (I ounce each) semi-sweet
  chocolate
6 tablespoons water
2 tablespoons margarine *or* butter

2 cups sifted confectioners' sugar
I teaspoon vanilla
⅛ teaspoon salt

In medium saucepan, combine chocolate, water, and margarine. Over medium heat, cook and stir until chocolate melts and mixture is smooth. Remove from heat; stir in sugar, vanilla, and salt.

PECAN PIE BARS

BEST FOODS, A DIVISION OF CPC INTERNATIONAL INC.

Makes 4 dozen bars

Bar Cookie Crust (see below)
4 eggs
1½ cups Karo® Light or Dark Corn Syrup
1½ cups sugar

3 tablespoons Mazola® Margarine,
  melted
1½ teaspoons vanilla
2½ cups chopped pecans

Preheat oven to 350°F. Prepare Bar Cookie Crust. In large bowl, beat eggs, corn syrup, sugar, margarine, and vanilla until well blended. Stir in pecans. Pour over hot crust; spread evenly. Bake 25 minutes or until filling is firm around edges and slightly firm in center. Cool completely on wire rack before cutting.

BAR COOKIE CRUST

2½ cups flour
1 cup cold Mazola® Margarine, cut in
  ½-inch pieces

½ cup confectioners' sugar
¼ teaspoon salt

Preheat oven to 350°F. Grease 15-by-10-by-1-inch baking pan. In large bowl with mixer at medium speed, beat flour, margarine, confectioners' sugar, and salt until mixture resembles coarse crumbs; press firmly and evenly into prepared pan. Bake 20 minutes or until golden brown.

CAKE MIX COOKIES

GENERAL MILLS, INC.

Makes about 4 dozen cookies

1 package Betty Crocker® SuperMoist® Cake Mix (any flavor except fudge marble or carrot)

½ cup shortening

⅓ cup margarine *or* butter, softened

½ teaspoon vanilla

1 egg

Preheat oven to 375°F. Mix about half of cake mix (dry), with shortening, margarine, vanilla, and egg in large bowl until well mixed. Stir in remaining cake mix.

Drop dough by rounded teaspoonfuls about 2 inches apart onto ungreased cookie sheet. Bake 9 to 11 minutes (centers will be soft). Cool 1 minute before removing from cookie sheet.

VARIATION

Mix ½ *cup* chopped nuts into dough. Shape dough by scant teaspoonfuls into balls. Place on ungreased cookie sheet. Bake 9 to 11 minutes (centers will be soft). Cool 1 minute before removing from cookie sheet.

GIANT SKIPPY® OAT COOKIES

BEST FOODS, A DIVISION OF CPC INTERNATIONAL INC.

Makes about 24 cookies

1¼ cups flour

1 teaspoon baking powder

1 teaspoon baking soda

¼ teaspoon salt

2½ cups quick oats

1 cup Mazola® Corn Oil Margarine

1 cup Skippy® Creamy *or* Super Chunk® Peanut Butter

1 cup sugar

1 cup firmly packed brown sugar

2 eggs

1 teaspoon vanilla

Preheat oven to 350°F. In medium bowl, stir flour, baking powder, baking soda, and salt. Mix in oats. Set aside. In large bowl with mixer at medium speed, beat margarine and peanut butter until smooth. Beat in sugars until blended. Beat in eggs and vanilla. Add flour/oat mixture; by hand, mix until well combined. Shape into 2-inch balls. Place 6 balls on ungreased cookie sheet; flatten each to 3-inch diameter. Bake 15 to 17 minutes or until golden. Remove from cookie sheet. Cool completely on wire rack. Store in tightly covered container.

BEST EVER PEANUT BUTTER COOKIES

BEST FOODS, A DIVISION OF CPC INTERNATIONAL INC.

Makes 6 dozen cookies

2 cups quick oats
1¼ cups unsifted flour
1 teaspoon baking powder
1 teaspoon baking soda
¼ teaspoon salt
1 cup Mazola® Margarine

1 cup Skippy® Creamy *or*
   Super Chunk® Peanut Butter
1 cup sugar
1 cup firmly packed brown sugar
2 eggs
1 teaspoon vanilla

Preheat oven to 350°F. In small bowl, stir oats, flour, baking powder, baking soda, and salt. In large bowl with mixer at medium speed, beat margarine and peanut butter until smooth. Beat in sugars until blended. Beat in eggs and vanilla. Add flour mixture, beat until well blended. Drop by rounded teaspoonfuls 2 inches apart on ungreased cookie sheets. Bake 12 minutes or until lightly browned. Remove from cookie sheets. Cool completely on wire rack. Store in tightly covered container.

WHOLE-WHEAT ORANGE PEANUT BUTTER COOKIES

BEST FOODS, A DIVISION OF CPC INTERNATIONAL INC.

Makes about 3 dozen cookies

1¼ cups unsifted whole-wheat flour
½ teaspoon baking powder
½ teaspoon baking soda
⅛ teaspoon salt
½ cup Mazola® Margarine
½ cup Skippy® Creamy *or* Super Chunk®
   Peanut Butter

⅔ cup firmly packed
   light brown sugar
⅓ cup sugar
1 egg
2 teaspoons grated orange peel
½ teaspoon vanilla
Sugar

Preheat oven to 350°F. In small bowl, stir together flour, baking powder, baking soda, and salt. In large bowl with mixer at medium speed, beat together margarine and peanut butter until well blended. Beat in sugars until well blended. Beat in egg, orange peel, and vanilla. Add flour mixture; beat well. Cover; refrigerate 1 hour. Shape dough into 1-inch balls. Roll in sugar. Place on ungreased cookie sheets 2 inches apart. Flatten with lightly sugared fork, making crisscross pattern. Bake about 12 minutes or until lightly browned. If desired, score with skewer after 5 minutes of baking. Cool on wire rack. Store in tightly covered container.

VARIATION

Reduced-Sugar Whole-Wheat Orange Peanut Butter Cookies: Omit ⅓ cup sugar. If desired, roll in additional sugar and flatten with lightly sugared fork.

HONEY NUT PEANUT BUTTER OAT BARS

BEST FOODS, A DIVISION OF CPC INTERNATIONAL INC.

Makes 39 bars

2 cups quick oats
1½ cups unsifted flour
1 teaspoon baking powder
¼ teaspoon salt
⅔ cup Roasted Honey Nut™ Skippy®
   Super Chunk® Peanut Butter

2 tablespoons Mazola® Margarine
1 cup sugar
⅓ cup Karo® Dark Corn Syrup
2 eggs
1 teaspoon vanilla
2 cups raisins

Preheat oven to 400°F. Spread oats in 15½-by-10½-by-1-inch jelly-roll pan. Bake, stirring occasionally, 8 to 10 minutes or until lightly toasted. Cool. Turn down oven to 350°F. Grease 13-by-9-by-2-inch pan. In small bowl, stir together flour, baking powder, and salt. In large bowl with mixer at medium speed, beat peanut butter and margarine until well mixed. Beat in sugar, corn syrup, eggs, and vanilla until well blended. Beat in flour mixture until well mixed. With wooden spoon, stir in oats and raisins. Spread evenly in prepared pan. Bake about 25 minutes or until cake tester inserted in center comes out clean. Cool completely on wire rack. Cut into 3-by-1-inch bars. Store in tightly covered container or wrap individually in plastic wrap.

VARIATION

Reduced-Sugar Peanut Butter Oat Bars: Reduce sugar to ¾ cup.

PEANUT BUTTER RAISIN BARS

NABISCO FOODS GROUP

Makes 2 dozen bars

½ cup firmly packed light brown sugar
½ cup light corn syrup
½ cup peanut butter
6 Nabisco® Shredded Wheat Biscuits *or*
   3 cups Spoon Size® Shredded Wheat,
   coarsely crushed

¾ cup seedless raisins
½ cup chopped dry-roasted
   unsalted peanuts

In large saucepan, over medium, heat brown sugar, corn syrup, and peanut butter until smooth and bubbly, stirring occasionally. Quickly stir in cereal, raisins, and peanuts; press evenly into greased 8- or 9-inch square baking pan. Cool. Cut into bars; store in airtight container.

To microwave: In 2-quart microwave-safe bowl, blend brown sugar, corn syrup, and peanut butter. Microwave at HIGH 1 to 1½ minutes until bubbly; stir until smooth.

PEANUT BUTTER CHIPS AND JELLY BARS

HERSHEY FOODS CORPORATION

Makes about 18 bars

1½ cups all-purpose flour
½ cup sugar
¾ teaspoon baking powder
½ cup (1 stick) cold butter *or* margarine

1 egg, beaten
¾ cup grape jelly
1⅔ cups (10-oz. pkg.) Reese's® Peanut
   Butter Chips, divided

Heat oven to 375°F. Grease 9-inch square baking pan. In large bowl, stir together flour, sugar, and baking powder; cut in butter with pastry blender or fork to resemble coarse crumbs. Add egg; blend well. Reserve half of mixture; press remaining mixture onto bottom of prepared pan. Spread jelly evenly over crust. Sprinkle with *1 cup* peanut butter chips. Stir together remaining crumb mixture with remaining ⅔ *cup* chips; sprinkle over top. Bake 25 to 30 minutes or until lightly browned. Cool completely in pan on wire rack; cut into bars.

DATE ALMOND FINGERS

DOLE FOOD COMPANY

Makes 18 bars

1½ cups Dole® Chopped Dates
Zest and juice from 1 Dole® Orange
¾ cup brown sugar, packed
½ cup margarine
2 eggs

½ teaspoon almond extract
1 cup whole wheat flour
½ cup Dole® Whole Natural Almonds,
   toasted, and ground
2 teaspoons baking powder

Preheat oven to 350°F. Mix together dates in *½ cup* hot orange juice in small bowl for 5 minutes. Purée in blender until smooth, 1 minute. Beat sugar and margarine until fluffy. Beat in eggs, *1 tablespoon* orange zest, and extract. Stir in date mixture. Combine flour, ground almonds, and baking powder. Add to date mixture. Stir until blended. Spread batter in greased 13-by-9-inch baking pan. Bake 20 to 25 minutes. Cool in pan 15 minutes. Turn onto wire rack to complete cooling. Cut into finger bars.

FRUIT AND NUT COOKIES

DOLE FOOD COMPANY

Makes about 4 dozen cookies

1 cup margarine
1 cup granulated sugar
½ cup brown sugar, packed
2 eggs
1 tablespoon grated orange peel
2 teaspoons grated lemon peel
2½ cups all-purpose flour

1 teaspoon baking soda
1 teaspoon ground cinnamon
¼ teaspoon ground nutmeg
1 package (12 ounces) Dole® Raisins
1 package (8 ounces) Dole® Chopped
   Dates
1 cup Dole® Chopped Almonds, toasted

Preheat oven to 375°F. Beat margarine and sugars until fluffy. Beat in eggs and orange and lemon peel. Combine flour, baking soda, cinnamon, and nutmeg. Beat into margarine mixture until blended. Stir in raisins, dates, and almonds. Drop by heaping tablespoon onto lightly greased cookie sheets. Spread slightly with back of spoon or fork. Bake 10 to 13 minutes. Cool on wire rack.

To toast almonds: Preheat oven to 350°F. Place in a shallow pan and bake for 10 minutes. Toasting time will vary depending upon the size of the almonds.

JUNGLE BARS

DOLE FOOD COMPANY

Makes 32 bars

2 ripe, medium Dole® Bananas, peeled
½ pound dried figs
½ pound dried apricots
½ pound Dole® Whole Pitted Dates
½ pound Dole® Raisins

2 cups granola
½ pound Dole® Chopped Natural
    Almonds, toasted (see below)
1 cup flaked coconut

Combine bananas, figs, apricots, dates, raisins, and granola in food processor, or run through food grinder. Stir in almonds. Press mixture into greased 13-by-9-inch baking dish. Sprinkle with coconut. Cover; refrigerate 24 hours to allow flavors to blend. Cut into bars.

To toast almonds: Preheat oven to 350°F. Place almonds in a shallow pan and bake for 10 minutes. Toasting time will vary depending upon the size of the almonds.

THE FIRST CEREAL FLAKES
The Story of W. K. Kellogg

Like so many great discoveries, the first breakfast cereal flakes were created accidentally. After long days as business manager at Michigan's Battle Creek Sanitarium, a Seventh Day Adventist institution with a regimen of vegetarianism, fresh air, sunshine, and water therapy, Will Keith Kellogg had been experimenting with ways to make grains more nutritious and digestible for the patients. He was running boiled wheat through rollers devised to create granola, one of the Sanitarium's previous breakfast discoveries. Distracted from his lab experiments one day in 1894, he left the cooked wheat exposed to air. The following day he decided to roll it through anyway. To his amazement, the rollers discharged a flake for each grain of wheat instead of a rolled sheet of wheat.

W. K. Kellogg and his brother, Dr. John Harvey Kellogg, the superintendent of the Sanitirium, believed that grains were very healthy foods. They served their creation to the patients, many of whom wrote after being discharged to ask for more of the breakfast treat they had eaten at "the San." This encouraged the Kellogg brothers to start a cereal company, The Sanitas Nut Food Company, to supply Sanitarium patients.

Here the corn flake was created in 1898. At first W. K. had trouble making corn flakes as appetizing as the wheat flakes, but he discovered that using malt flavoring and only the heart of the kernel created a much tastier flake.

While W. K. Kellogg was absorbed in his experiments, forty-two competitors also started cereal businesses in Battle Creek, many of them marketing Kellogg's own wheat-flake innovation. Only a handful of these companies would survive, and Kellogg had the business instincts to keep his company among the winners. He decided the way to fight these copycats was through consistent quality and effective marketing, advertising, and promotion.

Kellogg started his own Battle Creek Toasted Corn Flakes cereal company in 1906, soon to be known throughout the world as The Kellogg Company. The high demand for Kellogg products and W. K.'s desire to maintain quality prompted him to add this legend to each cereal box: "Beware of imitations. None genuine without this signature. W. K. Kellogg."

Kellogg's Corn Flakes® became an overnight triumph. W. K. Kellogg went on to earn his place among the movers and shakers and the great philanthropists of the early twentieth century—surprising achievements for a man who hadn't started his company until age forty-six, who once wrote in his diary, "Afraid I will always be a poor man."

CHERRY DOT COOKIES
KELLOGG COMPANY

Makes 5 dozen cookies

2¼ cups all-purpose flour
2 teaspoons baking powder
½ teaspoon salt
¾ cup margarine, softened
1 cup sugar
2 eggs
2 tablespoons skim milk

1 teaspoon vanilla
1 cup chopped nuts
1 cup finely cut, pitted dates
⅓ cup finely chopped maraschino cherries
2⅔ cups KELLOGG'S CORN FLAKES® cereal, crushed to 1⅓ cups
15 maraschino cherries, cut into quarters

Preheat oven to 350°F. Stir together flour, baking powder, and salt. Set aside. In large mixing bowl, beat margarine and sugar until light and fluffy. Add eggs. Beat well. Stir in milk and vanilla. Add flour mixture. Mix well. Stir in nuts, dates, and ⅓ cup chopped cherries. Shape level measuring-tablespoon of dough into balls. Roll in crushed cereal. Place on baking sheets coated with cooking spray. Top each cookie with cherry quarter. Bake about 12 minutes or until lightly browned.

EASY S'MORE TREATS

GENERAL MILLS, INC.

Makes 24 squares

¾ cup light corn syrup
3 tablespoons margarine *or* butter
1 package (11.5 ounces) milk chocolate
  chips

1 teaspoon vanilla
9 cups Golden Grahams® Cereal
3 cups miniature marshmallows

Grease rectangular pan, 13-by-9-by-2 inches. Heat corn syrup, margarine, and chocolate chips to boiling in 3-quart saucepan, stirring constantly; remove from heat. Stir in vanilla. Pour over cereal in large bowl; toss until completely coated with chocolate. Fold in marshmallows, 1 cup at a time. Press mixture evenly in pan with buttered back of spoon. Let stand at room temperature at least 1 hour or until firm. Cut into about 2-inch squares. Store, loosely covered, at room temperature, no more than 2 days.

To make 16 Treats: Grease square pan, 9-by-9-by-2 inches or 8-by-8-by-2 inches. Decrease corn syrup to ⅓ cup, margarine to 1 tablespoon, chocolate chips to 5.75-ounce package, vanilla to ½ teaspoon, cereal to 4 cups, and marshmallows to 1½ cups. Continue as directed above—except fold cereal gradually into chocolate mixture until completely coated. Fold in marshmallows. Press mixture evenly in pan with buttered back of spoon. Let stand at room temperature at least 1 hour. Cut 9-inch pan into 2¼-inch squares, 8-inch pan into 2-inch squares.

To microwave: Microwave corn syrup, margarine, and chocolate chips in 4-cup microwave-safe measure or medium, clear microwave-safe bowl, uncovered, on 1 minute, 30 seconds; stir until almost smooth. Microwave, uncovered, about 2 minutes, 30 seconds, or until large bubbles form on surface; stir in vanilla.

THE SWEET BEAN
The Story of Vanilla

Vanilla has long been regarded as the premier flavoring ingredient for pastries, cake mixes, soft drinks, candies, liqueurs, and other sweetened foods. What we think of as the taste of chocolate would not be possible without the addition of vanilla. The cacao bean itself has a bitter taste and needs to be married to the sweetness of vanilla to become the flavor that chocaholics crave.

Like so many of the world's important foods, vanilla was brought back from Latin America by New World explorers. In 1520, an officer of Cortés' expedition hesitantly accepted a taste of a frothy brew the Aztecs had prepared from ground cacao beans and corn, water, honey, and a flavoring agent they called *tlilxochitl*. Learning that the sweet new flavoring agent was from long, thin pods, the conquistadors called the additive *vainilla* from the Spanish word meaning "little bean."

The explorers liked the taste so much that they made room for vanilla on their voyage back to Spain. By the end of the sixteenth century, confectioners were blending chocolate treats flavored with vanilla. The apothecary of Queen Elizabeth I proclaimed vanilla to be a meritorious flavor with enough character to enhance foods on its own.

To keep up with increasing demand, the Spanish brought cuttings of the bean plant back to the homeland. The tropical plants flourished in greenhouses, but the fragrant orchid flowers never developed into bean pods. Finally, in 1836, a Belgian botanist, Charles Morren, discovered the reason for the problem. The bees and hummingbirds attracted to the orchids to pollinate the plants lived only in the New World. A method of hand pollinating the flowers with a bamboo stick was developed. This method is used for commercial cultivation to this day.

Most of our vanilla comes from the island of Madagascar, an island off the southeast coast of Africa that is three times larger than Great Britain. The vanilla beans are harvested by hand, then immersed in boiling water for two or three minutes. Daily the beans are spread to heat and dry in the sun, then wrapped in coverings to sweat until morning, for a period of ten to twenty days. A fermentation process occurs. The beans become dark brown, and the crystals that will frost the pods and impart the characteristic smell and flavor of vanilla begin to form. The beans are sun dried for up to six more months.

The Minister of Commerce of Madagascar meets annually with top worldwide purchasers of vanilla to discuss the annual crop and set prices. McCormick &

Company is the largest purchaser involved in these negotiations. McCormick's agent personally selects the choicest vanilla beans. Crates packed with vanilla are loaded onto coastal steamers from small wooden boats floating just beyond the coral reefs. The coastal steamers enter the two main ports of Madagascar where the vanilla is transferred to ocean steamers for shipment to New York.

In the McCormick laboratory, each batch of vanilla is treated in a time-consuming process. Vanillin and water content is analyzed. The production facility is told how much alcohol and water to add to extract the flavor from each bean batch in order to comply with government regulations. Then the beans are ground, packed into baskets, and placed in large stainless-steel percolators where the flavor is extracted much the same as coffee is processed through percolation. An aging process and conscientious testing are the final steps to assure the correct degree of flavor and the mellow sweetness of excellent vanilla.

GINGER BITES
MCCORMICK & COMPANY, INC.

Makes 12½ dozen 1-inch cookies

½ cup butter, softened
½ cup sugar
½ cup molasses
2 eggs
1 teaspoon baking soda
1 teaspoon McCormick/Schilling® ground
  Ginger

½ teaspoon McCormick/Schilling
  Cinnamon
3¼ cups flour
1 teaspoon McCormick/Schilling pure
  Vanilla Extract

Preheat oven to 350°F. Cream butter with sugar. Beat in molasses and eggs. Combine next 4 ingredients and add gradually, mixing well. Stir in vanilla extract. On board dusted with confectioners' sugar, roll out small amount of dough at a time, to ⅛-inch thickness. Cut out cookies using very small, 1- to 1¼-inch cutters, or use a knife to cut 1-inch squares. Bake on ungreased cookie sheets 5 minutes. Cool on wire racks.

MERRY MORSELS (HOLIDAY COOKIES)
MCCORMICK & COMPANY, INC.

Makes 14 dozen 1-inch cookies

1 cup butter
1 cup sugar
1 teaspoon McCormick/Schilling® pure
  Vanilla Extract
½ teaspoon McCormick/Schilling Imitation
  Rum Extract
2½ cups sifted flour

¼ teaspoon McCormick/Schilling Mace
¾ cup finely chopped green and red
  cherries (candied *or* maraschino that
  have been chopped and drained well
  on paper towels)
½ cup finely chopped pecans
¾ cup flaked coconut

Preheat oven to 375°F. Cream together butter and sugar. Stir in vanilla and rum extracts. Stir in flour, mace, cherries, and pecans. Chill dough. Shape into rolls 1 inch in diameter. Roll in coconut. Wrap in waxed paper and chill. Dough may be frozen at this stage and baked as needed. Slice ¼-inch thick. Place on ungreased cookie sheets. Bake 5 to 7 minutes or until edges are golden.

HOLIDAY WREATHS
KELLOGG COMPANY

Makes 16 wreaths

½ cup margarine
1 package (10 ounces; about 40) regular
  marshmallows
1 teaspoon green food coloring

6 cups KELLOGG'S CORN FLAKES®
  cereal
Red cinnamon candies

Melt margarine and marshmallows in large saucepan over low heat, stirring constantly until marshmallows melt and mixture is syrupy. Remove from heat. Stir in food coloring. Add cereal. Stir until well coated. Portion warm cereal mixture, using ¼-cup dry measure. Using buttered fingers, quickly shape into individual wreaths. Dot with red cinnamon candies.

To microwave: In large microwave-safe bowl, melt margarine and marshmallows at HIGH 2 minutes. Stir mixture and heat at HIGH an additional 2 minutes. Stir in food coloring. Continue as above.

CALIFORNIA WHITE CHOCOLATE FUDGE

KRAFT GENERAL FOODS, INC.

Makes about 2½ pounds

1½ cups sugar
¾ cup Breakstone's® Sour Cream
½ cup Parkay® Margarine
12 ounces white chocolate, coarsely chopped

1 jar (7 ounces) Kraft® Marshmallow Creme
¾ cup chopped walnuts
¾ cup chopped dried apricots

In heavy 2½- to 3-quart saucepan, bring sugar, sour cream, and margarine to full, rolling boil over medium heat, stirring constantly. Continue boiling 7 minutes or until candy thermometer reaches 234°F, stirring constantly. Remove from heat; stir in chocolate until melted. Stir in remaining ingredients until well blended. Pour into greased 8- or 9-inch square baking pan. Cool several hours or overnight; cut into squares.

(Note: To easily remove marshmallow creme from jar, remove lid and seal and microwave on HIGH 30 seconds.)

Preparation time: 30 minutes, plus chilling

VARIATION

Substitute macadamia nuts for walnuts.

MICROWAVE TRUFFLES

MCCORMICK & COMPANY, INC.

Makes 50 truffles

24 ounces semi-sweet chocolate pieces
2 tablespoons butter
2 tablespoons dairy sour cream
½ teaspoon McCormick/Schilling®
  imitation Brandy Extract
½ teaspoon McCormick/Schilling imitation
  Rum Extract

½ teaspoon McCormick/Schilling pure
  Vanilla Extract
Cocoa
Flaked Coconut
Finely chopped pecans

To microwave: Put chocolate, butter, and sour cream in 3-quart covered heatproof glass casserole. Heat in microwave oven on HIGH 2 minutes. Stir thoroughly. Heat 1 minute longer. Stir. Divide mixture into three portions. Add one extract to each portion and mix well. Shape into 1-inch balls and roll in cocoa, coconut, or chopped pecans. Store in airtight container.

FOOLPROOF DARK CHOCOLATE FUDGE

BORDEN, INC.

Makes about 2 pounds

3 packages (6 ounces each) semi-sweet
  chocolate chips
1 can (14 ounces) Eagle® Brand
  Sweetened Condensed Milk
  (*not* evaporated milk)

Dash salt
½ to 1 cup chopped nuts
1½ teaspoons vanilla extract

In heavy saucepan, over low heat, melt chips with sweetened condensed milk and salt. Remove from heat; stir in nuts and vanilla. Spread evenly into waxed paper–lined 8- or 9-inch square pan. Chill 2 hours or until firm. Turn fudge onto cutting board; peel off paper and cut into squares. Store, loosely covered, at room temperature.

To microwave: In 1-quart glass measure, combine chips with sweetened condensed milk. Cook on HIGH 3 minutes. Stir until chips melt and mixture is smooth. Stir in remaining ingredients. Proceed as above.

FANTASY FUDGE

KRAFT GENERAL FOODS, INC.

Makes 3 pounds

¾ cup Parkay® Margarine
3 cups sugar
⅔ cup evaporated milk
   (*not* sweetened condensed milk)
1 package (12 ounces) Baker's®
   Real Semi-sweet Chocolate Chips

1 jar (7 ounces) Kraft®
   Marshmallow Creme
1 cup chopped nuts
1 teaspoon vanilla

Preparation time: 10 minutes   *Cooking time:* 15 minutes

To microwave: Microwave margarine in 4-quart bowl or casserole on HIGH 1 minute or until melted. Add sugar and milk; mix well. Microwave on HIGH 5 minutes or until mixture begins to boil; stir after 3 minutes. Mix well, scraping bowl. Microwave 5½ minutes; stir after 3 minutes. Gradually stir in chocolate until melted. Add remaining ingredients; mix well. Pour into greased 9-by-9-inch or 13-by-9-inch pan. Cool at room temperature; cut into squares.

Stir together margarine, sugar, and evaporated milk in heavy 2½- to 3-quart saucepan; bring to full boil, stirring constantly. Boil 5 minutes over medium heat, or until candy thermometer reaches 234°F, stirring constantly to prevent scorching. Remove from heat. Gradually stir in chocolate until melted. Add remaining ingredients; mix until well blended. Pour into greased 9-by-9-inch or 13-by-9-inch pan. Cool at room temperature; cut into squares.

VARIATIONS

Omit nuts. Substitute 1 cup peanut butter for chocolate pieces.

Substitute 4 cups Kraft® Miniature Marshmallows for Kraft® Marshmallow Creme.

Substitute 40 Kraft Marshmallows for Kraft® Marshmallow Creme.

Double recipe. Use 13-ounce jar Kraft® Marshmallow Creme and 5-quart Dutch oven.

Substitute 1 cup Kraft® Party Mints *or* Butter Mints for nuts.

Substitute 1 cup Kraft® Peanut Brittle, crushed, for nuts.

Omit nuts. Add ½ cup crushed peppermint candy.

Substitute 8 squares (8 ounces total) Baker's® Semi-sweet chocolate, broken in half, for chips.

FIVE-MINUTE FUDGE

CARNATION, NESTLÉ FOOD COMPANY

Makes 2 pounds

2 tablespoons butter *or* margarine
⅔ cup *undiluted* Carnation® Evaporated
   Milk
1⅔ cups sugar
½ teaspoon salt

2 cups (4 ounces) miniature
   marshmallows
1½ cups (9 ounces) Nestlé® Toll House®
   Semi-Sweet Chocolate Morsels
1 teaspoon vanilla
½ cup chopped nuts

In medium saucepan combine butter, evaporated milk, sugar, and salt. Bring to a boil over medium heat, stirring constantly. Boil 4 to 5 minutes, stirring constantly. Remove from heat. Stir in marshmallows, chocolate, vanilla, and nuts. Stir vigorously for 1 minute until marshmallows melt and blend. Pour into buttered 8-inch square pan. Cool. Cut into squares.

VARIATIONS

Fancy Fudge: Omit chopped nuts. Substitute ¼ cup toasted chopped almonds and ½ cup finely chopped candied mixed fruit.

Five-Minute Fudge Rolls: Make Five-Minute Fudge as directed above. Spread about 1 cup chopped nuts on waxed paper. Pour fudge mixture over nuts. As fudge cools, form into roll. Slice.

Peppermint Fudge: Sprinkle ¼ cup coarsely broken peppermint candy over top of fudge in pan.

Upside-Down Coconut Fudge: Spread 1 cup flaked, toasted coconut on bottom of buttered 8-inch square pan. Top with fudge.

Peanut Fudge: Substitute ½ cup chopped peanuts for nuts.

HERSHEY'S® VANILLA MILK CHIPS ALMOND FUDGE
HERSHEY FOODS CORPORATION

Makes about 4 dozen candies

1⅔ cups (10-oz. pkg.) Hershey's® Vanilla Milk Chips

⅔ cup sweetened condensed milk

1½ cups coarsely chopped slivered almonds, toasted

½ teaspoon vanilla extract

Butter 8-inch-square pan. In medium saucepan over very low heat, melt vanilla milk chips and sweetened condensed milk, stirring constantly, until mixture is smooth. Remove from heat. Stir in almonds and vanilla. Spread in prepared pan. Cover; refrigerate until firm, about 2 hours. Cut into 1-inch squares.

To toast almonds: Preheat oven to 350°F. Spread almonds on cookie sheet. Bake, stirring occasionally, until lightly browned, 8 to 10 minutes; cool.

CHOCOLATE PIZZA

KRAFT GENERAL FOODS, INC.

Makes one 12-inch pizza

1 package (12 ounces) Baker's® Real
   Semi-sweet Chocolate Chips
1 pound white almond bark, divided
2 cups Kraft® Miniature Marshmallows
1 cup crisp rice cereal
1 cup peanuts

1 jar (6 ounces) red maraschino cherries,
   drained, cut in half
3 tablespoons green maraschino cherries,
   drained, quartered
⅓ cup Baker's® Angel Flake® Brand
   Coconut
1 teaspoon oil

Melt chocolate chips with 14 ounces almond bark in large saucepan over low heat, stirring until smooth; remove from heat. Stir in marshmallows, cereal, and peanuts. Pour onto greased 12-inch pizza pan. Top with cherries; sprinkle with coconut. Melt remaining 2 ounces almond bark with oil over low heat, stirring until smooth; drizzle over coconut. Chill until firm; store at room temperature.

To microwave: Microwave chocolate pieces with 14 ounces almond bark in 2-quart bowl on HIGH 2 minutes; stir. Continue microwaving 1 to 2 minutes or until smooth when stirred, stirring every 30 seconds. Stir in marshmallows, cereal, and peanuts. Pour onto greased 12-inch pizza pan. Top with cherries; sprinkle with coconut. Melt remaining 2 ounces almond bark with oil in 1-cup measure on HIGH 1 minute; stir. Continue microwaving 30 seconds to 1 minute or until smooth when stirred, stirring every 15 seconds. Drizzle over coconut. Chill until firm; store at room temperature.

VARIATIONS

Substitute 1 cup chopped or halved pecans or walnuts for peanuts.

For smaller pizzas, shape mixture into four 6-inch rounds or twelve 4-inch rounds on waxed paper–lined cookie sheets.

Preparation time: 15 minutes, plus chilling

CARAMELS

PET INCORPORATED

Makes 81 caramels

2 cups sugar
2 cups light corn syrup
1/8 teaspoon salt

1/2 cup unsalted butter
2 cups Pet® Evaporated Milk
I teaspoon vanilla extract

In 3-quart heavy saucepan, combine sugar, corn syrup, and salt. Cook over medium-high heat until mixture reaches firm-ball stage (244°F), stirring occasionally. Add butter, and very slowly add evaporated milk so that mixture does not stop boiling. Stirring constantly, cook rapidly to firm-ball stage again. Remove from heat, add vanilla, and pour mixture into a buttered 9-by-9-inch pan *without* scraping sides of the saucepan. Cool thoroughly before cutting.

CARAMEL NUT CLUSTERS

KELLOGG COMPANY

Makes about 24 nut clusters

1/4 cup margarine or butter
1/2 pound (about 28) caramels
2 tablespoons milk

3 1/2 cups KELLOGG'S CORN FLAKES®
  cereal
1/2 cup chopped nuts
1/2 cup shredded coconut

In large saucepan, combine margarine, caramels, and milk. Stir over low heat until melted and smooth. Remove from heat. Add remaining ingredients. Mix well. Drop by rounded measuring-tablespoon onto buttered or waxed paper–lined cookie sheet. Cool.

NUTTY CHOCOLATE DROPS

KELLOGG COMPANY

Makes about 24 chocolate drops

I package (11 1/2 ounces; 2 cups) milk
  chocolate morsels

I cup KELLOGG'S CORN FLAKES®
  cereal
I cup chopped peanuts

Melt milk chocolate morsels in medium-size saucepan over low heat. Stir in cereal and peanuts. Drop by rounded measuring-tablespoon onto buttered or waxed paper–lined cookie sheet. Chill until set.

EASY CHERRIES JUBILEE

PEPPERIDGE FARM, INC.

Makes 6 servings

I package (10 ounces) Pepperidge Farm®
  Frozen Puff Pastry Shells
I can (17 ounces) cherry pie filling

2 tablespoons water
3 tablespoons brandy
Vanilla ice cream

Prepare pastry shells according to package directions. In mixing bowl, combine pie filling and water. In small saucepan, heat brandy until hot. Ignite and pour over filling. Stir until flame goes out. Spoon ice cream into pastry shells and top with warm sauce.

NAPOLEONS

PEPPERIDGE FARM, INC.

Makes 12 napoleons

I sheet Pepperidge Farm® Frozen Puff
  Pastry, thawed 20 minutes
I package (4½ ounces)
  instant chocolate pudding
I cup sour cream

I cup milk
I cup confectioners' sugar
I tablespoon milk
2 ounces semisweet chocolate, melted

Preheat oven to 400°F. Cut pastry into 4 strips, 2½ inches wide. Cut each strip crosswise into thirds. Bake strips on an ungreased baking sheet for 12 to 15 minutes. Prepare pudding according to package directions, susbstituting sour cream for 1 cup milk. Cut pastry rectangles in half, making a top and a bottom. Generously spoon pudding on bottom half and top with other half. Blend sugar and milk. Spread on top and drizzle with chocolate.

ELEPHANT EARS

PEPPERIDGE FARM, INC.

Makes about 32 pastries

I sheet Pepperidge Farm Frozen Puff
  Pastry, thawed 20 minutes
Granulated sugar

Cinnamon
I egg beaten with I tablespoon water

Preheat oven to 425°F. Unfold and cut pastry sheet in half. Roll out 1 piece to an 8-by-14-inch rectangle. Sprinkle generously with sugar and cinnamon. Fold the short edges of the pastry one-quarter the distance toward the center. Sprinkle again with sugar and cinnamon and fold short edges again toward the center, leaving a ¼-inch space between edges. Fold 1 side over onto the other, making an 8-layer rectangle. Chill 10 minutes. Repeat with another piece. Slice chilled rolls crosswise into ½-by-¾-inch pieces. Brush with egg mixture. Place on ungreased baking sheets and bake 10 minutes, or until golden brown. Remove immediately from baking sheets and let cool.

VARIATION

For appetizers, substitute grated Parmesan cheese for sugar/cinnamon mixture.

FRUIT 'N CHEESE DESSERT SALAD

SARGENTO CHEESE COMPANY, INC.

Makes 6 servings, 1 cup each

I package (0.8 ounces) sugar-free-cook-
  and-serve vanilla pudding
I can (15 ounces) pineapple chunks
  packed in juice, drained, with juice
  reserved
¼ cup orange juice

6 cups assorted fresh fruits, cut into
  1-inch chunks
¾ cup (3 ounces) Sargento® Preferred
  Light® Fancy Shredded Mozzarella
  Cheese

In a saucepan, combine dry pudding, reserved liquid from pineapple, and orange juice to make fruit glaze. Heat over medium, stirring constantly until thickened, about 1 minute. Cool. Gently toss fruit glaze with pineapple chunks and fresh fruit chunks. Cover and chill until ready to serve. Top each 1-cup serving with 2 tablespoons cheese.

WHIPPED TOPPING
NESTLÉ FOOD COMPANY

Makes 3 cups

½ cup ice water
½ cup Carnation® Nonfat Dry Milk
1½ teaspoons unflavored gelatin
2 tablespoons cold water

2 tablespoons boiling water
¼ cup confectioners' sugar
1 teaspoon vanilla

In mixing bowl, combine *½ cup* ice water and nonfat dry milk. Chill bowl, beaters, and nonfat dry milk mixture. In small bowl, combine gelatin and *2 tablespoons* cold water. Let stand 3 minutes. Add *2 tablespoons* boiling water. Let cool to room temperature. Whip chilled nonfat dry milk mixture until stiff peaks form. Add gelatin, confectioners' sugar, and vanilla. Whip until well blended. (Note: If whipped topping develops an airy appearance, simply stir vigorously to restore smooth appearance. For best results, prepare same day as serving).

NUTMEG BRANDY SAUCE
NESTLÉ FOOD COMPANY

Makes 1½ cups

½ cup sugar
1 tablespoon cornstarch
½ teaspoon nutmeg
⅝ cup (5-ounce can) *undiluted* Carnation®
   Evaporated Milk

½ cup apricot nectar
2 tablespoons butter
4 teaspoons brandy
½ teaspoon vanilla

In small saucepan combine sugar, cornstarch, and nutmeg. Gradually stir in evaporated milk, apricot nectar, and butter. Cook over medium heat, stirring constantly, until mixture comes to a boil; boil 1 minute. Remove from heat. Stir in brandy and vanilla.

Serve warm or chilled over fruit, ice cream, or cake.

INDEX

More great cookbooks from Ten Speed Press

THE SEATTLE CLASSIC COOKBOOK
by the Seattle Junior League

More than 500 classic recipes from the Pacific Nortwest, where fresh natural ingredients and casual elegance have shaped the cuisine. "The 'classics' here are fish, seafood, and game ... All courses are covered and there are 18 different menus ... a posh collection." —*Booklist* magazine
$13.95 paper or $21.95 cloth, 320 pages

WHITE TRASH COOKING
by Ernest Matthew Mickler

"That is the most delicious cookbook I have encountered—and it seems that my diet in childhood was all white trash!"
—Helen Hayes

This celebration of Southern food and folks, with its down-home recipes and wonderful color photos has been praised by *Vogue* magazine, author Harper Lee, NPR radio, the *New York Times*, and thousands of happy readers. $14.95 paper or $19.95 cloth, 192 pages

EATING WELL IN BUSY WORLD
by Francine Allen

Forty delicious, healthful menus are proof positive that people on the go don't have to eat fast food. Well-organized shopping lists, chef's secrets and shortcuts, and clear, realistic timetables (the average menu takes 30 minutes start to finish, some as little as 15!) combine to make cooking fun again. $8.95 paper, 128 pages

THE POTATO EXPERIENCE
by Lisa Tanner

The simple potato is easily transformed into spicy appetizers, homey salads, light diet meals, and hearty main courses. This beautifully hand-lettered and illustrated cookbook starts with plain potatoes (and a few yams and sweet potatoes) and creates hundreds of inexpensive yet impressive dishes. $11.95 paper, 240 pages

THE BROWNIE EXPERIENCE
by Lisa Tanner

Brownie lovers have been known to cook their way through this book from cover to cover, sampling every one of the more than 100 variations ... including traditional brownies and exotic ones, no-bake, health food, and frozen ones and even chocolate-free brownies. $7.95 paper, 168 pages

GET YOUR BUNS IN HERE
by Laurel A. Wicks

One hundred mouthwatering recipes for cookies, cakes, pastries, brownies, sweet rolls, candies, muffins, pies, tarts, and other goodies that kept patrons lining up at a small but very popular bakery in Wyoming. $9.95 paper, 144 pages

TEN SPEED PRESS
Box 7123
Berkeley, CA 94707

Available from your local bookstore, or order direct from the publisher. Please include $1.25 shipping & handling for the first book, and 50 cents for each additonal book. California residents include local sales tax. Write for our free complete catalog of over 400 books and tapes.

For VISA and Mastercard orders call (510) 845-8414